TO BE FRANK

The Politics and Polemics of a Radical Russell

Ruth Derham

SPOKESMAN

To John G. Slater and Kenneth Blackwell,
with gratitude

Published in 2022 by
Spokesman
5 Churchill Park, Nottingham, NG4 2HF, England
spokesmanbooks.org
Spokesman is the publishing imprint of the
Bertrand Russell Peace Foundation Ltd.

A catalogue record is available from the British Library.

Printed and bound in Britain

ISBN 978 0 85124 911 7

Contents

Illustrations

Preface

The idea for this book developed during the writing of my biography of Frank Russell (1865-1931) – *Bertrand's Brother: The Marriages, Morals and Misdemeanours of the 2nd Earl Russell* (2021). During my research I gathered a huge amount of both archival and published material – journals, articles, letters and speeches by Frank – that underpinned my writing but could not be quoted at length. Much of it was rich material. Was there not some way in which I could share it? A selection from the desk of Frank Russell seemed the likely answer. Discussions with Ken Blackwell and his subsequent acceptance of my bibliography of Frank's writing and speeches for *Russell* provided the impetus; the bibliography's reception on publication – the surprise at Frank's diversity, humanity and thoughtful commentary on social issues of the day – gave further encouragement; and conversations with Tony Simpson of Spokesman Books afforded the means. Such consideration Frank has rarely received.

When Frank died suddenly in March 1931, his one-time personal secretary, the lawyer and writer E.S.P. Haynes, writing in regard to divorce law reform, expressed the hope that 'whenever the cause is won full justice will be done to Lord Russell as a pioneer in this movement, as indeed he was in several other movements.'[1] Across the spectrum of Frank's campaigns this hope is yet to be realised. His name is familiar to pockets of enthusiasts for his contribution to their specific field; or is recalled in relation to his unfortunate yet vastly entertaining 'peccadilloes' which I explored in *Bertrand's Brother* and which have been the principal cause of his appearance in other biographical works. He is remembered as the older brother of polymath Bertrand Russell who kickstarted his younger brother's mathematical career by teaching him Euclid in his youth, or for having been Bertrand's contact with the outside world on his incarceration in Brixton in 1918. Otherwise, Frank Russell has been largely ignored.

There are several possible reasons for this. One is a simple issue of timing. Frank did not live to see many of his campaigns come to fruition and history is not so good at remembering such pioneers, especially when others took up the banner at a critical moment. Lord Gorell Barnes' famous pronouncement in *Dodd* v. *Dodd* (1906), for example, his elevation to the peerage in 1909 and subsequent chairing of the 1910 Royal Commission tasked with investigating

1

the divorce laws have largely wiped from memory the groundwork done by Frank between 1902 and 1908. In other causes, Frank was one voice among many or took a background role. Women's suffrage, birth control, worker's rights and the plight of conscientious objectors all fall into this category. Still further, Haynes suggests that Frank's status may have been a factor:

> Our modern world is not perhaps sufficiently grateful to anyone who in an age of standardized democracy has the courage of his opinions and will go to prison (which must be most unpleasant for a confirmed smoker) without perturbation. The type is becoming more rare as the aristocratic ideal becomes more unfashionable and every citizen is levelled down to the same mediocrity.[2]

Here Haynes refers to the grand finale of Frank's very public involvement in the ten-year *cause célèbre* in which he desperately tried to extricate himself from his first unhappy marriage in the face of some incredible allegations by his wife and mother-in-law which culminated (after he took the law into his own hands) in his being tried for bigamy in the House of Lords in 1901 and imprisoned in Holloway for three months. Despite his official pardon in 1911 this event attached a certain stigma to his name. Before the pardon it prevented him taking a prominent position in the Divorce Law Reform Union (1906) and afterwards, in the Society for Constructive Birth Control (1921). It may have influenced his career in other ways. It has been suggested that it prevented him taking office in the first Labour Government but this is perhaps a narrow reading of events. Frank did not naturally ingratiate himself with others. He was considered something of a loose cannon who 'never thought of taking refuge in any obscurity of phrase or misleading euphemism'[3] and was 'too defiant to have recourse to propitiatory tricks'.[4] Word around the campfire was that he and Ramsay MacDonald 'don't love each other'.[5] Either way, it is generous of Haynes to suggest that Frank risked his liberty simply for the strength of his convictions when by his own admission it was a 'desperate expedient'. Yet Haynes' allusion to the 'aristocratic ideal' in relation to Frank is not misplaced. Despite his personal imbroglios, there *was* something of Plato's virtuous seeker after truth in him. He was a rationalist with a utilitarian morality; social injustice moved him profoundly; and he held his birthright in healthy contempt. 'I am very aristocratic,' he wrote to George Santayana in 1891, but it is nothing 'to be proud of or to encourage.'

Before elaborating on what a reader might expect to find in this selection, it is worth considering the influence of Frank's upbringing on his career. In particular, the place of religion, so influential in late-Victorian society and the object of so many of his polemics.

Frank had been raised by radical freethinking parents far from the influence of London society in an atmosphere completely devoid of religious dogma. He had been given an extraordinary amount of freedom. When he was ten and Bertrand not yet four, the brothers suddenly found themselves orphaned and in the care of their devout grandparents, Lord and Lady John Russell. Bertrand was kept at home and educated by a succession of governesses and tutors while the rebellious and troublesome Frank was sent to school – Cheam and subsequently Winchester College. There he succumbed to the orthodox religious atmosphere. His beliefs would go through various transitions before ostensibly settling, as did Bertrand's, on non-belief. In his memoirs, Frank wrote:

> The evolution of my belief may be traced thus. In the High Church period [at Winchester], a narrow sectarian practice, but with a rather more generous belief. I thought any Christian might be saved, and had my doubts about good Pagans, in spite of what Heine says of Socrates. I believed firmly in the Incarnation, had a personal love for Christ (which, indeed, I have not lost) and did really feel at Holy Communion that I was attended by Angels and Archangels and all the Company of Heaven. So comforting! Such blessed soporific poppy and mandragora! Buddhism [at Oxford] gave a wider outlook, a less limited circle, and it was not necessary to believe Buddha himself to be more than a teacher. Moreover, while it included the whole world of believers and unbelievers in its scope, making the only difference between them that the initiated knew and consciously trod the Way, while the unenlightened stumbled haphazard, it made the results depend in each case on individual effort ... The last step which comparatively few take, not only denies personal immortality and looks for mere annihilation at death, not only denies a particular or any supreme Being, but also a purpose, and regards the world of human beings as purely fortuitous. I believe the formation of the world to be more accurately described by Lucretius ... and I see no reason why it should not end as fortuitously either in the conflagration of a collision, or in the cold of interstellar space.[6]

The reasons he gave for his conversion were twofold: the tendency of science to confirm the axiom *Ex nihilo nihil fit* (nothing comes from nothing) and his freethinking conclusion that all gods are the product of human conceit. He came to regard the soporific effect of religion as an impediment to human development and the influence Church wielded over State as pernicious. On this, too, he and Bertrand were in accord; so much so that the article that best expresses Frank's attitude – his scathing attack on Anglican bishops in 'The Difficulties of Bishops' – was erroneously ascribed to Bertrand in Lester Denonn's bibliography published in 1963.

The pivotal moment in Frank's career appears to have been his aforementioned incarceration in Holloway at the age of thirty-five. While as a young man the title 'Earl Russell' was something he would rather have forgone, as he matured he began to see how his status could be employed for the betterment of society. *Lay Sermons* (1902) – an agnostic's perspective on religious doctrine largely written in Holloway – marks the transition. Its very existence raises questions about the extent to which it was written with his own future in mind. Its opening chapter is a 'Call to Arms'; its second addresses 'Labourers in the Vineyard'. In it, Frank wrote that, alongside country vicars and principled politicians,

> ... reformers receive the contemptuous tolerance accorded to visionaries, and on the career of one and all the word 'failure' appears to be written, and 'ineffectual' to be the only comment on their lives. But the harvest is not yet, and when, after seed-time the grain is lost to sight in the ground, no man can say how it may be germinating, what roots it is striking, or what the ultimate crop shall be.[7]

3

Was this Frank using his confinement to consider and fully embody the role he would play on his release? Was he addressing himself as much as his readers when he wrote that any honest labour, however late it is begun or however 'successful' it is deemed, is worthy of its penny and gives its own reward? 'Character is the thing that tells,' he continued. 'We must determine then to keep our eyes up to a high standard.' Certainly Frank left prison full of reforming zeal and from this point onwards his letters to editors appeared frequently in national newspapers, his uncompromising speeches were heard in towns all over the UK and in the House of Lords, his opinion on social issues was reported in the press and he had articles published that were well researched, direct and honest. Though undoubtedly he did waste energy tilting at windmills, he worked hard to prove he was no vacuous aristocrat. An acknowledgement of his labours appeared on the occasion of his forty-eighth birthday in the *Daily Citizen*. Lord Russell was, it said:

> ... the embodiment of strength and purpose. Once he has decided on a line of action there is nothing can make him swerve from the path. Yet there is nothing of blind obstinacy in his determination ... every opinion, every phase of the situation to be fought is carefully and honestly considered in making up that mind ... no week passes but he spends at least four days in his study delving deep into all manner of social and scientific subjects.[8]

The body of work that Frank produced to earn this accolade is probably uniquely diverse. It is difficult to think of another person who could have written or spoken with equal authority on such disparate subjects as the domestic uses of electricity, prison reform, wireless equipment and religious dogma. While I thought it important to reflect something of the whole spectrum of his industry in this selection, the pieces I considered likely to be of greatest interest to a modern reader were those that best reflect Frank's ethics and social policy: his politics and his polemics. As such, some of the spheres within which he operated – motoring and its laws for example – are less represented here than may be considered proportionate. Some of this work is covered by other publications: Piers Brendon's *The Motoring Century* (1997), for example. On some subjects he spoke little but his interest permeated his work. Frank's 'idea' of science falls into this category. Others – much of Frank's technical work, for example – I considered to be of too specialist interest to be included. Frank wrote articles on wireless technology, road building and traffic regulations. He spoke on the use of medical evidence in the courtroom and the relationship between medicine and the law. Latterly, he became one of the few Labour government representatives in the House of Lords; or, as Frank genially put it, their 'maid of all work'. Open access to his significant contribution is available in *Hansard* online. Interested readers can find details in the appended bibliography of everything I have been able to discover Frank did outside the House of Lords and his major contributions within it.

The final selection for this volume has been organised chronologically with endnotes for each chapter kept intentionally to a minimum – to aid understanding or identify individuals but not overwhelm the text. Variant spellings – recognise/recognize, etc. – have been silently standardised across the volume. As regards chronology, the single exception is Chapter 5 containing motoring articles which were written concurrently with the pieces in Chapter 4. Amusing though it is to think of Frank standing up in the House of Lords arguing for divorce law reform one day and sitting down to write his motoring column for *The Graphic* the next, it did not make for fluid reading to combine them. In all other instances the strict chronology assists in understanding the development of Frank's thinking. It also seemed necessary from a historical perspective.

For historical interest and the sheer pleasure of reading them, I have begun with a couple of juvenile letters and select entries from Frank's journal of his second year at Winchester College. Frank's travails with his brand new stylographic pen, his struggles against indolence, the rituals of the school and its jargon and the seriousness with which the boys took sides during the 1880 General Election are as entertaining as they are informative. Extracts from his Oxford journal, which includes the summer before he went up, spent with Bertrand and the Russells at Pembroke Lodge and Haslemere, give an insight into his early scientific interests, his religious and academic development and the opportunities afforded a young earl in the 1880s. Frank's university career was cut suddenly short in 1885 when he argued with the vice-chancellor Benjamin Jowett over his relations with another undergraduate in a mysterious episode that would haunt Frank for the rest of his life. He was sent down by Jowett and by the Russells to America on a very modern 'grand tour' to allow the dust to settle. The letters he wrote home demonstrate the psychological impact of Frank's sending down: his resolve under attack and sense of isolation. In their frank observations they give an impression of the new world in the late nineteenth century: its people, industry, policy and sheer magnitude. They include some delightful period notes, such as the occasion Frank knocked on the door of the White House to arrange an interview with Grover Cleveland and his detour to Camden to visit Walt Whitman. In editing the letters and journals I have extended abbreviations, standardised dates and silently corrected the occasional spelling mistake.

The period following Frank's return from America was largely taken up with establishing his electrical engineering business and finding himself embroiled in marital woes. Chapter 3, then, contains a rather eclectic mix of writings and speeches. I have included the speech he made in mitigation of his sentence at his bigamy trail which was often recalled as an early example of his eloquence when his reputation as an orator grew.

After his blistering critique of the history of Christianity in *Lay Sermons* came his audacious rewriting of the divorce laws as presented to the House of Lords. In our more permissive society, with its liberal divorce laws, it is perhaps difficult to comprehend the consequences of an unhappy marriage in an age of 'respectability', when unmarried partners were stigmatised, when livelihood depended on a good marriage – particularly for the working classes and for women – and an abusive or renegade spouse was difficult if not impossible to break free from. Frank protested against these draconian laws on a number of platforms: in both serious and popular journals, in speeches to societies and to the bishops and peers in the House of Lords who so vociferously upheld them. Examples of each type are included in this selection. Following which are some cogent arguments for women's suffrage and commanding defences of the rights of such diverse groups as motorists, workers and conscientious objectors. On social policy, Frank and Bertrand had numerous points of congruence such that the pieces in this section will interest and inform Russell scholars as much as the earlier letters and journals that elucidate the mutually respectful aspects of their relationship.

After a lifetime spent protecting his autonomy, vociferously resisting any attempt to restrict his personal freedom and upholding the same right for those on whose behalf he fought, in December 1912 Frank joined the Fabian Society and announced himself a 'candid friend' of the burgeoning Labour Party. He was the first peer to do so. Ostensibly he took this significant step to formalise his support for nationalisation. Fabian ethics dovetailed with his own in its animating principle of raising the fortunes of the working man, not by the pity of benevolence, but by 'the freest and fullest development of human quality and power'.[9] Sidney Olivier (1859-1943) wrote in *Fabian Tracts*, 'So far as man has attained freedom to do and be as he desires, he has attained it only through the evolution of society' and society's development in accordance with socialistic principles allows the individual 'to live in the best way conceivable' for the good of the whole community.[10] In a talk to the Portsmouth Fabians in 1913 Frank supported this principle, stating his belief that trade unionism would advance the cause of the working man palliatively as a temporary measure but that ultimately it came down to each individual to improve his lot through better education. I am, he wrote in 1916, a 'strong individualist and socialist'. His actions and the selection that follows prove it.

This book is dedicated to two gentlemen who have so enthusiastically supported and encouraged all my work on Frank Russell: John Slater and Ken Blackwell. I must also thank Ken for his invaluable contribution to the bibliography in Appendix I and John for reading many of the pieces I considered for this selection and for offering constructive advice. His emailed critiques became a regular early morning gift on opening my inbox. I'd like also to thank Bill Bruneau for similar treasures and for many thought-provoking conversations. Also, Ken Blackwell and Andy Bone for their assistance in annotating the 'Letters to Bertie'; Winchester College Archivist Suzanne Foster for her help deciphering the more obscure references in Frank's Winchester journal and letters to 'Mrs Dick'; the Warden and Scholars of Winchester College for permission to include the letters in this volume; John Lenz and Jared Hanson-Park for Greek translations; Tony Simpson for his guidance and advice in editing and compiling the book and for suggesting its subtitle; Tom Unterrainer for editing the final draft; and my husband Ian for proof-reading and for everything else he did in every way imaginable to support me through this project.

Throughout this work I have referred to the Russell brothers as 'Frank' and 'Bertie', principally to avoid confusion, but also to be consistent with the manner in which they addressed each other. In his lifetime, Frank was known to the world as 'Russell' but his better-known brother is also more usually referred to by this title. No offence is intended and hopefully none caused.

Notes

1. E.S.P. Haynes, 'The Late Earl Russell and Divorce Law Reform', *Saturday Review*, vol. 151 no. 3933 (14 Mar 1931), p. 369.
2. *ibid.*
3. Address given by Lord Snell at Telegraph House, 30 March 1931 (Add MS 58556).
4. Desmond MacCarthy 'Books in General', *New Statesman*, 3 Mar 1923, p. 632.
5. Laurence Housman letter to Frank, 4 Apr 1924, RA1, Box 7.32, 080202.
6. MLA, p.338-9.
7. *Lay Sermons*, p.15. The Parable of the Vineyard Workers is at Matthew 20: 1-16.
8. 'H', 'The Man As He Is: Earl Russell', *Daily Citizen*, 13 Aug 1913.
9. Ball, p.74.
10. Olivier, p.97-99.

1. Frank and Rachel, *c.* 1871-2.

1.1 Frank at Winchester College, 1881.

Chapter 1

Formative Years

Juvenile Letters

For Christmas 1870, Frank's grandmama, Lady Stanley of Alderley, sent him Lear's *Book of Nonsense*. After listening to his parents making up their own, the five-year-old Frank had a go himself and sent the result to Maude Stanley:[1]

Dear Aunt Maude
There was an old man of Surat who was always eating a cat
When once by mistake he ate up a rake
That greedy old man of Surat.
Frank Russell
1870

In summer 1873, the Amberleys employed Douglas Alexander Spalding as a tutor for Frank on the recommendation of John Stuart Mill. Spalding's main area of interest was biological science. Frank was allowed to assist in his experiments. Spalding's influence is evident in the eight-year-old Frank's letter to Lady Stanley:[2]

3 September 1873

Dear Grandmama
I was stung to-day on the sole of my foot, by a bee.
I go barefoot & I like it.
The wasps & bees are fighting vigorously, the wasps are eating the honey & even the bees themselves all except their heads. They eat the bees alive.
We took a hive of honey today without killing the bees.
Thank-you very much for the watch you sent (to) me. It does not go, but Mr Spalding will take it to a watchmaker. He does not think there is much the matter with it. It went for 64/32 of an hour after it came. It was not going when it came.
I was stung just before I began this letter; I am quite well now.
Frank Russell

A Winchester Journal

Frank's mother, Kate, and younger sister, Rachel, died in 1874. After the death of their father, Johnny, Viscount Amberley, in 1876, Frank and Bertie were sent to live with their Russell grandparents at Pembroke Lodge ('PL'). For Frank, the experience was not a happy one. After two years trying and failing to control him, the Russells sent him to Cheam preparatory school and then Winchester College. Frank's 'private' Winchester journal gives an amusing insight into life in the school begun by William of Wykeham in the fourteenth century and the preoccupations of the average 'Wykehamist'. The language used is strictly that of Winchester – the so-called Winchester *notions* that every boy had two weeks to learn when he first arrived and would then be examined on. All notions in the following extract are italicised and a glossary provided for non-Wykehamist readers on p. 22. Frank had high hopes for writing a book of notions. He discussed it with the headmaster on 6 November 1883, but it would be overtaken by events.

This extract from Frank's journal begins in January 1880 and finishes at Easter with the highlight of the year: the general election. Frank was an able but somewhat lackadaisical student. Classes were organised by performance rather than age and Frank had just moved up to the senior division of 'Middle Part', with all 'Senior Part' still ahead of him.

January 1880
23: ... Gallery roll came down today: I am still in Upper Six...
24: There was a *jaw* about our mission in the East End of London[3] to hear which I *sociused* Charlesworth jnr. ...
26: Began our first lesson of Homer this evening: it is not much more *swink* than Phoenissae...
28: Can't *jockey up* in Toye's[4] div. now I suppose 'cos I haven't *mugged* decently yet...
30: ... I have *firked* my Stylographic Pen[5] to be mended, the point broke off about a fortnight ago in my pocket.
31: ... Jockeyed up 8 places today at Livy. Begin reading *The Newcomes* by Thackeray. Have finished *Jane Eyre* by one Currer Bell.

February
1: Sunday. ... Bummer[6] preached in chantry this evening: a very good sermon about doing our best to keep up our ignorance of evil & our shame of doing wickedness as being shields which God has given us to resist them. He also said how awful a thing it was to teach others the knowledge of good and evil. 'Better were it for that man that he had never been born.' ... Root[7] preached in middle chapel but as I was engaged in watching the sun moving on the wall I did not hear much of the sermon...
4: ...I am 27th in the *Cuse* and 11th junior *up to books*.[8] ... I took 1 ¼ hours tonight to do 15 lines of Homer but I find our verses fairly easy.
5: ... I have read about 200 pages of *The Newcomes* there are 800 nearly altogether...
6: ... Got my stylographic pen back today and am writing this with it. It has been mended very successfully as far as I can make out but when they sent it me it had a horrid sort of purple ink in it which I have just replaced with black. It is 'bleeding' furiously at this moment but no doubt that will be

remedied in time…

7: …Toye gave us a sort of examina paper today on the Horace and Homer we had been doing… Got 40 out of 48 in verses this time…

9: Ye old stylograph is doing very well…

10: Knew my Homer awfully well this morning got every question right & knew my history better than I *tugly* do. … I have been using this pen up to books today with the most perfect success and my notes look much clearer than the pencil ones…

11: … In *toy-time* tonight we have a Verse Task, 20 Morning Lines, Homer and History all to be known before 10 a.m. tomorrow: Toye does put on the pressure.

13: … Have just finished *Charles O'Malley* by Lever. Am reading a book at Wells' called *Hugh Russell at Harrow*. Am still very low up to books. I am sitting in Lea's *toys* and in other ways I feel much more swagger than formerly. Perhaps it is 'the knowledge of evil, like a god' alas!! how dear it costs!!

16: …24th in Cuse = 3rd junior a rise of one place…

17: *Tick* 1s 9d at Octo's[9] in the course of the afternoon… Hang about shops most of the afternoon… Am getting on slowly with *Newcomes*.

18: Five weeks more to end of term! hurrah! I have *grubbed* a frantic lot today and am *grubbing suction* at this moment. Sit in Lea's toys nearly every night. … *Shirk* into shops pretty often now but haven't been nailed this half…

19: … Went down river in an old tub with Dumas… Found Wigg [and others] at boat-house. *Tight-nailed* by Wigg with *boots* on; wonder if he expects me to pay.[10]

20: Had to pay Wigg a bob this evening for fines… Toye was awfully *frout* this morning at Livy *croppled* about 6 men and didn't let us out till nearly 12:15…

21: …Toye saw my stylographic pen but grumbled at it rather: I think he pressed too hard when he used it…

23: …Have finished *Newcombes*. Am reading *Henry Esmond*.

March

1: … 23rd in Cuse: have *jockeyed* Dickinson snr at last…

2: …Jockey up the morning lines eight places, one place more for Homer, lose five places in history…

5: …Jockey up in *stinks* this afternoon…

7: Sunday. Got a note from Mrs Jahra before breakfast: *leave out* to dinner. …Having got myself as decent as I could & being in a beastly funk I laid my hand on Jahra's gate exactly as college struck one.[11] … Ridding was very amusing and my coyness did not last long. He said that he had been tied to school-life his whole existence except one year after he took his degree & his father was a schoolmaster before him. … Mrs Jahra is hardly *cud* but I thought, ladylike. …Was higher up to books yesterday than I have in this term namely 9th senior…

8: … Am reading *Gil Blas* in French. … Lawrie in our div. has started a stylographic pen.

10: … Jockey up from junior to second senior for knowing that *cubit* is derived from *cubitus*, the outstretched arm, and when I get there Toye sees my notes among Livy pages which he thinks at first are *welching* notes but finds they aren't. His expression when he sees them is 'What in the name of fortune have you got there? Russell!'...

11: ... There are liberal placards up everywhere saying 'vote for Baring' etc. etc.[12] No conservative ones have appeared yet.

12: ... Freshfield[13] takes some Tory placards to cloisters this afternoon. Old Scrunter tears one down gets awfully groaned...

13: ... Begin paying off ticks in shops. David Horndon and some other men attack a man carrying some liberal placards, one of them gets paste pot over his head and clothes. ... Any amount of conservative placards are pasted up over commoners and several hung up in Stoney's classroom.[14]

15: ... At stinks I wrote on my blotting-paper 'Plump for Baring', 'Down with Dizzy' so Allan started an opposition bit with 'Dear old Dizzy, Down with the reds' which Kitty Hill[15] nailing gave him to write out. ... 'Beaconsfield for England' is a new conservative placard...

16: ...On rising this morning a liberal placard appeared posted on Root's house. But after chapel it had disappeared. Owing to my daring to express a feeling of joy on seeing it there I got smitten on the head: under which blow I still smart. ... A liberal bill sticker is attached in King's gate street by a mob of the school...

17: Gladstone made 5 speeches on his way from London to Edinburgh yesterday and made the train an hour late. There is a blue placard on further end of Racquet Court which the Reds have not yet pulled down. We have defaced all their red ones. There is a staunch liberal butcher in King's gate street who hangs up 3 blues in his shop and guards them zealously...[16]

18: ...There are some red placards on Fearon's *fives* court which I propose to have down. Root has started a *bobby* between 5 to 6 to keep his men from splicing stones at the *cads*...

19: ... Latin questions this morning, Euclid in the afternoon. ... Get last *English Mechanic* I shall have this term.[17] Notion: cads are going to mob us as we go to the station next Wednesday...

20: ... Root's Bobby took Wigg's name yesterday as he saw him tearing down a blue placard. ... Parliament's last sitting today. ... Take *Middlemarch* out of the library; have finished *Vicar of Bullhampton*, good but stretched rather long.

23: ... Results at 2:30: 50th in French, 28th in Stinks, 14th left down.[18]

24: No cad *mill*, as everyone expected so that my new *roker* bought for the occasion proved useless. ... Reach PL about 11:30... Play draughts with Bertie and chess with granny in evening. Read *Dr Thorne* by Trollope on my journey...

25: ... At 7:00 go to great Liberal meeting at St James's Hall for Sir A Hobhouse & Mr John Morley...[19] Very enthusiastic and amusing...

27: Saw in *Surrey Comet* this morning that Uncle Rollo was hissed at a Tory meeting in Richmond last night... Uncle Rollo spoke at a working men's meeting in Richmond today...

30: ... Uncle Rollo brings up some Liberal placards & ballot papers to show how to vote... Go in evening to Wimbledon to Liberal meeting to hear Stern...[20]

April
1: ... Go to meeting at 4 o'clock this afternoon at Petersham School. Uncle
Rollo in the chair. Lasted an hour. Very good one. Bertie goes. Drive
afterwards with Bertie and Uncle Rollo to Ham on Stern's drag: do some
canvassing on the way. Bertie enjoyed it tremendously. Splendid day for
everything.
2: ... Go to Herbert Gladstone's meeting at Twickenham... Uncle Rollo
chairman 8 min. speech. Meeting rather noisy: asked many questions:
Herbert answered them all & spoke splendidly, wonderful...
5: Drove down to the polling in Richmond to-day with Granny & Bertie &
Uncle Rollo & Auntie. I walked right into the polling place: saw the ballot
boxes & the places where they put their crosses. Then Uncle Rollo and I
went to Red Lion Square to hear the result of Middlesex announced...
Gladstone (L) out: beaten by 4,000. He seemed not at all dispirited. Polling
for Midlothian today: if Gladstone senior gets in for Mid-L he will resign
Leeds & perhaps Herbert may contest it... Heard Midlothian at 9:30 p.m.
Gladstone in by 211... hurrah! hurrah! hurrah!!![21]

Frank's journal for the summer term at Winchester was much taken up with
sporting events, exams and turbulent friendships. The next extant diary is for
1883. As Frank approached his eighteenth birthday he spent an eventful
summer employed in four characteristically diverse occupations: telegraphy,
theosophy, cramming for his Oxford entrance exam and teaching Bertie
Euclid's propositions.
    In the summer of 1879, Frank had set up his telegraphic system at PL, which
he then described thus:

The line wire is 500 yd of No 11 B.W.G. galvanized iron wire fixed to the
trees by staples 1 1.2 in. long. The instruments are needle, and it is worked
by a 4-cell Daniell at one end, and a 2-cell Leclanché at the other: though
one cell is sufficient to produce a marked deflection. Earth is made by a
wire would round water pipes.[22]

In the summer of 1880, on his way back to PL, he made purchases to improve
it:

July 31st. ... went with Aunt Maude to Dale & Crampton & bought 2
Anderson patent cells, 2 Leclanché, 2 dozen insulators, a small magnet,
some chemicals & two bell pushes & told him to send them to Richmond...

But not until the 1883 diary do we find a more detailed account showing his
enthusiasm for it, oddly juxtaposed with his being 'so much more occupied in
revolving new ideas of the universe in my mind' than he was about Oxford.

July 1883
28: [London] ...called at the Garden Mansions, left *Zanoni*, St George was
out, but I found and carried off *The Occult World*...[23] [PL] did some work in
my laboratory & charged my 10 cell Daniell.
29: Sunday. ... I worked a good deal in the lab & fitted up 5 of Granule cells
& set up a galvanometer... Finished *The Occult World* & strange to say I half

13

believe in it.

30: Mugged this morning, then repaired the leading in wire at the stables with Phillips' assistance & have made a good job of that. Taught Miss Bühler the elementary parts of telegraphing on my Sounder today...[24]

August

1: The Parcels Post came into operation today & Uncle Rollo received a book from Bickers tonight by it... Read Homer in the morning: then gave Miss Bühler a telegraph lesson, in which she did very well. Tested the line today, found the resistance about the same as it used to be, 36w. Set up 4 small cells which I find work the instrument all right through the line. ...I am reading the Reports of the Psychical Society which are very interesting, especially those on Thought transference... I have been working my Sounders through line today & they go very well. Dale's cell though a little troublesome to set up is really very powerful & constant when set up.

2: Sent some SN coils to Dale today to fit up as telegraph instruments as I have always been unable to get the needle to swing well... Miss Bühler had a lesson with the Sounders in separate rooms today & we got on perfectly. Finished the 5th book of the *Iliad* this evening.

3: Did some Homer till 10, then carried 4 chloride cells over to the stables with Phillips & set up the other instrument there. At 11 to 12:15 I had a long telegraphic conversation with Miss Bühler in which we succeeded admirably... After luncheon I walked down to the station to meet Carew... [25] I shewed him all my electrical apparatus & Miss Bühler kindly telegraphed a sentence from the stables to show how it was done...

4:. ... Carew and I went to London about 9, called on St George at the Garden Mansions: he lent me *A Strange Story*[26] and some other books... We then walked on to St Paul's had a look in there, and then went to hear some cases in the New Law Courts which I had never been inside before... After [tea] we wound some bobbins for my new Sounder with the sewing machine... [and] paraffined some coils...

5: Sunday. ... Worked in my laboratory all the afternoon, tried my new electromagnet that I am making for a Sounder...

6: ... I exploded a bottle of oxyhydrogen by the spark this morning for Carew's amusement, which I had decomposed by electricity on Sunday.

8: Did a good deal of telegraphing this morning & put new keys onto the Sounders far nicer than the old ones. I lent Carew the Psychical Reports... went with St George to Bishopsgate Street where at the house of a Mr Smith we held a séance. Present: Prof Henry Sidgwick[27] [and others]... All that we obtained after sitting for a long time in darkness in a very stuffy room was movement of a light table & raps, but it would not move without contact...

9: ... I telegraphed with Miss Bühler: we have got on wonderfully & I can read pretty well & quickly when she sends without stopping between each letter. I gave Bertie his first lesson in Euclid this afternoon – he is going to come to me to learn it by Hawtrey's method[28] & is sure to prove a credit to his teacher. He did very well indeed & we got half through the definitions.

10: Another good spell of Homer this morning, got through 450 lines! Then some telegraphing: when we tried again in the evening we could not succeed & I failed to discover the cause. One of the battery wires at the stables has been eaten away five times so I am going to put a GP wire there.

I rewound my magnet coils on the Sounder here with finer wire yesterday – it works much better. ... I have finished & returned *A Strange Story*...

11: ... altered the arrangements of the wires & led them in in a far neater & safer fashion so that I think they will not now get out of order easily. In the afternoon came the schoolchildren to celebrate my birthday, 9 boys & 9 girls... Miss Bühler & I exhibited some telegraphy to them which I think interested them. At 7 they sung a few songs, cheered me & then departed.

12: Sunday. I attained the age of 18 today & half sorry I am to be so old though I feel quite that age. I got a pretty jug from Granny, Carlyle's [*On the*] *Choice of Books* from Auntie, a toolbox the result of Bertie's first attempts at carpentering with Figg's aid...

13: ... Bertie's Euclid lesson after luncheon: we did Prop. 1 in which he was naturally very much interested & did very well...

14: Did 400 lines of Homer this morning then showed the telegraph to Martha Bennett, the clerk of Petersham Post Office, whom I had asked to see it...

15: Did 200 lines this morning and finished the five books I want for smalls. Then I *thoked*. We had our last telegraph lesson this morning & then I took it down & set it up so that Miss Bühler might practice in my room by herself [while Frank was away visiting the Howards at Naworth Castle].

28: ... I read two chapters of Madam Blavatsky's *Isis Unveiled* a very interesting book on astral science which St George is reading...

September

1: [Haslemere] ... I began my work today & did the whole of the 3rd Philippic...

4: Jowett wrote to Granny a short time ago just to say he hoped I was reading with a tutor & this has so perturbed their ignorant minds that they have forthwith hustled up & down till they got one by Jowett's aid & the man called Owen is coming tomorrow...[29] Did the 3rd Prop. with Bertie this morning, he is getting along well with his Euclid... I had a long conversation with Auntie on astral subjects this afternoon, she was very perverse and quite content with an attitude of unreasoning disbelief. She seemed quite surprised at my now firm belief in thought reading & was altogether very obstinate.

6: ... Took Bertie in the 5th Prop. this afternoon but I was hasty & he was dull & so we did not manage to do it very well...

7: ... Bertie successfully mastered the Pons Asinorum this evening, & in fact did it very well... Received some books from Wells[30] today, *Esoteric Buddhism, Occult World* & a splendid new book on Electricity & 'de Amicitia'[31]...

9: Sunday. ... I read a great part of the *Heir of Redclyffe*[32] today, a very touching & beautiful part, Philip's illness and Guy's death. I began *Esoteric Buddhism* by Sinnett this evening: it is a book of the deepest interest but it is very hard to grasp its meaning...

11: ... Got to the end of the 11th Proposition with Bertie tonight – Granny has exaggerated fears of half-an-hour at a time injuring his mind by overwork!...

12: ... Props X and XI with Bertie tonight.

13: ... The amount of telegraphic conversation we have now is enormous &

we often send without an acknowledgement between the words…
14: … I did the 12th Prop. with Bertie tonight & so finished Hawtrey's book: he has gone through them all with great success & seems to me to thoroughly understand them. I am very proud of my pupil…
16: Sunday. … We went to Church at Haslemere in the morning… Sermon a little better than last Sunday but very poor: the curate said that he could not think that reverence of spirit could exist without reverence of form or that prayers could count if not said kneeling! …
18: … I finished *Esoteric Buddhism* last night, I have been very deeply interested in it but cannot yet give its doctrines my complete adhesion. I was amused to hear them laughing at the Occult World today as if their knowledge was so complete![33]
20: … I have read nearly 200 pp. of Nasmyth's *Autobiography* today: & some new books came, the most interesting of which are Jennings' *Rosicrucians* & Mallock's *Is Life Worth Living?*[34] I hear the most fearful wailing going on next door from Bertie & Miss Bühler at their approaching separation: there is one of the chief evils of the governess system… The wailing is really terrible & very prolonged.
21: … I got a letter from St George today about the absurdity of the general anthropomorphic conception of God, which I answered to say that I thoroughly agreed with him & gave in my belief to Esoteric Science or Religion.
22: … I have begun reading Spencer's *Study of Sociology*[35] & imagine it will be very interesting…

September saw 'the last of Owen', which was followed by a trip to Winchester during which Frank shared his newfound Buddhist beliefs with the closest friend of his final year there, Lionel Pigot Johnson (1867-1902), poet, critic and founder member of the Rhymer's Club (1890).

An Oxford Journal
In early October Frank sat his 'smalls', during which he found himself on one occasion alone in the library where 'I read Max Müller's preface to his translation of Kant's *Kritik der reinen Vernunft*[36] & was quite carried away by it & made intensely anxious to read the book'. He matriculated on 15 October to become a Balliol man. The following day he attended his first Agamemnon lecture delivered by his tutor Evelyn Abbott ('very good'). Most of his early journal is concerned with socialising. Two events stand out:

October 28: Sunday. … Varsity sermon at 10:30. Butler of Harrow preached, mediocre… second sermon by Boyd Carpenter,[37] which was quite magnificent & which I enjoyed thoroughly. … [in the afternoon] to my great pleasure Boyd Carpenter came as Aunt Maude had warned me. He did not stay long, but talked about *Esoterica Buddhism*. I however rather avoided going deeply into it, considering how little I knew him & how we must differ. It was very kind of him to come & I was delighted to see him…

November 27: The Warden of Keble kindly asked me to meet Gladstone, who is staying with him, at tea, so I joyfully went. I did not have the chance of doing much more than saying *salve et vale*, but I was able to look at him.

He seemed much older than I should have thought. I had a bit of a talk with Max Müller about Buddhism there & he was very interesting but hopelessly esoteric.

In his end of year summary, Frank laid out his religious conversion:

> To me a far more important event [than his first term at Oxford] has been my conversion from Christianity to what I first called Buddhism but now Theosophy or Esoteric Truth... Briefly what I believe now is this: that all faith is the result of intuition or spiritual perception, that this is the only infallible guide & the one thing to be most carefully cultivated by the moral life & by abstinence from meat & wine among other things: I also accept the philosophy of Devachan, Nirvana & successive reincarnations & believe in the possibility of knowing all things by going the right way to work. All these ideas have become clearer to me by constant meditation & have brought me a firm faith & a peace that cannot be taken away, besides by making me realize the infinite littleness of this life giving me that much justly praised αταραξία or tranquillity of mind. Of course this has resulted in moral improvement & I am beginning through my conceit to see how much room there is for more...

His 1884 journal, though still mostly concerned with daily comings-and-goings, has some interesting entries demonstrating Frank's developing critical faculty, his interests and opportunities afforded by his status. The academic year ended with an epic bicycle tour of the south-west of England ending in Winchester in time for that great cricketing event of the year: Eton Match. The tour spanned 250 miles over 7 days without the benefit of pneumatic tyres!

January
19: [Oxford] ... Saw Abbott and arranged my lectures – I am going to Robinson's Inductive Logic, Papillon's de Corona and Paravi's Juvenal... Read and got Darwin's *Descent of Man* out of the Union library...
25: ... Have at last finished *Progress & Poverty*[38] – it has been very interesting & gives one plenty to think about...

February
24: Sunday. ... assembled in my rooms Maurice, Hobhouse, Charley, Louis Mallet, Jackson & Newbolt to form a Reading Society.[39] I was President as they met in my rooms: we passed some rules, meet on Sundays at 9, read each for 10 mins, appointed Newbolt permanent secretary, limited numbers to the present 7, etc. Then we fell to read, Charley read Byron's 'Dream': Anak[40] some Carlyle: Jackson Wordsworth's 'Intimations of Immortality': Mallet some Swinburne: Hobhouse some of Spencer's *Principles of Psychology*: I read from *Light of Asia*: & Maurice some Emily Bronte: it was very pleasant & successful...

March
4: ...Wrote to Wigg[41] for an hour, & sent 8 pages – I had received 16 from him this morning as he had been alarmed at my last letter in which I apparently said conscience was the only intelligible guide: I answered with

a discourse on righteousness, . . .,[42] God indefinable, incomprehensible, morality leading to religion, not vice versa. This promises to be the beginning of an interesting correspondence...

6: ... Went on to the Max Müllers and there met [Henry] George: he is very American in speech but his words are good and I was glad to meet him. He is a short man, full of his subject...

7: ... I went to [Henry] George after Hall, he was lecturing in the Clarendon rooms.[43] The meeting was a very noisy... George spoke very vaguely, utterly failed to answer the questions Marshall[44] put to him, as well as many others. I came away at 10 & went for a walk round Professoropolis to air myself...

20: [Marlborough College] Went to breakfast with Beesly,[45] one of the dons, who was to have taken us in but refused, because according to Maurice being a violent radical, he was afraid of being laughed at for taking a peer into his house!...

21: ... My general opinion of Marlborough is that it is not a school or place I should ever get to love, that their dormitories are too crowded, & toilet arrangements insufficient, the studies & other divisions separate the various parts of the school from each other too much: the arbitrary & strange division into houses strikes a stranger but I suppose acts all right: the outhouses seem too much cut off – the college buildings & chapel are quite hideous. The whole system of management seems to me a curious mixture of Oxford ideas with private school ways...

22: [PL] ... I began Bertie's Euclid again – he seems to remember it very well...

April

20: [Oxford] ... We had a lively meeting [of the Unconventionals] with less doleful pieces than usual. I read a grand bit of 'In Memoriam' near the end: Charley read some *Autocrat*...[46]

27: It was quite unusually interesting at Hawkins' – Boas, Spender, Bruce & Saunders[47] talked philosophy & discussed materialism & utilitarianism quite seriously & soberly. ... The Unconventionals met tonight... I read the last few pages of Myers' *Modern Essays* on the religion of Beauty.

May

2: ...Col. Olcott[48] & Willy[49] turned up at luncheon after which we sat & smoked till after 4 talking about various things. I maintained the theory of Christianity against which he [Olcott] was much too bitter & of much of which he seemed to take a very prejudicial view: & in some things appeared actually unable to grasp their meaning. At 8:30 came to meet him Eliot, Spender, Maurice, Hobhouse & Charley, bringing with him Haverfield, Northcote & Edwards of Merton, his new *pax*.[50] Eliot & Haverfield were rather bitter opponents but went away about 10:30 after which he seemed more at his ease & talked for another hour. I think the discussion was a success on the whole... The conclusions I came to about him were, that he was as far as I could see, sincere & meant what he said, very wide minded & quite ready to understand that he must expect opposition: he is not refined, but he does not thrust himself forward as much as Americans generally do, though he seems to me to have far too great an idea of his own personality for a true 'contemplator' of so vast a system. I do not like his antagonism of Christianity which I think he regards in an unfair light though it may have been that I did not make plain the difference between my idealised Christ, & the dogma of the Churches.

18: Bertie's 12th birthday, height 4'6" – didn't give him anything…

30: … Looked over my paper against Bishops in the House of Lords today & read it to the Palmerstone in the evening. I am afraid it was what Hobhouse would call priggish & too like a sermon but they seemed pleased with it & I was most unexpectedly pleased at the very liberal tone they adopted in discussing it afterwards…

June

1: Sunday. … Left the Unconventionals at 9:45 & went in to the Master's party as he had asked me… talked a good deal with Sir R Morier & Lowell the American minister,[51] who is very pleasant, honest & amusing… I had a rare experience afterwards, at about 11:15 as the Master asked me at Morier's suggestion to come to the smoking room… I argued long on the duty of preaching tolerance there with Hardinge of Balliol, fellow of All Souls:[52] he is a very nice young man but hopelessly conventional. The Master went to bed at 12 but I stayed there till nearly 1 before I said goodnight. I enjoyed myself immensely & had a lot of very interesting talk, & was pleased to listen to Lowell, felt like a happy heathen when I went to bed.

3: … I have been reading a great deal of *Leaves of Grass* lately, a book by an American, Walt Whitman, written in lines as if meant to be poetry, but with no scansion or even rhythm. It breathes of nature & is a very catholic production, embraces all creeds, religions, & races: in spite of this I cannot trust it because of the strong undercurrent of sensuality I seem to detect all through it…[53]

8: Sunday. We went to 'Varsity sermon at New College by Dean Burgon:[54] the best treat I have had since I have been up here, he preached in quite the old orthodox personal God style, assuming literally from Genesis cc. 1-3: talking about the Deity's counsels, decrees & hints in the calmest way. It sounds incredible to us nowadays but after all it is only the logical Church position, though it exposes more clearly than most sermons how little right the present Church has to remain. He went on to deprecate women's higher education as violating a divine decree, & regretted that no provision was made for Church Catechism in our honour schools, etc. … Poor man! he was so earnest that one could not help being sorry that he was so blind…

10: Have been reading Virgil steadily lately, finished the *Aeneid,* as also Aeschylus' *Choephorae.* I have arranged my bicycling tour today: it will lie through PL, Rochester, Sittingbourne, Canterbury, Charing, Cranbrook, Lewes, Brighton, New Shoreham, Worthing, Arundel, Chichester, Cosham & Botley to Winchester where I shall arrive in time for Eton Match after 250m riding…

18: … Started on my bicycle at 11… crossed Magdalen Bridge & left Oxford. I had several hills to walk after Benson, & found roads loose everywhere. I lunched at Maidenhead & after starting from there, the wind against me added to all else[55] made me so exhausted that I turned into a pub about 9 miles from home & drank 5d of whisky which just got me home at 5:30...

19: [PL] My people are rather in a ferment about Marson the nice new curate. He preached a sermon against Christ's bodily ascension which was complained of, so the Bishop of Rochester has inhibited him. Good for the Church! We are petitioning, etc. but I don't suppose will succeed...

20: Marson saw the Bishop of Rochester today – it is hopeless, they cannot agree: the Bishop believes in heaven as a locality! & thinks Marson ought to too! I think on the whole the quintessence of inanity in religious matters may be looked for in a bishop.[56]

21: Longest day: I am off on the beginning of a week's bicycling tour, to Rochester tonight........ I have had a most enjoyable tour & will try to give some account of it now it is all over... My first day's ride started from Vauxhall which I had reached by train was dull & almost disheartening – it began with 6 miles of paved & crowded street, with tramways all along it. Climbed over Blackheath & up Shooter's Hill, it gave me quite a new idea of London making it look much more like old bird's eye views of it than anyone can imagine now. Riding was pain & grief to me till Dartford where there was a charming little church with nice black oak stalls & an old oak carved pulpit. Gravesend was funny as were all the glimpses of the Thames I got, with its shipping & its ever widening mouth. After Dartford, the roads were better though very loose all the way. All the Kent characteristics appeared, brick kilns, windmills, corn, chalk, all except hops. Smoked my pipe on top of the hill at Rochester & talked to an old inhabitant. 'Tis a pretty little town to look at but the Cathedral is poor with the exception of one gate. There is a nice piece called the Castle Gardens where I sat after supper while a band played & the townspeople promenaded up & down.

22: Sunday. Through Sittingbourne which is a poor place, up a long hill at Chatham on starting, over roads still very loose & country still bearing on it the stamp of Kent. I made my way to Canterbury. I washed & went to Cathedral – found myself in time for the anthem & sermon. Smoked a pipe in the precincts after service & was just going to call on the Parries in great trepidation when I met Sydney who invited me cordially to supper – Mrs Parry was very kind & absolutely insisted on my staying there which I was very much pleased to do though looking rather odd in my bicycling clothes.[57]

23: *Thoked* steadily all morning. Sydney who is between his Greats papers and viva came to the Dane John[58] with me & we basked in the sun talking & smoking. Started at 3 p.m. had a long pull uphill to Challock but fairly easy riding & very pretty lanes. Charing which I flew through at a great pace looked very nice. Got to Cranbrook towards suppertime & got there some letters. Took a walk round about in the evening – it is very lonely & seems to have a school there.[59] Plenty of windmills but I am in the Weald of Kent & see more trees than chalk, a state of things I prefer.

24: Hard uphill work soon after starting followed by a dull road along the crest of a range of hills, got very stony near Lewes with strong headwind (it having of course changed at Canterbury) which made my last few miles hard tiring work. Nice inn the 'Bear' in Lewes – one drawback, but I believe it quite accidental, viz that there were several bugs in my bed – there is no need for me to describe what has often been done before, suffice it to see I did not sleep much – ugh! There are very nice confectioners' shops here.

The town lies in a hollow, I don't care for it much on the whole: it has a castle which I went over.

25: Very pleasant riding all day today. I succeeded in avoiding the greater part of Brighton & rode afterwards along the shore, where I was much invigorated by the sea air. Lunched at Worthing & had a very pleasant bathe in some seawater baths. From there to Arundel, very good road & very good pace. The old castle is not much but there is a most magnificent new Catholic Church built by the Duke of Norfolk[60] which a man kindly showed me over: it is enormous & very tastefully designed – the various altars were lovely. Talked to some discharged soldiers who were tramping, told them to go to the Charity Organization & gave them a severe jaw, but of course gave way in the end & relieved them – I hope not wrongly. Had tea at Arundel & started for Chichester about 7, went a tremendous pace & did 10 ½ miles in 45 mins. i.e. a rate of 14 m.p.h.! I am getting stronger everyday & feel very healthy & happy. The weather has been perfect throughout.

26: I purchased at Chichester at an old bookshop 15 volumes bound in beautiful red Morocco containing the whole of Dickens in very good paper & ink: I am delighted with them. Was shown over the Cathedral this morning by a nice old verger – it is extremely interesting inside – though poor externally. We talked about Dean Burgon & he said he was very hard to get on with & always irritating people but so kind that one could not be angry with him long. I went to morning service, choir not [*missing word*] saw Burgon there. Rode to Cosham where I lunched, found my journey on from there to Botley 3 miles longer than I had expected so had to put it on to be in time for Kelsall[61] who was to meet me there. Was only 10 mins late, average today 12 m.p.h. Had a bath at Botley then Kelsall & I went for a stroll, then came in & had a feed, a large vegetarian grub, & then went out again & I had a smoke. He left about 10:30 & I went to bed. Was glad of his conversation: my spirits are rising fast as Winchester draws near.

27: Rose & breakfasted early, oh! such a glorious day: got into Winchester at 9:35…

Glossary of *Notions*:[62]

Bobby: policing.

Boots & Leather: a peel of the commoner bells.

Cad: another term for *fags* or juniors who were sweated to run errands for seniors.

Croppled: to be punished with additional work for not preparing for lessons.

Cud: pretty.

Cuse: the weekly division order posted by the master assessing the boys in classics - 'cuse' (to rhyme with 'use') taken from the last syllable of 'classicus'.

Firk: to send or send away (from Anglo-Saxon, *fercian*).

Fives: Winchester Football, 5-a-side.

Frout: angry, hence terrifying (from Anglo-Saxon *froht*).

Gallery: dormitory.

Grubbing: eating; *grubbing suction*: eating sweets.

Jaw: a lecture.

Jockey up: to gain a place.

Mill: a fight

Mug: to study or work.

Pax: an intimate friend.

Roker: a stick or poker.

Shirk: skiving or going somewhere without leave.

Socius: to walk with.

Stinks: science.

Swink: hard work.

Thoke: to be idle.

Tick: credit.

Tight: the worst there is

Toy-time: evening study or prep. Derived from *toys* – a cabinet that opened into a desk and shelves at which senior boys sat to work and which held all their paraphernalia.

Tugly: ordinarily (*tug* was something common or regular – derivation unknown).

Up to books: in lessons or classes, in which benches the boys sat on were called 'books' and the boys literally moved up or down according to their performance.

Welching: cheating.

Notes

1. DSA 175/2. Kate Amberley wrote that she had used 'Surat' in her own rhyme. Otherwise, the ideas were all Frank's.
2. DSA 104/2.
3. The School Mission was established by headmaster Revd Dr George Ridding (1828-1904) in 1876 in Bromley-by-Bow, East London.
4. Arlingham James Toye (1842-1899), the only master apparently without a nickname.
5. The 'stylo' was the first mass produced fountain pen – a recent invention, patent 1875. The writing tip consisted of a metal tube containing a fine wire to regulate ink flow. Frank's was a Christmas gift from Lady Stanley. In the early 1880s stylos were quickly superseded by the nibbed fountain pen (https://vintagepens.com/stylos.shtml, accessed 21 Jul 2021).
6. This unfortunate nickname appears to have been ascribed to the minister of the School Mission, Mr Dunne.
7. Revd John Trant Bramston (1843-1931) was nicknamed 'Root' as in 'the root of all evil'.
8. The lower ranking in *Cuse* suggests Frank was less good at classics than his other subjects.
9. Octo's was a popular confectioners and cakeshop which allowed the boys up to 10 shillings *tick* or credit.
10. Wigg was Frank's gallery prefect, so the entry suggests Frank got caught where he shouldn't have been and expected to be punished accordingly!
11. 'Jahra' was the headmaster's nickname; hence, his wife was 'Mrs Jahra'.
12. Francis George, Viscount Baring (1850-1929), liberal candidate for Winchester.
13. Edwin Hanson Freshfield (1864-1948), a particular friend from Frank's House.
14. William Liscombe Stonhouse (1837-1907). Frank was in his division in his third term.
15. Revd Arthur Du Boulay Hill (1850-), tutor of natural sciences.
16. National uniformity of political party colours dates from the mid-twentieth century, prior to which there were many regional variations. Gladstone favoured blue, while the conservatives campaigned under banners of red, white and blue, but generally favoured red, the colour of the Crown (Lippiatt, pp. 37-39).
17. *English Mechanic and World of Science* (1865-1926).
18. End of term results were read out by the Master for each div. Frank was 14th overall in his division – 'left down' meant he did not move up to the next division the following term.
19. Arthur Hobhouse (1819-1904) and John Morley (1838-1923) both contested Westminster, unsuccessfully.
20. Sydney James Stern (1844-1912) contested Mid-Surrey, unsuccessfully.
21. Herbert Gladstone won in Leeds and became his father's private secretary. Gladstone snr. became prime minister for the second time and chancellor of the exchequer for the fourth. 'Auntie' is Agatha Russell.
22. Description from 1879 diary, quoted in *MLA*, p.80.
23. Frank's Stanley cousin St George Lane Fox-Pitt (1856-1932) introduced Frank to theosophy and lent him numerous books – in this instance Edward Bulwer-Lytton's *Zanoni* (1842), a fictionalisation of a manuscript of the 17th century spiritual sect the Rosicrucians, and Alfred Percy Sinnett's recently published *The Occult World* (1883).
24. Phillips was a navy pensioner employed as watchman in the park who lived above PL's stables; Dora Bühler was Bertie's governess.

25. Edward Arthur Carew-Gibson (1868-1931), a *pax* of Frank's from Winchester.
26. Another novel by Bulwer-Lytton (1850).
27. Henry Sidgwick (1838-1900), Professor of Moral Philosophy, Cambridge.
28. Revd Stephen Hawtrey, *An Introduction to the Elements of Euclid* (1874).
29. Edward Charles Everard Owen (1860-1949), later a master at several Oxford colleges and then Harrow. Frank studied Cicero, Virgil and Demosthenes with him.
30. P&G Wells of Winchester.
31. 'On Friendship' by Cicero (44 BC).
32. By Charlotte Mary Yonge (1853).
33. Lady John hosted a garden party that afternoon and appears to have made light of Frank's new beliefs.
34. James Nasmyth, *James Nasmyth Engineer: An Autobiography* (1883); William Hurrell Mallock, *Is Life Worth Living?* (1879); Hargrave Jennings, *The Rosicrucians* (1879).
35. Published 1873. Herbert Spencer's work was much admired by the Amberleys.
36. F. Max Müller, *Immanuel Kant's Critique of Pure Reason* (1881).
37. Revd Dr William Boyd Carpenter (1841-1918), later President of the Society for Psychical Research (1912).
38. Henry George, *Progress and Poverty: An Enquiry into the Cause of Industrial Depressions and of Increase of Want with Increase of Wealth: The Remedy* (1879). Frank was introduced to the author on 6 March.
39. The so-called 'Unconventionals' (*MLA*, p. 98). Members were Maurice Llewelyn Davies (1864-1939), Leonard Trelawny Hobhouse (1864-1929), Charles Edward Sayle (1864-1924), Louis du Pan Mallet (1864-1936), Arthur Aubert Jackson (1864-1946), Francis George Newbolt (1863-1940), and Frank.
40. Newbolt's unexplained nickname.
41. Revd Montagu John Stone-Wigg (1861-1918), Frank's gallery prefect at Winchester (see fn.10), then curate of St Andrews, Westminster and later Bishop of New Guinea.
42. . . . : Literally, If (any)one wishes/will, etc. Frank quotes from John 7:17. In context, when the Jews questioned Jesus's teaching in the temple, he answered that the doctrine he preached was not his but God's, and that '*If any man will* do his will, he shall know of the doctrine, whether it be of God or whether I speak of myself.'
43. George's lecture is reviewed in full in *Oxford Chronicle*, 15 Mar 1884, p. 6.
44. Alfred Marshall (1842-1924), Lecturer & Fellow, Balliol 1883-4; Professor of Political Economy, Cambridge, 1885-1908.
45. Augustus Henry Beesly (1839-1909), Assistant Master. Maurice Llewelyn Davies, an old Marlburian, had taken Frank on a tour of his old school. Frank had taken Maurice to Winchester the previous December.
46. Oliver Wendell Holmes, *The Autocrat of the Breakfast Table* (1858).
47. Anthony Hope (Hawkins) (1863-1933), author; Frederick Samuel Boas (1862-1957); John Alfred Spender (1862-1942), later editor of *Westminster Gazette*; George Lewis Bruce (1862-1955).
48. Henry Steel Olcott (1832-1907), first president of the Theosophical Society, founded in New York, 1875.
49. Frank's cousin, William Augustus Lane Fox-Pitt (1858-1945).
50. Francis John Haverfield (1860-1919); George Russell Northcote (1863-1920); Osman Edwards (1864-1936). 'Eliot' is possibly Charles Norton Edgcumbe Eliot (1862-1931).
51. Sir Robert Morier (1826-1893), British Ambassador to Spain; James Russell Lowell (1819-1891), poet, critic and American Ambassador to England, 1880-85.
52. Sir Arthur Henry Hardinge (1859-1933).
53. *Leaves of Grass* (1855) was recommended by Lionel Johnson. On 4 Aug Frank

noted: 'I like the book better every time I read it.'

54. John William Burgon (1813-1888), Dean of Chichester Cathedral.

55. Frank had started feeling unwell the previous day.

56. The episode ended with the Bishop lifting his inhibition but the parish priest then refusing him the curacy, about which, Frank noted, Lady John expressed 'fumes of indignation'.

57. Head of the Parry household was Edward Parry (1830-1890), Bishop of Dover. Mrs Parry was Isabella, 4th daughter of the 1st Baron Stanley of Alderley and therefore Frank's great-aunt. Their 2nd son, Frederick Sydney Parry (1861-1941) of Winchester and Balliol was later private secretary to Prime Minister Alfred Balfour.

58. Dane John Gardens: a historic park within Canterbury's city walls.

59. Cranbrook (formerly Queen Elizabeth's) was founded in 1518 and received its royal charter from Elizabeth I in 1574.

60. Arundel Cathedral, commissioned by Henry, 15th Duke of Norfolk, in 1868 was opened on 1 July 1873.

61. John Edward Kelsall (1864-1924), another Balliol man whose family lived in nearby Fareham. Later, vicar of St Mary Magdalene, New Milton, Hampshire.

62. All definitions taken from Stevens.

2. Frank in Salt Lake City, 1885.

Chapter 2

An American 'Exile'

In May 1885, Frank's Balliol career came to an abrupt end when he was sent down by vice-chancellor Benjamin Jowett, supposedly for writing an 'improper letter' to another undergraduate. The Russells reacted by sending Frank on a six-month tour of the US to allow the dust to settle. Frank travelled with his tutor Graham Balfour (1858-1929). He wrote many letters home. Of those extant, the first two, addressed to the wife of the Second Master at Winchester, Sarah Richardson – 'Mrs Dick' – who was like a mother to Frank during his schooling and a lifelong friend thereafter – provide an insight into Frank's reaction to his expulsion. Thereafter, the letters – all bar one to Mrs Dick – cover the whole time Frank was in America. They reveal his growing sense of isolation in his 'exile' while simultaneously providing an amusing and informative account of young aristocrat's impressions of the New World in 1885.

1.

Ferishtah[1]
24 July 1885

Dear Mrs Richardson,
Thank you so much for your most kind and generous letter. I am more than all sorry to have distressed you so. But I have not the least intention of giving up my aspirations & hopes & ambitions, & as you say of ceasing to endeavour to do *exactly* what is right – as I see it. It is true I was tempted to renounce the struggle & when they all reviled & abused me I had a moment when I felt as if it were no longer worth doing right & that I might as well justify their abuse. But it has passed & I am going steadily, unswervingly, and unflinchingly to do that which seems to me right in God's sight, whether men approve or condemn, misunderstand or not – even if it costs me all my friends. I will not be untrue to myself, my Master, & I do not think I could really suffer for doing right. Certainly in spirit I feel free & honest & honourable – though I have made mistakes.

You & those like you it is who enable me to bear up in spite of much misconstruing: for I doubt if even I should have the strength to stand firm if everyone disbelieved in me.

27

I should like to see you immensely & like you to see this place: but you can hardly drive down from Bayswater: it is 10 miles. You might come by train from Clapham Junction to Hampton – about 35 minutes journey: or change at Richmond from Metropolitan. If you prefer it I will come & see you, except that I should like you to see the house. Just as you like to arrange.
Ever yours gratefully,
Russell

Earl's Court: 3.59 p.m.
Richmond: 4.27, 4.33
Hampton: 4.50

2.

Ferishtah
1 Sep 1885

Dear Mrs Richardson
It's awfully good of you to write to me again so soon; especially as I had not answered your last. I will try to make amends by telling you what I have been about. In the first place, accept my thanks for the Second Master's photos;[2] we admired them very much. Above all too, I thank you for your very kind words about Lionel;[3] it is a very great loss to me practically as I was always inclined to submit myself to his judgment, & to a great extent to take his advice, & I *do* love & respect him, though I may not always think it necessary to say so. But I can wait: little as we have seen of each other, I believe there exists a mutual attraction & respect which a year or so will not destroy, though things seldom last long in this life.

Do you know, I have gone into an odd habit lately of surveying myself from the standpoint of a critical, cool-headed outsider with tender leaning for myself? It is amusing & I find the ideas about myself resolve into a kind of sorrowful pity: I look at myself & feel so awfully sorry for myself: such a good sort of fellow, but never able to run smoothly in harness. It is laughable enough, but at the same time occasionally painful; & I feel as if I should like some to know me inside, & explain to the world that I am not such a villain as I appear on the surface. There: that is enough psychology for one letter.

Hurrah for the prospect of your being back on the 10th; I hope you will let me know: perhaps you would even be able to come down here? I am so sorry you feel tired & not active: I wish I could lend you my useless vigour. Glad you liked Ferishtah. Give my love to Waterfield[4] & tell him not to write unless he has time. Your name for the cat & pipe is grand.

I am dreadfully sorry for what you say of Mallie;[5] I had no idea he was so thoroughly ill as that; it is awful to think of the poor Daker[6] without him, he will be terribly crushed.

Several of my friends are here now & they are very merry & I am glad to see them so; but I always have an oppressive feeling of being prematurely aged which keeps me mournfully placid. Besides, the summer has passed now, & I am very much affected by the laughing or weeping of the trees.

Don't pity me; I am not unhappy, for I have not yet lost the vision of the brighter dawn to come; when I do that I shall be an atheist indeed & of all men most miserable.

Remember me to the Second Master, & believe me,

Your most affectionate,

Russell

3.

University Club, Madison Square
c/o Kings Sons & Co., New York
22 October 1885

My dear Percy,[7]

You will learn my plans from Harry.[8] I hope you will answer this in a fortnight, i.e. Nov. 5th & will stick to Thursday for your day.

We have been to Coney Island & Manhattan Beach, on Long Island. It was horrible; full of dreadful wooden buildings painted a ghastly green, & advertisements of drinks & sausages.

The people all drink iced things here to a terrible extent; & live in such a dry heat. Hotels, ferries, railroad cars all have hot dry air from stoves. It is enough to wither one up. Baseball seems the favourite game: & the boys are pleasant. This is an island & you have some trouble getting off it by rail to go west. Things – i.e. cabins, entrances, cars labelled 'Ladies' mean simply quiet – not a bit ladies only. They seem rather Evangelical & Puritanical here; when they have any religion at all. Still, I am told there are thousands of Catholics.

I am deadly sleepy: it is so hot & my head is nodding. If you like abbreviations you would get plenty of them here. B'way, 4th Av., Mfg. Co. etc. etc.

The rattle & clanging is awful: the locomotives have large bells which sound like a church steeple, a powerful reflector in front & a cowcatcher. They look very odd – generally with small wheels and bogey-trucks. Gradients and curves are nothing to this line. Ice creams are very good – but oh! the perpetual iced water. Each car has a vessel of it, with fancies & many lamps & a stove; char-à-banc benches – not nearly so nice as English. Am more than half asleep so forgive,

Yours ever

Russell

4.

New York
Sunday 8 November 1885

Dear Mrs Richardson

Thank you so very much for your letter of October 17 with the cross & Lionel's words which came by the same post. My best thanks are due to you for conniving at the iniquity of some grateful lines from my dearest friend! I shall not write to him, but am meditating an attack on his father soon, though I know Lionel would say it was useless.[9]

I wear a St Cross cross already, which is to me full of memories of Winchester & you,[10] but I will keep yours gratefully, & consult you later about a fitting disposal of it. The photos have not come yet, but two or three steamers are expected in a few days, so no doubt they are en route. I hope you are exchanging news with Marillier, as I find it easier to write often to various friends, than to compose one long epistle.

I should like to know about Mallie: I have heard nothing of him since I started. Give my love to the Daker, & remember me to any friends in College who care to be remembered – Jack Stainer & Waterfield & little Jim Palmer.[11]

Balfour & I went to a meeting of the Century Club last night, & I met Moncure Conway[12] who was glad to talk about you. I was so very glad to get the opportunity of a few words with him, as I knew how much you admired him. We leave here tomorrow for Albany & Niagara, & then away West. We came from Philadelphia yesterday morning, where we had seen a good deal, and been shown all American hospitality. The doorsteps & so forth there are all of marble which produces a very funny effect at first. It is a standing joke against the town. I spent a good deal of time about the wharves & docks, watching the shipping & the sailors, some leaning back lazily smoking or chewing, & others busy in unloading all sorts of cargoes. They look frank & pleasant to talk to, though I've no doubt one would think them brutal at first. There are huge ferry-boats in this country, which frequently transport freight trains entire; there being a paucity of bridges.

I had a very pleasant stay at Boston: everyone was very kind & did all they could to help us. I also saw a certain amount of the University at Harvard, & of the way they live there. The young men – 'fellows' as they call them – seemed to me a much better set than I had expected.[13] But then my introductions were from a quiet and intellectual New College American, of my acquaintance;[14] & I've no doubt they really vary as much as at Oxford. I begin rather to wish that I was still at Oxford, or saw any chance of going back there: such a sudden cutting off from all my pleasant societies & kind friends seems a little harsh. Still, what really strikes me is that the world is so much better & truer than I thought, & that so many – in fact, *all* my real friends – have stood so kindly by me & refused to drop me in misfortune. People *are* very good, & it makes one feel it worth trying & well worth living to have the joy of being loved & making one's friends happy. Though I fear that is not what I have done so far.

I think kindness & sympathy are the source of happiness & well-being to oneself and others: and the lesson my troubles have taught me is that one can never be too kind, too forgiving or long-suffering, or do harm by allowing oneself to be sympathetic. It is only an attempt to repay some of the kindness oneself has experienced. And so one ought always to present oneself as joyful as possible, to lighten other people's cares. Do you not think so? I know you do.

I look forward to brighter days, & to a time when I shall see Winchester again, & be free. A mist is breaking: man cannot live alone, nor offend his community & go unpunished, for we are all subject to one law. You will know what I mean, & how I bear you all with me through this land of unrest.

Ever yours affectionately,
Russell

5.

Cincinnati, Ohio
22 November 1885

Dear Mrs Richardson

Again my turn to write to you comes round, but I have no letter to answer.

I wish these horrible people wouldn't call one 'Mister'. A horrid little boy just came up to me in the hall, & shouted 'What time is it, please, Mister!' I never thought of myself as having a military appearance but within the last week I have been so hailed, once as 'Colonel' & the other time as 'Captain'. Perhaps it's partly because I've got more into the ways of the country now, and assert myself vigorously whenever I want to get anything done, by these infernally unattentive people.

They are very curt in their ways of putting things but I don't know that they mean to be rude: perhaps the best excuse is that they are only half-civilized & have not acquired the amenities of life. Two notices will exemplify what I mean – 'Dump No Dirt'; and on a door 'STOP! Only workhands upstairs'. They are so unpleasantly direct – 'American Burial Case Co.', 'trainman', 'horsecar', 'bellboy', 'Boot Room', 'Wash Room', newsagent, ticket-scalper, etc. rather than coffin, tram & so forth. A sort of German enumeration of the parts making up the thing indicated.

Most Americans are 'hell on grass' as they phrase it. You frequently see an apparently respectable citizen suddenly elevate a stalk of lettuce about two feet long, & make it disappear down his throat like a sword-swallower giving a performance.

We have been to Niagara, which I enjoyed & admired very much. The Falls impressed me as they should, and I was glad to begin calculating how much electricity they could be made to supply to New York & cities en route if they were kept constantly at it working dynamos. It seems a pity that so much power should go to waste!

From there we went to Buffalo & I saw a large grain elevator, capable of distributing grain around at the rate of 20 thousand bushels a day. It does it credit.

The best thing in the machinery line I've seen yet was at Pittsburgh. There we went over Edgar-Thomson Steel Works, belonging to Andrew Carnegie, a fairly well known man. Here we saw the whole process of manufacturing steel rails, & I was very much pleased by the quiet, easy way in which all the machinery worked at its great labours: almost by itself, taking very few people to keep an eye on it.

We have seen no people in these last towns & they have been dull, dirty & uncomfortable. Here we have come to a better hotel, & the town is cleaner, but very dusty: and all today there has been cold & rain. But if the weather is fairly decent we shall get on better after this: & see a little of the Ohio & Mississippi, at Louisville & St Louis before we reach Chicago. After that Omaha, Denver, Colorado Springs & Leadville, at which places we shall have real cold, Utah & Mormons, freeze in crossing the Rocky Mountains at 8,000 ft. elevation in January, but begin warm climate the other side at Sacramento & San Francisco on the Pacific Coast.

How is Mallie? & what's the Daker doing? no one has written to me for some time & I am absolutely without news of anything in England later than October 20th – about my friends, that is. I hope things are quiet in

Cincinnati
Ohio.

22 Nov. 1885.

Dear Mrs Richardson

Again my turn to write to you comes round, but I have no letter to answer.

I wish these horrible people wouldn't call me 'Mister'. A horrid little boy just came up to me in the hall, & shouted 'What time is it, please, Mister!' I never thought of myself as having a military appearance but within the last week I have twice been so hailed, once as 'Colonel' & the other time as 'Captain.' Perhaps its partly because I've got more into the ways of the country now, and assert myself vigorously whenever I want to get anything done, by these infernally unattentive people.

They are very curt in their ways of putting things but I don't know that they mean to be rude; perhaps the best excuse is that they are only half-civilised & have not acquired the amenities of life. Two

2.1 Letter to Mrs Richardson from Cincinnati, 22 Nov 1885.

college & that you are not having troubles or worries of any sort; also that your health is good, because I think it's a shame you should be ill. I wonder what has happened in Fifteens, & what will in Sixes:[15] it seems strange to be so far away from it all. And this is not one of the cases where distance is necessary to lend enchantment to the view; still less does out of sight mean out of mind. Ah well! my love to Lionel, and in fact everyone; & all good wishes to you from
Yours affectionately,
Russell

'I met a fool – a fool i'the forest – a fool, a fool, a motley fool.'[16]

6.

> Chicago, Illinois
> 7 December 1885

Dear Mrs Richardson

I was not able to write to you yesterday afternoon but will try to run in a letter now, just before starting on a 21 hour journey to Omaha & Council Bluffs. We got up at six this morning & went down to the Stock Yards to see the pigs & cows killed; but I am glad to say the frost made such a steam that we could see nothing. But ugh! the smell was enough to make me all but ill – & I feel quite sick still. Ask Lionel to translate you some of Aeschylus' remarks on human slaughter-houses & the reek of blood: it was all that. We saw cows shot down in their pens by a man walking along over their heads with a Remington rifle: that was more or less satisfactory, death being painless and instantaneous. The sights & smell of blood were awful. Fortunately the cold was intense, and that made it more tolerable. Thermometer was below zero at 9 a.m. -36° of frost, think of that! All one's breath froze as we went along, but we felt it wonderfully little, chiefly owing to there being no wind. It was unendurable Saturday & Sunday nights when there was a bitter wind.

I wanted to answer your last letter, but all my things are packed & I can't get at it. The journey will be pleasant enough, as the cars are very comfortable, and kept hot enough to suit even Lionel.

I never meant to suggest that Lionel should write to me without his father's permission: it's not that I'm conscientious enough to think it morally wrong – any more than I do the revolution in Bulgaria: but as a book on the American constitution says 'When a rising against the existing government succeeds, it is called a revolution, when it fails, a rebellion'! A humorous & true way of putting it.

We have been very well looked after here by a young Harvard man, Mr Sturgis[17] (cousin to Julian Sturgis) who is paymaster of the CBL railway, by which we go to Denver. He is a thorough gentleman, quiet & well-bred, which things it is rather rare to find in this country. I guess now the cold weather has set in, we shall have to endure it as well as we can till we cross the Rockies, which will only be a month from now.

Oh! I suppose by the time this reaches England you may not be at Winchester. I send you & the Second Master all Xmas & New Year greetings & good wishes and Margaret[18] too, if you see her these holidays.

We went from here the other day to the town of Pullman, & saw all the beautiful sleeping & parlour cars being manufactured, which was very interesting. It is a model town, and in one man's hands, who gives his workman good cottages & allows no drink. There is a very luxurious theatre, & everything is clean, orderly & comfortable. But they grumble, as Plato knew they would, at too much government & go to the next village for their drink.

I am rather glad the Liberals are coming in after all, but very much pleased at their having had a severe slap in the face about Disestablishment. Long live the Church! cries the whilom Buddhist.

I hope everyone is not going to pander to & cower before the Irish: let them have what is just, but let us give it them like men, soberly; & not throw it as a sop while we run away. Excuse the political diatribes, & believe me Ever yours affectionately,
Russell

7.

El Paso Club, Colorado Springs
22 December 1885

Dear Mrs Richardson
I am very sorry to be two days late, but neither Sunday nor Monday have I had a moment, & even this is only snatched between a lunch & a dinner. Need I say how much obliged I was to you for the pleasant sight of Lionel's handwriting you afforded me, and of the messages sent me therein. I am surprised that he is not going into the Church: if he means by it a refusal to preach a half-truth when he sees a wider, I am sincerely glad; but if he does it through desire of dilettantism & shirking of hard work, I am sorry. Probably I shall following him, however, to whatever profession he leads. I am glad your letter came just in time to prevent my writing to his father. I hope all *will* be right when I come back, though except as regards my friends I doubt it. I fear I did not make myself clear about Marillier: I did not mean to suggest that you should write to him about me, but only that he should send you my letters to him & other friends, so that you might know what I was doing. However, I have told him now to send them to Lionel, who will read you anything you would care to hear about my doings. Again I thank you for the very kind idea of letting him be your secretary.

Your description of his friends and their doings was very amusing. (It is your letter of November 21 I am answering.) Yes, I know when I return – I shall land *Deo volente*[19] about the 23rd of May, or a few days earlier.

The weather is perfectly splendid here: temperature from 50° to 60° outside today, have been living without coat or gloves, am writing at open window: I only hope Lionel will show or send you some of my other letters to see how we've been enjoying ourselves. I am glad to hear of Mallie & should wish to think there was hope – do keep me informed.

We ascended Pike's Peak yesterday, over 14,000 feet high, it was difficult to breathe at that height, & we had hard work dragging our horses through the snow & over the stones; it is 3,000 ft. above timber-line. The 10 miles took us nearly 6 hours to do, & I am very stiff today, not having been on a horse for 2 or 3 years. It is a month later than tourists have ever ascended before, & I should certainly not have believed in England that you would

find me trusting my precious carcase on a horse over a wretched path of
breaking timber, shingly sand, snow and ice on a precipitous hillside!
Though it is called a 'trail' here. However here I am with all my limbs, &
glad I've done, and recovered from the terrible shooting pains in my head
which the snow-glare & thin air (barometer *18* inches!) gave me. Otherwise
it was most pleasant up there – bright, warm, sun, not much wind, &
perfectly clear air – view 300 miles in extent! Excuse further descriptions
now, you'll find them in other letters. Happy New Year & love to all from
Yours most affly
Russell

Excuse this beastly paper: it's the best in the Club.
We are staying at Manitou now: only in here for the day.

8.

> Salt Lake City, Utah
> Sunday 3 January 1886

Dear Mrs Richardson
Many thanks for yours & Lionel's of December 6th. I am dreadfully sorry
about Mallie,[20] & for the Daker: it will be such a terrible sorrow to him.
Mallie was so good, so lively & yet so thoroughly in earnest: no long-faced
Methodist, but a bright, laughter-loving worker for God. Ah! the world is so
full of bitter losses, & one doesn't know what to make of them, as one hugs
the ice ever nearer to one's heart. Resignation is all – God's will be done.
I shall try & write to the dear Daker, though I hardly know what to say.
    You need not be afraid of our weather: compared to the miserable
driviling [*sic*] cold I have been told of, we have had bright, clear, crisp, &
sometimes even warm days. I have had several different colds – but what
of it? Your account of the Dickling in Sixes was very amusing.[21] I am so glad
the Second Master & Freddy[22] are both in good health: I do hate to see
people worried by work. Remember me to Alise, if she is still within your
ken, to Margaret, & all my friends in College: & my love to Lionel (you
don't know how glad I am that you have learnt to like him now). I thank
you for the sheet from him, but I warn you, if it goes on, I shall be tempted
to reply same day – *et puis?*
    I shall wait till this evening when I may be able to write more sensibly,
to go on.
9 p.m.
    Writing by an electric arc-light is not much fun, anyway. I enclose you a
little handkerchief entirely of Utah manufacture – the silk-raising being an
experiment here. It's not up to much, but perhaps you may find it
interesting, as a reminiscence of Salt Lake. We went to service in the
tabernacle (much like any Dissenting Shop) from 2 to 4 today, a beehive
shaped building (of which the Mormons are the busy bees).
    The English & ordinary idea of them is very incorrect. They do not
revenge themselves on apostates, but are a homely, domestic, agricultural
& peaceable people: very like the Jews living under Mosaic dispensation,
on whose model they fashioned themselves, as to the duty of raising
children, living peaceably, having ecclesiastical courts, and so forth. Their
faith intellectually is bosh – but their practice produces a community as

vigorous & patient, & materially prosperous as Israel. Perhaps Lionel will read you parts of other letters, in which I have said more about them. Just at present, they are grossly oppressed – nominally, because of their polygamy: in reality, because 'Gentiles' are thirsting for the lands *they* have made fertile! And the government encourages it – in this *free* country! The intolerance in every subject of these Americans is as bad as that of the Middle Ages! Free indeed!

Ah well! my heart is in dear old England, & I shall be jolly glad when my body's there too. This prosaic & go-ahead place wearies me terribly: it needs much imagination and a lively poetic eye to strike out of it the strong wild music of Walt Whitman.

Ever yours affectionately
Russell

Kings Sons, New York is my only address.

9.

San Francisco, California
Thursday 21 January 1886

Dear Mrs Richardson

I am sorry to be so far behind my regular time, but perhaps you will forgive me when you hear what I've been doing. We have been 8 days away from the City, riding to the Yosemite Valley from Madera. 185 miles riding, & 44 hours in the saddle! And very hard work it was too: going, there was the trouble of not being used to riding, and having high mountain ranges to cross – but coming back we had cold, snow 18 inches deep, and torrents of rain to contend with: and we are glad to be back! Even so I would have written to you, but my precious bundle, containing your letter, writing paper & ink, fell off the horse unobserved & was lost irretrievably in the snow: not to be found, my guide assures me till spring-travel & the melting time come – which is cheerful.

So far the Californian weather has not proved much, & though naturally warmer than the Rocky Mountains, has not been really fine. Still I enjoyed the actual riding once I got used to the saddle; & the Yosemite Valley itself is very fine. We climbed on foot over some very long trails to the Vernal & Nevada Falls – well worth seeing. Our other expeditions were however cut short by the snow which came down heavily on the 2nd morning after our arrival & lasted all day. The trip, we find, is considered quite a feat at this time of year. It takes two days hard riding to reach the valley from the railway, & the same time to return, so that with only about 6 days were expended in actual travelling. It was fun – but most fun now we are back. I think Lionel would have enjoyed riding all day through those mountains and rainstorms!

I have seen little of San Francisco yet, but hope to do so before I leave. The Chinatown, Mint etc. are all very interesting if I can get properly introduced to them.

I am glad to hear that Lionel has got off to New [College] all right, & 2nd too!

We stayed a couple of days in Sacramento on the way here. It is a pleasant, quiet place, but without anything to see in it.

Here everything is reckoned in 'bits' (8 bits = 1 dollar): the theory being that any coin under sixpence is too small to be handled or spoken of. However 'nickels' (= 5 cents = 2 ½ d) have now come in for newspapers & tram fares, & no doubt in time the East will introduce 'red' cents. Still if a thing is one 'bit', you can have it for 10 cents: but if you tender a quarter, you still only get 10 cents change, thus paying 15. It is very ridiculous to Eastern & English ideas, but comes from the old days of mining prosperity, when quarks were broken up into two bits, to make small change – there being none.

Perhaps all this is dull, in which case forgive me. The terrible storms we passed through have done great damage to this ever-flimsy country. There are wash-outs on the railways, trains 16 hours late or not running at all, & all telegraphic communication with this city has been suspended for 24 hours. I think we may be proud & very glad of having got here through it! Yours affly
Russell

10.

Hotel del Monte, Monterey, California
Sunday 31 January 1886

Mr dear Mrs Richardson
I have yours of January 3rd from Bonchurch.[23] I hope you have been enjoying yourself there much as we have here: this being the great seaside season of the Pacific Coast. I am sorry I have never mentioned Balfour, but whenever I say 'we' it's meant to include him. I hope you may see him when we come back – in the end of May. How nice it is when the day comes round for writing to you, to know that another fortnight's passed, & that my exile is drawing nearer to its end.

Thank you for your kind remarks about our idolizing people – I quite feel what you say. But I am sorry you are so severe on Waterfield – I don't think he at all deserves it – Matt. xiii. 6. is a libel on him.[24] He is undoubtedly very narrow-minded, but that, though an irritating misfortune, is hardly a crime: and I think he has plenty sturdy strength to stand up for the right as he conceives it. Though I may not agree with him in theory, I cannot but admire uprightness & loyalty to one's own ideals.

Now of Johnson I should say that he was very wide-minded & great in theory, but without the earnestness & endurance to put it into practice. I think perhaps Lionel has yet to learn his 'duty to his neighbour'. 'If any man love not his brother whom he hath seen . . . . .'[25] and love implies action as well as feeling.

How is Lenny Morshead getting on in College?[26] I like him very much though I think he barely knows me.

I wish you had the Daker with you – I knew you would do him good: give him my love when you see him.

Please accept my thanks en masse for all your other school news & believe me that I devour every item with the greatest eagerness. Young Bilbrough has proved a very regular correspondent[27] – ask the Second Master if he remembers how noisy & troublesome we used to be in his mathematical div.?

We came down here on Wednesday & leave next Tuesday, for Los

Angeles, where we shall arrive Thursday. Then Santa Barbara, El Paso, San Antonio and New Orleans are our stopping points. Thence ship to Tampa in Florida arriving about March 3rd.

This is a lovely place, warm as on English early summer days, with a beautiful blue sea just over the sand-dunes, and a large & well-kept garden around the hotel, full of walks and birds. Armies of Chinese are forever clipping, trimming, sweeping, raking just like an English garden. The village of Monterey is a delightful tumble-down old fishing village. Of course all this coast was settled by Mexican Spaniards 100 years ago & there are Catholic missions everywhere. It makes the State quite respectable – though of course these progressive Americans despise the Mexicans as lazy rascals and horse-thieves. (Anywhere west of Colorado a man found stealing horses is liable to be shot down on the spot by the aggrieved party!)

I don't care much for the people here, but they can't spoil the lovely climate & the pleasant air of tranquillity over everything.

Ever yours affectionately
Russell

11.

El Paso, Texas
Sunday 14 February 1886

Dear Mrs Richardson

I am sorry I cannot write myself, but I have an evil finger, which hurts vilely, and 'The Kind Balfour' is writing for me. I don't wonder that you are going to fetch Margaret back from Germany, but after all she has not been very long there.[28]

Perhaps I more or less agree with you about Lionel, but only more or less. I had a very pleasant letter from the Daker: he sent me the sermon he had preached about Mallie – please thank him very much for me.

No, you don't repeat your news. You apologized before, but you haven't done it.

I think I remember lively Miss Lyndon,[29] who you say is with you.

I enjoyed my stay at Monterey very much. The place is charming, & the natives delightfully lazy.

Spent another day with the dentist in San Francisco on leaving; 22 hours journey then a night in Los Angeles; on the next evening by a most miserable bug-infested freight-steamer to Santa Barbara.

Here we found comfortable hotel, delightful climate, and some friends of Bilbrough's, whom I had missed in New York – the Patons and their party. We had a very jolly time with them; & the manager & the proprietor of the hotel are both delightful people, and arranged very pleasant expeditions for us.

Though Balfour is writing this, I can't help saying that it was a very great pleasure to get someone new to talk to for a bit; – he quite agrees with me.

We drove out 16 miles to Col. Hollister's ranche,[30] & the adjacent one – Mr Cooper's.[31] Both very well kept, especially the latter; we had a jolly picnic lunch at Hollister's, & enjoyed some native Californian champagne. There were orange trees off which we ate nice ripe oranges; & date palms, & olive & flowers, & innumerable eucalyptus trees. Some of the views were also very lovely.

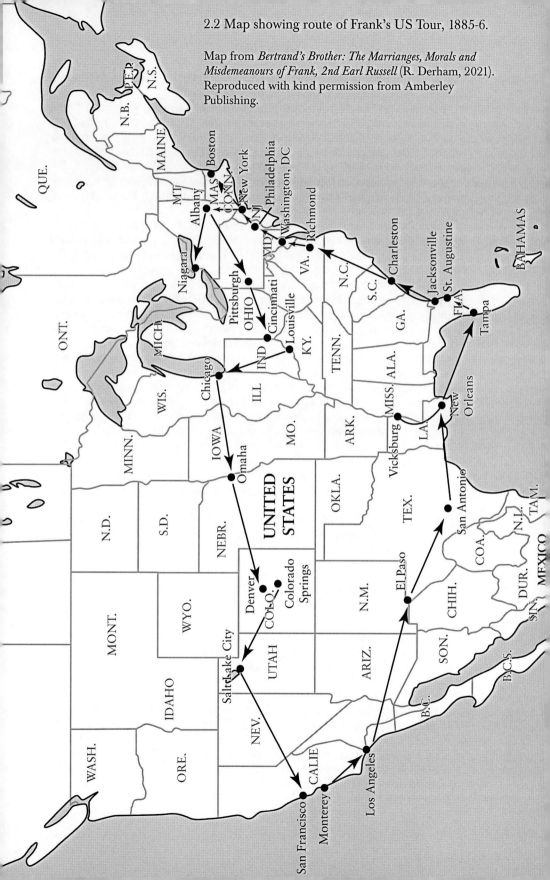

2.2 Map showing route of Frank's US Tour, 1885-6.

Map from *Bertrand's Brother: The Marriages, Morals and Misdemeanours of Frank, 2nd Earl Russell* (R. Derham, 2021). Reproduced with kind permission from Amberley Publishing.

It is very warm all along this coast: thermometer begins about 60° in the morning, & goes up to 70° or 80° in the day.

After only too short a stay, we said farewell on Thursday night, & had a really decent passenger steamer to transport us. Had about 3 hours at Los Angeles, then took the Southern Overland – very poor sleeper, irregular meals, irritating changes, & bumpy track – but ultimately arrived here at the convenient hour of midnight last night.

You can imagine that in addition to my finger, I am feeling pretty tired; & have been worried all day by an infernal wind, which raises clouds of dust all over the place. The hotel also is beastly.

So far I entirely agree with the Yankee pedlar, who gave as his deliberate opinion of this State: 'Well – if I owned Hell and Texas, – I should I guess *let* Texas.' But perhaps this is prejudice, as I have only been one day in the State so far.

In spite of my headache, the ruthless Balfour insists on dragging me on tonight (it's true there's nothing more to see). We leave in the middle of the night, & hope to reach San Antonio Tuesday morning. These long journeys over alkali deserts, where nothing grows but the cactus, & not always that, are very tiresome, & the amount of dust is frightful.

We took a tram car across the Rio Grande into El Paso del Norte, Mexico this afternoon. The church was a wretched hole, with only two or three worshippers; but we found the rest of the populace at a cockfight, summoned thither by a loud tattoo on a drum. We watched one fight but I don't think it's a very edifying exhibition – & consider the crowd who thus sought their Sunday amusement was the most villainous lot I have seen.

After a week in New Orleans we go through Florida and hope to make Washington about March 12, staying there a fortnight.

Of course this place swarms with Mexicans in picturesque costumes; and a cross between them and the Indians: and is full of Spanish notices & people talking Spanish.

I think that is all I had to say & hope you won't mind my not writing it myself, but my finger's very bad.

Yours affectionately,
Russell

12.

On the Mississippi, State of Louisiana
Sunday 28 February 1886

My dear Mrs Richardson

Many thanks for yours & Lionel's of January 31. I am glad his week at Portsea has done him good[32] – I hoped it would make him a little more *really* sympathetic with us poor mortals instead of putting us off with artistic dreams.

Many thanks for all the Winchester news given in your usual lively style! Young Bilbrough is a very regular correspondent, & seems to miss Willie very much. I don't wonder you feel lonely with both gone – but I quite decline to admit that anyone in the Second Master's house is 'old & grumpy'. Thanks for the line to Johnson – it is cheering to see his handwriting even where there isn't much in it.

Excuse my writing, but these Mississippi steamers have high-pressure engines which go off in explosions, & are notoriously shaky so that my paper keeps jumping. We left New Orleans 5 p.m. yesterday & go to the historic Vicksburg (arrive tomorrow afternoon) about 400 miles upstream. We make the trip to see what the Mississippi is like & it's certainly very big & very, very dull! There's more in a mile of the Thames than a hundred of this! Nothing but a broad sheet of filthily muddy water, low banks, & small trees crowded very close together. The boat is a huge flat-bottomed thing (carrying cotton on her down trips) drawing very little water, & every now & then running right into the banks to leave some barrels, or boxes, or mules or even human freight. She is immensely large & yet goes right in anywhere in a way that's surprising. There was a fog & mist when we started but it's fine now, though not very warm, & oh! so dull!

We spent 4 days at San Antonio after leaving El Paso. That was very dull but we met a pleasant English captain there, & had a rest. One day more brought us to New Orleans & there we have found some good friends. It's a jolly city but a horrible climate, & we being very tired & rather seedy have hardly done anything this last week. Still we've been introduced at the Club, seen a Cotton Mill, listened to speculations on the Cotton Exchange, and been to the Exposition – this last a miserable lifeless survival of a really good exhibition last year. The people & customs are more French – ergo pleasant & civilized: the streets are vilely paved & rather dirty: & the Americans think only of cotton & sugar. In this backward State, lotteries & gambling are allowed, there are no factory & no compulsory education laws, the State legislature is very corrupt, the City police venal! Still it is pleasant to live in, I should say.

There are crowds of black, hopelessly ignorant, Southern n****rs everywhere. To me they seem to have a sort of craven self-assertion, an I-am-free–I-hope-you-won't-kick-me look about them; as if in spirit they had not yet cast off the yoke of slavery.

I have been able to finish in peace owing to our being now at a landing. I sail from New York on 8th of May in the Cunard Liner *Umbria*.
Ever yours affectionately
Russell

13.

St Augustine, Florida
Sunday 14 March 1886

Dear Mrs Richardson
I have yours of February 14. I have also had news of the photos you sent me some time ago, which seem to have been returned to Richmond for some reason. I have written for them. I am delighted to hear that you keep getting younger: you may look in the glass & call yourself 43 as much as you like, but you shall not frighten any of us away!

I wonder if Mrs Bloxam[33] has ever pardoned me for my attempt to improve that drawing room? I am glad to hear Mrs K[34] is well, & I don't wonder she's liked.

Since I last wrote we have left New Orleans – unhealthy place – on the 4th of March in a little steamer. We didn't reach Tampa, on the west coast of this State, till Sunday morning. I was very ill on the journey with headaches & things – not sea-sickness. Sunday afternoon we took the train to Sanford & slept there, crossing the river – 5 miles – to Enterprise next morning. Wednesday morning at 7.30 we left Enterprise on a fast steamer down the St John's River, arriving Palatka at 5 p.m. The country is all full of swamps, pines, maples & cypress: the rivers are a collection of lakes & very shallow in most parts. All the vegetation is luxurious & tropical – a curious horsehair growth 2 or 3 ft long hangs from the trees – the rivers are full of alligators, snakes, turtles, & beautiful birds. The deadly moccasin snake very common here, as also the rattler.

Thursday morning we left Palatka in a little square tub with a small stern wheel worked by steam, & proceeded up the Ocklawaha River to Silver Springs. This river is very narrow, full of the sharpest curves, with no banks – swamp extending ½ mile back among the trees – and a strong current. How on earth we ever got up it at all, even at 6 miles an hour, I don't know. The water is a lovely brown colour, & the fresh green of the trees, which often brushed the boat on either side, was delicious. I thoroughly enjoyed the trip. We reached Silver Springs about 8 a.m. Friday. They were just beautiful: the clearest crystal water to a depth of 50 ft., whence you saw the whole stream issuing. The water was tepid and nasty to drink.

We got away about noon, & spent the whole day in constant changes of train & ferry to make 100 miles to this place, which we reached 8 p.m.

Here we make an enforced halt for washing. The hotel is full, so we have been shoved into a not very comfortable cottage – taking meals of course at the hotel, which is excellent, like most in this State.

The town has a fort & was founded by the Spaniards; is, I am told, 330 years old, but I have been too busy writing letters & too lazy to investigate yet. This State is called a summer resort but since I've been in it, the wind has been very cold, & I've been very glad of my fur coat.

We are once more on the Atlantic Coast – hurrah for the 8th of May!
Yours affectionately
Russell

14.

Washington, D.C.
Sunday night, 1 a.m. 28 March 1886

Dear Mrs Richardson
I have so much to do here in seeing people, dining out & so forth, that this is the first chance I've had today of writing to you. I have yours of February 28th. I am very sorry indeed to hear of Cripps' critical state,[35] but I hope I shall find Bilbrough's improved report continued in your next. I hope Waterfield is all right by now. Do let me know of Cripps – he is such a jolly boy.

I have met your friend Mrs Dyer here.[36] She is delightful & it was so pleasant to be reminded of you, & to find someone in this exile who knew Winchester & Lionel – & to whom one could talk. She has also told me of Senator Edmunds & his wife,[37] whom I showed over College last June. I had quite forgotten it but I hope to go & see them this week.

We have been doing so much that I hardly know where to begin. I spent 3 very pleasant days at Richmond, Virginia where the Southern gentlemen were very kind to me & showed me everything worth seeing. I liked them & their ways very much & hope to spend some time in Virginia if I ever come back here. We got here last Tuesday. Forgive me, I can write no more tonight I am so tired & the gas is flickering badly.

Monday.

I still feel rather sleepy & my eyes are bad, as is only natural. We have dissipated a great deal here; seen the President (Grover Cleveland) whom I rather liked, Secretaries Bayard, Whitney, Senators Evarts & Aldrich, Governor Wetmore of Rhode Island, Sir Lionel West the British Minister & his daughter,[38] & Mr & Mrs Field, an old Philadelphia couple who have been a great deal in England, Messrs Hay, Brown, Schuyler, Loring, Hardinge, Wharton & crowds of others, ladies & men.

We have dined with the Farnams, some New England friends of ours; & last night with a pleasant English party at the British Minister's. Tonight we go to Secretary Bayard: the poor man has lost wife, daughter & 2 other relations in the last six weeks – so of course the party will be quiet. He is a beautiful man, both in face and character; & I look forward eagerly to meeting him privately.

I am proposing to make a steam-launch expedition in July along the rivers of England from Thames to Trent with some of my friends. Do you think Lionel's father could ever be got to let him come? Of course I should like it immensely if he would, & moreover it would do Lionel so much good to be dragged away from books for a month: for we both dislike to watch him killing himself. Perhaps you would ask him what he thinks about it?

Ever yours affectionately
Russell

P.S. I am quite serious – only I fear Captain Johnson will never be got over.

15.

Philadelphia, Pa.
Sunday 11 April 1886

Dear Mrs Richardson

At last our long tour is ended, & here we are at last in a city we have seen before, & where everything is not strange, unknown & new. It feels quite homelike after such perpetual changes. And now we have only 18 days in Boston & a week in New York, before we sail: and the *Umbria* will take us on her next trip. How glad I am to be getting back!

I have yours of March 14th – I am very glad to hear of the improvement in Cripps & am looking forward to having it confirmed in your next which ought to have been here by now.

Thanks, my finger is all right & I have not had to cut it off.

I am so sorry you have not been well, & how you must have been worked & worried with all the sick ones in your house! I wish I could have been there to try to help you.

Lionel has not added his line for some time & I miss it: he does not emulate your wonderful goodness in writing so regularly.

I am so sorry the Second master is turning grey – I do not like to see all my friends getting old.

I have not been able to keep to my Vegetarianism in the West, because I should frequently have been starved if I had. But now I have come back here where one can get good vegetables, I am beginning it again.

I wish I could be with you: I wonder when I shall see Winchester again?

I don't think I have yet told you that I met Mrs Elisha Dyer at Washington. Of course we foregathered at once & made great friends over you: & I am to go down to Providence & see her again. Did I tell you before?

We had such a nice time at Washington, & the Farnams & the Fields were very good to us: Mrs Farnam quite taking me under her wing.

We spent two days at Baltimore pleasantly, & saw several good pictures at the Walters Art Gallery.

Here we have done wonders. Mrs Moore took us to see the Keely motor, which actually worked & astounded me considerably.[39] We then dined with her & went to the play, having been at one on our own account the day before. Friday visited a school also, in the morning.

Yesterday I was given a ride on a locomotive in the morning & shown the system of signals: took a ride of 15 miles in the afternoon on a horse, & dined with a vulgar banker – ugh! This morning I went over to Camden, but Walt[40] wasn't in – & we leave tomorrow morning for Boston.
Yours affectionately
Russell

Seems to me on reading this that I never saw a letter with so many *I*'s in it!

16.

Somerset Club, Boston
Easter Day, 25 April 1886

Dear Mrs Richardson
I have your letters of March 28 & April 4 & 10. I will certainly go to see the Sellars[41] when I reach New York which will be May 1st, and Elisha Dyer says he will call too.

Dear Fred Morshead! I hope he has not been having worries. I like and admire him as much as anyone I know. I was very glad of my letter from Waterfield, & have written to him in answer to it. Lionel has given up: I am very glad at your prospect of managing Captain Johnson, though hardly hopeful. What does Lionel say?

It would be just perfect if he could & would come. It has just occurred to me though that your term doesn't end till August, & I was thinking of going in July. *Mais nous verrons.*

I do want to hear at last that Cripps is better – what a terrible illness it is! & what will be the end?[42]

We went down to Providence yesterday & spent the day with Mrs Dyer. I like her fairly, but I still think you are right in your last remarks about her. (Curiously enough I got the letter just as I started for her house.) Governor Dyer, the aged one, begged to be remembered to you. Elisha 3rd was there & his brother George whom I much preferred.

A man at Harvard named Gammell had met Freshfield[43] in the Yellowstone! isn't it funny?

3 weeks from today I hope to be in Liverpool.

This is Easter at last, after the dragging weariness of Lent. I went to Early Service this morning, having found a High Church here: but when I returned for 10.30 service, I found the doors besieged by a crowd bustling & pushing, & though I came early & waited half-an-hour, it was impossible even to reach the door. So I have had to do without my Church. How different from our lovely, peaceful Winchester.

Well, I hope I may see you again soon & College too. Give my love to the Second Master & to Popsey[44] & to everyone else you see.
Yours ever affectionately
Russell

Notes

1. Determined not to return to PL after his sending down, Frank took a house in Hampton-on-Thames and named it 'Ferishtah' for Browning's recently released *Ferishtah's Fancies* (1884).

2. Second Master: Revd George Richardson (1839-1904), AKA 'Dick'. Sarah Richardson (née Porter, 1843-1906) was his wife.

3. All mentions of 'Lionel' concern Lionel Johnson. The nature of his relationship with Frank is examined in *Bertrand's Brother*.

4. Reginald Waterfield (1867-1967), then a college man at Winchester; later Principal of Cheltenham College (1899-1919) and Dean of Hereford (1919-1947).

5. Malise Archibald Cunninghame-Graham (1860-1885), Curate of St John's, Winchester.

6. Revd Henry Compton Dickins (1838-1920), vicar of St John's (1871-1920), nicknamed 'The Daker'.

7. Letter addressed to Percy Umfreville Henn (1865-1955), an Oxford friend of Russell's, later an educationalist and clergymen (RA1, Box 6.28, 080056).

8. Henry Currie Marillier (1865-1951) was at Peterhouse, Cambridge when Frank was at Oxford. They met through mutual friends. Marillier became managing director of Morris & Co. (1905-1940).

9. Captain Johnson had banned all communication between Frank and Lionel after Frank's sending down.

10. The Church and Hospital of St Cross, Winchester, a charitable foundation established by Henry of Blois c.1132.

11. Both then college men, John Frederick Randall Stainer (1866-1939) later became a composer, and Edwin James Palmer (1869-1954), Bishop of Bombay (1908-1929).

12. Moncure D. Conway (1832-1907), American abolitionist, freethinker and writer.

13. One of these 'fellows' was cosmopolitan philosopher George Santayana (1863-1952) who would become a lifelong friend.

14. Edward Perry Warren (1860-1928) who went from Harvard to New College in October 1883.

15. 'Fifteens' and 'Sixes' are Winchester inter-House football tournaments, named for the number of players.

16. Frank quotes from memory *As You Like It*, Act 2, Sc.7, presumably still dwelling on his own predicament.

17. Charles Inches Sturgis (1860-1952), nephew of George Sturgis (1817-1857). George was the first husband of Santayana's mother. Santayana was named after him.

18. Margaret Richardson, their daughter.

19. God willing.

20. Mallie Graham died on 26 Nov 1885.

21. William Porter Richardson (1868-1949), their only son, was affectionately known as 'The Dickling'.

22. Frederick Morshead (1836-1914), Frank's Housemaster.

23. Near Ventnor, Isle of Wight.

24. Reginald Waterfield (fn.4). From the Parable of the Sower (Matthew 13:1-23): the seed that fell on stony ground had 'no deepness of earth: And when the sun was up, they were scorched; and because they had no root they withered away' (v.5-6).

25. Frank quotes from memory 1 John 4:20-21: 'If a man say, I love God, and hateth his brother, he is a liar…'

26. Leonard Frederick Morshead (1868-1936), son of 'Freddy', Frank's Housemaster.

27. Harold Ernest Bilbrough (1867-1950), later Bishop of Dover (1916), then Bishop of Newcastle (1927-1941).
28. Margaret had been sent to school in Neuwied am Rhein in September 1885. The reason for her possible withdrawal is not known but her letters reveal she was still there in April 1886.
29. Eleanor Lyndon (1856-1924), schoolmistress.
30. Colonel William Welles Hollister (1818-1886) gave his name to the city of Hollister in San Benito County and had by this time relocated to Santa Barbara where extensive land purchases included the 26,000 acre Rancho Nuestra Señora del Refugio from José Francisco de Ortego.
31. Ellwood Cooper (1829-1918) moved to Goleta, Santa Barbara in 1870 on Hollister's advice and purchased 2,000 acres where he planted 400 acres of fruit trees; an area still known today as 'Ellwood'.
32. The school mission was moved to Portsea in December 1882.
33. Jessie Findlay Bloxam (née Porter, 1851-1926), Mrs Dick's sister.
34. Gwendoline (née Hall, 1849-1941), wife of Colonel Edgar Kensington (1842-1923).
35. Reginald Cripps (b.1868), another college man was suffering from pneumonia with pleurisy. The Headmaster's Report 1886 shows there were 17 cases of pneumonia and rheumatic fever at the school that spring, no doubt accounting for concerns over the health of the others.
36. Mrs Nancy Dyer, wife of Lieutenant Colonel Elisha Dyer Jr. (1839-1906), later Governor of Rhode Island.
37. George F. Edmunds (1828-1919), Senator of Vermont, and his wife Sarah (1831-1916).
38. Thomas F. Bayard (1828-1898), Secretary of State; William Collins Whitney (1841-1904), Secretary of the Navy; Senators William M. Evarts (1818-1901), New York, and Nelson W. Aldrich (1841-1915), Rhode Island; Governor George P. Wetmore (1846-1921); Sir Lionel Sackville-West (1827-1908), British Ambassador to the US, and his daughter, Victoria (1862-1936).
39. John Ernst Worrell Keely (1837-1898) spent a dozen years developing his motor, which supposedly harnessed the power of 'etheric vapour'. He attracted substantial investment and exhibited his invention on several occasions, claiming in March 1886 it achieved 2,700 psi from a single pint of water. Keely died with the secret of his invention undisclosed. In 1899 it was revealed to have been a 'delusion and deception', the 'mysterious' forces created being 'the result of trickery' (*New York Times*, 20 Jan 1899).
40. Walt Whitman (1819-1892). Frank succeeded in meeting his idol on another occasion and describes the experience in *MLA*, p. 119.
41. Possibly American merchant David Plenderleith Sellar (1833-1901) and his wife Mary.
42. Frank heard of Cripps' recovery on his return.
43. Solicitor Edwin Hanson Freshfield (1864-1948) was another of Frank's Winchester friends.
44. 'Popsey' was Margaret Richardson's nickname.

3. 'An Earl's Matrimonial Affairs', *Penny Illustrated Post*, 20 Jul 1901.

Chapter 3

From America to Holloway

In the years immediately following Frank's 'exile' friends became concerned that Frank lacked direction. In August 1888, Lionel Johnson wrote to Santayana, 'I incline to think it time for his drama of life to become critical in some way... he does not appear to progress.[1] Santayana, it appears, expressed a similar opinion to Frank, provoking the following letter. At the time of writing, Frank had recently established an electrical engineering business with James Swinburne. In July 1892 he left the company to form Russell & Co. which he promoted with an article in *National Review*.

Letter to Santayana[2]

Amberley Cottage
10 August 1891

My dear Santayana,
How unreasonable you do continue.

I consider that the study and advancement of science are among the noblest aims possible. I entirely differentiate that from keeping accounts which I will admit is a slavery and which I will discontinue as soon as my firm is rich enough to pay a hireling to do it. At the same time while admitting that it is beneath me, what I do I try to do as well as I possibly can: & I should not presume to write an essay on Walt Whitman when I had only read a tiny portion of him! In the meantime it is a distraction & keeps me out of mischief.

I am very aristocratic. Quite true: but it is an accident of birth & surroundings. I do not look on it as a thing to be proud of or to encourage: & although the society of a person who is vulgar is in a thousand way disagreeable to me, I think that rather a reprehensible fastidiousness. I believe in Christianity, not in the House of Lords.

If I ever do become a leader of men, be very sure you will think me more vulgar than you do, for it will be as a ranter & extremist of one kind or another.

Remember that to the best society among the Jews Christ must have appeared very vulgar, & 'not at all a person one could ask to dine, my dear'.

As a rule you show intelligence but in dealing with me you sometimes seem to have the most curious blindness. Pray continue this discussion verbally, it is too long to write. I willingly admit that I am not yet *rangé*: but shall I ever be? By nature I am a lotus eater.

There is no news & I am

Yours ever,

Russell.

Electricity in Country Houses
(with B. H. Thwaite), *National Review*, February 1893

Electricity, the progress of which has already caused its areas of application to be wider than Faraday, or Volta, or Ampère, dreamed of, possesses possibilities which, if we could see into the middle of next century, would surprise us. Until now one of the imperfections of country life has been the inadequacy of artificial illumination. Our final resort is to paraffin lamps or to wax candles. Before the invention of incandescent electric light the establishment of a small private gas-works would probably have been the best solution of the problem. A few country houses have been equipped with private gas-works; but the cost is prohibitive to the general. Now at length the development of science has given us the means by which, through a system of co-operation, the resources of electricity may be economically utilized.

The beauty and the utility of the electric glow lamp is recognized. Then, the electric light, with electric motor fans for ventilation, does not exhaust the atmosphere. Electricity has many other pleasing properties, which will readily occur to those who visited the Electrical Exhibition at the Crystal Palace. Such of them as witnessed the experiments in electric cooking must have had their imaginations stimulated. As if by magical influences, all the processes in the preparation of food flowed from an ingenious adaptation of the electric current. For coffee-grinding, a labour always necessary in the household, we have a procedure at ease; the movement of a handle sets in vigorous rotation the laundry mangle and the domestic washer; the current heats the ironing instrument; and, to set the wheels of the sewing machine in motion, the seamstress has only to press a button or to turn a switch. Boots can be cleaned by a similar device, which, besides, will polish the knives and brighten the tarnished plate. Ventilation in the sick-room is achieved by a miniature fan; and, without any danger of fire, the couch of the invalid can be warmed, and heat can be applied to any part of his person. An even temperature can be automatically maintained by the employment of electric appliances.

In the conservatory we have an enchanting application of the electric force. A small 500-candle-power arc light emits a luminous glow as if from the face of the sun, and the rays are sufficiently checked by ground or semi-opaque glass. The beam is chemically active, and has, in a measure, the sun's influence on life. Crocuses, tulips, magnolia, and other flowers, are marvellously affected. They spring as it were from death. Most vegetables are affected similarly. Dr Oliver, of Kew, considers it now established that the growth of vegetables can be appreciably accelerated by the judicious use of the electric arc light. It only remains for the horticultural capitalist to apply the principle extensively. Henceforth no country house need be flowerless at any time. The artificial cultivation of fruit and flowers would be a profitable enterprise. We could rear them in greater abundance than they are reared in France itself. At Boston, USA, there is, it is said, a man who has trebled his crops by a judicious use of electricity. There can be no doubt that many gentleman farmers and intelligent yeomen could modify their lack of prosperity by following that American's example. In farm-buildings the electricity is available for many services. A motor at the end of a conveniently-placed shaft, or mounted on a truck, would drive all the farm machinery. There are other operations in farming, especially in harvesting, to which the force can be applied.

How, it will be asked, can such wonders be economically produced? Before answering, we must look back upon the results of an experiment in Germany fifteen months ago. The Government equipped an installation for ascertaining what percentage of an initial force could be transmitted between Lauffen and Frankfort, a distance of 110 miles. It was found that energy equivalent to nearly 200 horse-power could be transmitted through bear copper conductors suspended overhead like telegraph wires for the entire distance, and with a loss of only some 26 to 28 per cent of the initial force. In other words, out of the 190 horse-power introduced at one end of the conductor the energy actually available for work at the other end equalled 138.9 horse-power; and that on a rainy day. This extraordinary result marked an era in the industrial development of the world, and is an event of great importance in its influence on the future of Europe. Although these long-distance tests were initiated by a Frenchman, M. Depretz, the culminating test was carried out by German skill and under the patronage of the German Government. The principle fact was the application of the Multiphase and high-pressure current; to which, combined with the method of oil insulation, the high efficiency realized was credited. The energy available at the Frankfort end of the line was utilised for lighting, pumping, and driving ventilating fans and other machinery. The Lauffen-Frankfort demonstration proves that, by co-operation, residents in the country within an area comprised in a circle of from ten to fifteen miles may have, in each house, the modern resources of electricity at their service. It has been shown that electric energy can be transmitted over a distance of 100 miles with a loss of only some 28 per cent. For the longest distance in a fifteen-miles area, there would be only about one-seventh of the loss.

Our proposal is that the owners of country houses should combine for the purpose of establishing at some fixed place (say near a railway station) a station at which to generate the force. A skilled working electrician should be engaged to supervise the generating plant and that involved in the utilization of the energy. Each house could be connected with the generating station, which would become a 'telephonic exchange'. For any ordinary householder in the country, the plant and the skilled labour required would involve costs and inconvenience too heavy to be borne; but the central-station system would reduce the cost sufficiently. At the station a steam-engine, or a fuel-gas engine, would drive two alternating dynamo machines. The electro-motive force developed at a low pressure would be transformed into one of greater pressure, and suitable for the distance to be traversed between the station and the houses. The pressure of the current would be reduced at each house to the measure appropriate to the character of the work to be done. Each householder would be supplied with a meter, and the electric energy used would be charged against him. The allocation of the units for light and heat could be made the basis of the proportion of the first cost. Thus the largest investor would have the largest supply. A simpler principle might be found in the adoption of the Joint-Stock Acts, with certain limitations as to maximum rates to be charged and maximum dividends to be earned. The projects could be carried out so that there could be no dispute as to the liabilities.

Correspondence with George Bernard Shaw

Aside from his engineering ventures, much of the next ten years was taken up with Frank's personal problems. Yet during this period Frank also began to turn his attention to social issues, becoming a local councillor in 1894 and taking his seat on the London County Council (LCC) in 1895. This first communication between Frank and Shaw was triggered by Frank seeking Shaw's opinion on the divorce law amendment bill introduced into parliament by William Alexander Hunter, Liberal MP for Aberdeen, on 10 February 1892. Shaw replied:

'It is so hard to get any political party to risk meddling with the marriage laws, that I doubt if anything serious will be done until the increase in the number of women able to earn their own living leads to an increase in the number of free unions, known to all the friends of the parties, but not supposed to be. If people only realized before marriage that they might come to dislike one another, and that to have to live with one whom you dislike is penal servitude of the worse kind, they would face anything in the way of social ostracism sooner than run such a risk. But as a matter of fact there is no need to be found out by people who do not want to find you out, and who will wink at anything provided it is not officially mentioned. Consequently I am inclined to think that the upholders of the marriage contract will eventually be forced to lighten & loosen the chains in order to prevent their falling out of use altogether. I am of course quite in favour of Hunter's Bill.'[3]

Frank, whose own divorce case had been tried the previous December, responded:

> Amberley Cottage, Maidenhead
> 16 Apr 1892

Dear Mr Shaw

Many thanks for your letter which is of great interest to me. I will not say that I have always thought, but I must say that I now think that a free union between a man & a woman, disguise it how you will, is cowardly on the part of the man on account of its unfairness to the woman. I am very far from holding any superstitions in regard to the sanctity of the ceremonial marriage per se; at the same time the fact of social ostracism remains and its brand falls heaviest on the woman. Very few men have such nobility of character and very few women such whole-souled devotion as to prevent such a union being broken sooner or later. And when it is broken the chief hardship falls on the woman.

But knowing the facts of life to be such as they are, I do firmly believe that any relaxation of the marriage laws if supported by popular opinion, must be conducive to morality.

Yours faithfully,

Russell

A few years later Frank gave his first public talk on the subject of morality, delivered to the Newington Reform Club on 5 Jun 1895. It was reported as follows:

'Moral Questions: Earl Russell Lectures at Newington'
South London Press, 8 June 1895.

'What is Morality?' is the subject upon which Earl Russell, LCC, gave an address before the members of the Newington Reform Club on Wednesday night. Earl Russell was content to make his definition 'the course of conduct which tends to the ultimate happiness of the individual and of society.' The more repressive policy of the Pharisee did not in itself sum up morality – tended, in fact, to discredit the higher life. The earl is no believer in asceticism; he regards it as an accidental growth upon Christendom, the product of the licentious world in which the new religion found itself. Nor is the world a vale of tears, but a place to be made better. All this, of course, was very unorthodox. A healthy contempt for the scourge and the hair-shirt ran naturally to a condemnation of monasticism as an attempt to escape moral damage by shirking the battle of life. So, too, celibacy. Was it, asked the earl, right or natural for any man or woman to remain unmarried? Let them, he suggested, read Mr Grant Allen's latest novel and ask themselves whether they considered that those persons had lived the fullest life possible to them and had not been stunted in their growth?[4] On cases of ordinary immorality, the obvious comment was that they were wrong because they involved selfishness and disregard for consequences to the individual and to society; and though Earl Russell does not say that the state of society is right which makes early marriages immoral, immoral they are for precisely the same reasons. But we have a good deal yet to learn he declared, regarding our marriage laws, where the formalism of the Jew still moved – of the Jew who held his wife a slave – and made adultery a condition of divorce or left ill-matched husband and wife to live stunted lives. That old formalism cropped up in the over-recurrent Sunday observance question, the oft-heard condemnation of the working man for his trip to Gravesend, or his game of skittles on his only holiday. Was there no one in the present day whose short cut to prayer – not like that of the old Jews – consisted chiefly in carrying a prayer-book to church? The root of the matter was this – that formalism was out of date, that questions of sexual as well as other morality must be approached in a very different way. Was the human body the Temple of the Holy Ghost or the devil? The earl declared that the mind which found indecency in bathing boys, in nude statues, in pictures of the nude was on the same level as the mind of the City Clerk who went to see women in tights for the sake of the suggestion of indecency he could draw from them. And so for crime, for repression of speech, for violence of propagandism, for lying

– the new touchstone for all these moral questions was wrapped up in the old Commandment, 'Thou shalt love thy neighbour as thyself.'

Frank's views on marriage and divorce were further expounded in a letter to Bertie of 1900. The letter was written on Frank's return from America after his elopement, migratory divorce and Nevada marriage with Mrs Mollie Somerville (née Cooke, c.1859-1942). Bertie later described his lack of sympathy with Frank in this as 'temporary' and 'indefensible', though not purely conventional but personal:[5]

Letter to Bertie

Telegraph House
12 June 1900

My dear Bertie

I am aware that Aunt Maude is a purely conventional person, but I hope you do not wish me to include you among the people who are horrified! It seems to me that to those who believe in divorce at all, one divorce should be as good as another from the moral point of view, otherwise you confound legal subtleties as to domicile with ethics. I have broken up no happy home, seduced no confiding girl, but simply announced to the world that I have taken a woman to be my wife in every moral sense & domestic relation, and with all the legal formalities possible under the circumstances.

The Ecclesiastically ridden laws of this country give me no divorce from Mabel Edith, a foul minded music hall character who has blackmailed me for 10 years. They give no freedom to my wife in spite of all the cruelty of her home life. We invoke what human laws are available to sanction the course which commends itself to our consciences & morals: & at last I obtain domestic felicity & a home and happiness. From you & Alys at least I was entitled to expect congratulations – not silence.

When I went to Paris years ago at Granny's instigation to talk to you about Alys, I did not ask myself whether she was the most desirable match in the world for you, or what her conduct had been. All I knew of her was that she was your choice. The question I did ask myself was whether your marriage to her was necessary to your happiness. I was convinced that it was, & from that moment I was in its favour. Your happiness was what I cared for – why now should you be indifferent to mine? As I am glad you are happy in your married life (even in your secluded & lecturing about the country way which in some respects would not be my way!) why should you not rejoice in my happiness?

Well – I don't often appeal for sympathy, but I care for yours, and frankly, I do not understand your attitude.

Ever yours affectionately,

F.

The law took an equally dim view of Frank taking matters into his own hands. He was tried for bigamy in the House of Lords and sentenced to three months' imprisonment in the first division. His speech in mitigation was regarded as 'manly' and often recalled as his reputation as an orator grew. Left to his own devices, Frank would have said something rather different.

Earl Russell's speech to the Lords during his trial for bigamy, 18 July 1901

My Lords, it is, I need hardly say to your Lordships, with the utmost reluctance and distaste that I have pleaded guilty to this indictment, but I have done so on the advice of my Counsel. And in saying that, my Lords, I do not wish it to be supposed that I reflect for one moment upon my Counsel or upon their advice; for more devoted, more painstaking, and more loyal advisers than I have had in this Case, no unfortunate prisoner could wish for.

My Lords, I find myself here pleading guilty to this indictment within one month only of my apprehension upon this charge of bigamy. I am told, and I must accept it as a fact, that I was mistaken in supposing that I had a defence to the charge. I thought, my Lords, that I had acquired a proper domicile in Nevada, – a sufficient domicile. I believed, my Lords, in the goodness of the Decree in Nevada and in the righteousness of my marriage there.

My Lords, I spent in Nevada something like eight months, for the purpose of obtaining that Decree, and for the purpose of obtaining that residence which gives one a domicile according to American Law. I should not have spent so long a time there if I had not supposed that the result of the proceedings would give me a valid opportunity of giving a social and legal sanction to a new home.

I am told, my Lords, that I am mistaken, and I am told so now not for the first time. When I came back from Nevada proceedings for Divorce were instituted by my wife, Mabel Edith, and I was anxious to defend those proceedings. The charge was one of bigamy and adultery, and I then took the advice of my Counsel and I said, 'I want to set up my Decree of Divorce in Nevada as a defence to that charge.' I was then told, my Lords, that I could not do so – that I could not establish to the satisfaction of an English Court; from the point of view of English Law, such a charge of domicile as would justify me setting up that Decree.

My Lords, for that reason, I did not defend those proceedings; and from that time, my Lords, I considered the Decree which I had obtained in America, and the marriage ceremony which I had gone through in America gave only a social sanction to the new union which I had contracted.

But, my Lords, when I was in America and when I first came back to this country, neither then, nor up till sometime after my return to this country, did I suppose for one moment that I was breaking the criminal law of this country. My Lords, I would not have broken the laws of this country willingly or defiantly. Your Lordships are not to suppose that it was in any spirit of bravado or in any spirit of defiance that I endeavoured to set myself above the laws of my own country. I did not know, and I venture to say that 99 laymen out of 100 would not know, that under any circumstances a second marriage in a foreign State could be punishable as bigamy in this country. Still less my Lords did I think that a second marriage which was valid and which is at this day undisputed in the State of Nevada, could be the subject of prosecution for bigamy here.

My Lords, I am advised I have made a mistake; and I have therefore pleaded guilty, and I am now, my Lords, only waiting until the dissolution according to the English law of my previous marriage has taken place, to marry again, according to the laws of this country, that lady with whom I went through the ceremony of marriage in Nevada. I shall then have contracted legally that union which I have now contracted not only illegally but I am told criminally.

My Lords, I am not alone in being under a misapprehension as to the possibility of the criminal effect of a marriage under those circumstances. I find even so great an authority as Sir William Anson in his book states that murder is the only offence committed outside the jurisdiction which can be punished within.[6]

My Lords, I have been in England for 13 months and I have now been brought to trial within one month. It is true Counsel have told you that I could not have successfully defended the domicile. There is much I could have wished to have explained to your Lordships which I feel I should not be justified in explaining now when no evidence has been given, and when no opportunity is afforded of testing my statement.

Twelve years ago this month, my Lords, when only 23 years of age, that series of misfortunes began, of which this trial today is the culmination. In July 1889, I was engaged to the lady my unfortunate union with whom Mr Robson has told you of. This, my Lords, is the end and the finish of that unfortunate engagement, twelve years ago, when I had not the experience and had not the judgment to guide me, which I have acquired by somewhat bitter experience since.

My Lords, I find that I had mistaken the Civil Law as to the validity of my divorce, and I find quite unexpectedly, and I assure your Lordships without any knowledge of it at the time, and without any conception of it, that I have made myself amenable to the criminal law of this country.

My Lords, there is no more for me to say, I can only now leave myself to the judgments of your Lordships, and ask for what indulgence your Lordships may see fit to give me.

Extract from *My Life and Adventures* (1923).

It was not the speech I should like to have made but it was the speech I was advised to make, and to that extent it served its purpose, for I am told it had a good effect.

What I should like to have said would have been that as there was no other way of getting rid of this horrible woman to whom I was tied I had adopted what appeared to be the only method for cutting the Gordian knot; that Mabel Edith knew all about the proceedings from the beginning and that my conduct did not harm or injure a single human being, and moreover that it was grossly unjust to pick me out for prosecution when another nobleman who had done exactly the same thing was not prosecuted because he was a favourite at Court; and that the real reason of my prosecution was merely because I was an unbeliever and a radical.[7]

On his release Frank gave one press interview and delivered a talk to the club he and Mollie had established on their return from America:

'Lord Russell's Release. Prison Experiences.
The Life of a "First-Classer".
Interview at his Chambers.' *Daily News*, 18 Oct 1901.

Yesterday morning, at eight o'clock, Lord Russell was liberated from
Holloway Prison on the completion of the term of three months'
imprisonment for bigamy to which he was sentenced by the House of Lords
on account of his marriage in Nevada after a divorce obtained in that State.
He drove straight home in a cab. In the afternoon (writes our representative)
I called at his chambers at Gray's Inn, where everything had been made
delightfully snug and comfortable for the Earl's reception after his long
period of wearisome seclusion from the world. The little room which he uses
as an office was alone in disorder, for to-day it was 'Begone, dull care!' and
into it had been promiscuously bundled the impedimenta from 'Holloway
Castle', a camp bedstead and huge portmanteau, for all the world as if his
lordship had just returned from a holiday tour. But amid the piled up
personal effects were things that spoke of anything but a holiday time. A few
volumes were there; one of them, I noticed, was the *Institutes of Justinian*, and
I speculated on the humorous question whether Lord Russell had beguiled
the tedious hours resulting from his mistake as to our marriage law by
studying the nice legal distinctions which existed in the tangled domestic
relations of old Rome. A pathetic touch was supplied by a chess-board and
a bundle of chess problems cut from the daily papers. What a life must it be
which would suggest such a severe recreation for the long days of summer!
But presently I was shown into the charming little smoking room, with its
richly coloured hangings and comfortable lounge, and in a few minutes was
taken to the large old-fashioned sitting-room, where I found the Earl and –
pace the Lord Chancellor – the present Lady Russell. His lordship was
enjoying his first smoke, and looked more fit and well than during the
anxious time before his imprisonment. His hair was massed in luxuriant curls
over his face, which beamed with smiles of amusement as he looked through
the pile of accumulated correspondence, of which he now obtained his first
glimpse. For during the three months he had only been allowed three letters
a week, and the allowance had been monopolised by Lady Russell herself,
in the days between the three weekly visits which she was allowed to make.
There were letters and telegrams of congratulation on his release both from
the Continent and this country; epistles of sympathy from various offenders
who had at one time or another experienced the hospitality of the Governor
of Holloway, and who evidently hoped that a 'fellow-feeling' would make
his lordship 'wonderous kind'; and formal letters from young men, who
began, 'My Lord,–I am a journalist', and promised themselves in this release
an opportunity for literary fame. A clergyman of the North of England wrote
a vigorous letter of sympathy and protest against the outrageous sentence
passed by the House of Lords; and there were anonymous screeds of abuse,
too malignant to be anything but funny.

'Well, My Lord,' said I, 'welcome back to liberty. I understand there is
rather more of you to welcome than when you went in.'

'What,' said Lord Russell, with a comical look of horror, 'do you notice –
–?'

'No, no, you look just the same to me, but I heard you had gained three

57

stones in prison.'

'Oh!" was the reply, given with much relief, 'I was afraid I was showing it. I did gain three stones, because the only exercise I got was two hours' walking, and none at all when it rained. But lately I have been dieting, and now I am only half a stone heavier than before.'

'What did you think of the sentence?'

'They tell me it was to have been six months but for my speech in the Lords. But three months seems to be the standard sentence for everything just now. We had one man in Holloway for three months for a serious offence under Stead's Act, and another who had been charged with murder and convicted of manslaughter. So whether it is a technical mistake or a serious crime, three months seems to be the fashion.'

'How do you like liberty?'

'I can hardly realise it yet. As I sit here and talk I cannot help feeling as if it is still prison, and the warder will come in at the door in a minute to stop us.'

'I suppose you were very well treated?'

'Yes, very well, so far as the regulations permitted. Things are much stricter now. Ten years ago visitors were allowed in the same room with a first-class misdemeanant. But I was only allowed to be visited three times a week, in a room divided into two by crossed wires so fine that only a lead-pencil could have been pushed through. The prisoner is locked in on one side, and the visitor on the other, and a warder walks back and forward outside, looking in at a glass door. The room being quite bare of furniture, all conversation echoes and reverberates most horribly, so that it is difficult to talk. It is impossible to keep on looking through the wires, it made my eyes so bad that in a short time I could not see.'

'Yes,' added Lady Russell, 'and when I got home if I went to my birds the very sight of their cages made me shiver.'

'Happily,' said his lordship, 'the Home Office allowed the grill to be abolished for one of my three weekly visits, but though this was done on account of the injury to my sight, they insisted on the wire grill being kept up the other two days.'

'What about your food?'

'Oh, I ordered it in myself. There is a place called 'The Cottage' nearby, where a contractor lives who is allowed to send in food to those prisoners who can order their own, the first-class misdemeanants and the remand prisoners.'

'Had you many visitors?'

'No, very few. I really did not mind that. For visitors unsettle me, and make the time seem long. It goes all the more quickly through the monotony when one is undisturbed.'

'What do you intend to do now?'

'To rest for a few days, and then resume my ordinary advocations. I suppose,' added his lordship, laughing, 'the public will think that means going about committing bigamy.'

'Will you marry again in this country?'

'As I said to the House of Lords, I am only waiting for my release by the Divorce Court to make my marriage legal. I look on a second marriage in this country as a purely legal formality, like the signing of a deed. But, of course, if it is necessary, I must do it. The divorce and marriage in Nevada were, and are, absolutely valid, and cannot be upset, notwithstanding what was said at the trial. I ought never to have been prosecuted at all, and they did not allow me time to get my evidence.'

A Peer's Prison Life, *St James's Gazette*, 27 Nov 1901.

In a lecture at the Pharos Club last night Lord Russell gave a graphic description of his life in Holloway Prison while serving the sentence of three months passed last summer by the House of Lords. When he went into prison the governor asked his religion, and he replied 'Agnostic'. That seemed to puzzle the governor, who said he supposed it was Protestant; at any rate it was not Catholic. And as 'Prot.' Lord Russell was entered on his 'door card'. He was given a debtor to act as his 'cleaner', or servant, and paid 2s 6d a week rent for his room, and sixpence a day for the cleaner's services. Of this sixpence the governor kept fourpence, giving 2d a day to the cleaner on his discharge. In conclusion Lord Russell praised the humanity of the officials and warders, but held that the life of most prisoners – twenty-three hours out of the twenty-four in cell – was terribly monotonous, and could do no good to young offenders.

Earl Russell on Prison Life, *Daily News*, 27 Nov 1901.

Earl Russell, who recently underwent three months' imprisonment in Holloway Gaol, last night delivered, before members of the Pharos Club, an address on 'Our Prison System'. Alluding to his experiences at Holloway, he said it was 'no fun' for him. On the whole, he found little fault with his treatment. Among the chief of his disabilities was the difficulty of obtaining articles of ordinary use and the insufficient exercise. With regard to the first it took three weeks of continuous application before he could get even a pair of nail scissors supplied to him and another three weeks to obtain his watch. He had found the prison warders very much more amiable than he had expected, but he could not say how they treated prisoners who were not members of the Peerage and not in the 'first class'. From what he had seen he did not think the warders were really rude to anyone. With respect to the sanitary condition of the prison Earl Russell said, 'While I was at Holloway there was a great deal of agitation with regard to vermin in the prison.[8] Now, that was all perfectly true, and the newspaper reports of the matter contained nothing which could really be called exaggeration. As a matter of fact the report of the whitewashing committee which was appointed to look into the matter was official rather than correct, and there was not much in it. But I know they were boiling some of the furniture afterwards.' He was much bothered by the continual clicking of the warders' keys in the locks as they made their nightly rounds, and he also found the consciousness of being under constant surveillance through the 'spyhole' somewhat disquieting. Despite his restrictions, however, his health did not greatly suffer, and he actually gained a pound or two, though this he ascribed principally to want of sufficient exercise, especially for a man who was used to activity. He could suggest no reform in the manner in which prisons were at present conducted.

Notes

1. *PP*, p. 303.
2. MS-3699, Box 3.8.
3. Shaw, p.336.
4. *The Woman Who Did* (1895), about a young woman who chose a Shavian-style 'free union' and had a child out of wedlock, was intended as a comment on the 'new woman'. It provoked much controversy and several answers – Victoria Crosse, *The Woman Who Didn't* (1895), Mrs Lovett Cameron, *The Man Who Didn't* (1895) and Lucas Cleeve, *The Woman Who Wouldn't* (1895), respectively about a woman who stayed with faithful to an impossible husband, a man who remained faithful to his wife, and a young woman who resisted seduction.
5. Note about Frank's letter (RA1 Box 6.27 46888), dated 1949 (RA1 Box 6.27 46887).
6. 'Only in the cases of murder and manslaughter and that by comparatively recent legislation can an Englishman who commits a crime abroad be tried for it in England' (Anson, 1896, p. 73). For the third edition, with reference to and as a direct result of Frank's trial, this appeared with the extension 'and the same rule applies to bigamy, though the second marriage has taken place "in England, Ireland, or elsewhere"' (Anson, 1907, p. 242).
7. *MLA*, p. 283.
8. See 'Visit to Holloway Prison: Are the Cells Verminous? Testimony of Warders: The Case of Earl Russell', *Daily News*, 5 Aug 1901, p. 3.

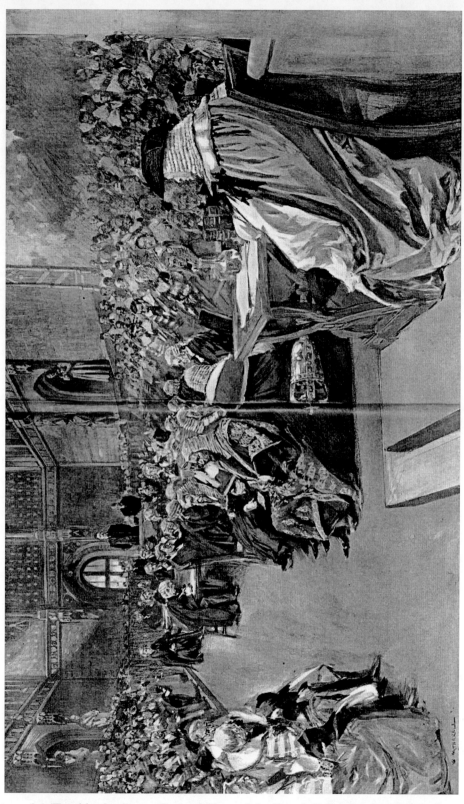

3.1 'Tried by his Peers: General View of the Royal Gallery at the House of Lords during Earl Russell's Trial for Bigamy', *The Graphic*, 27 July 1901.

4. Frank, 1901.

Chapter 4

After Holloway:
Proselytising Rationalism

Frank took advantage of his enforced solitude in Holloway to reread his Bible. He then began, as he put it, to develop some ideas he had long held. The resultant *Lay Sermons*, comprising twenty-two discourses on Christianity from an agnostic prospective, were published in November 1902. Their reception was mixed. Frank was undoubtedly still developing as a writer and the sermons needed panning for their gold. Few fully appreciated Frank's purpose. Of those who did, *Scotsman* commented that the sermons 'say many things that cannot but evoke sympathy and assent from readers repelled by the cast-iron antiquities of dogma'.[1] With each sermon his scathing analysis of the Church, its history and teachings intensified. They proved, continued *St James's Gazette*, 'that, whatever else Lord Russell may be, he is a man of courage.'[2]

Extracts from *Lay Sermons*

Love or Lust
'Whosoever looketh on a woman to lust after her hath committed adultery with her already in his heart.' – Matthew 5:28.

Christ was an inspired moral teacher of great fervour tinged with an ascetic revolt against the sensual conditions of his time. As such he was not perhaps best fitted to judge of the ordinary human relations between the sexes. From his earliest youth he had been occupied with the great questions of life, its conduct and its purpose, and had lived strenuously to draw others into the path of salvation, and to make the way plain. He had no time and no spare energy for domesticity, so that the life of the family, the natural mating of the sexes, the joy of wife and children, the slightly selfish heaven of an intensely happy home were to him altogether unknown experiences. In addition to this want of experience the morality of the age when the sanity of earlier Greek life had been succeeded by the orgies described by Paul in his epistles to the Romans and the Corinthians was such as to produce complete revolt against the body in the mind of the thinker and teacher, failing in a reaction of disgust to see any decency in any exercise of natural functions. We must further remember that the Jews among whom he had been born lived under laws which took a rather gross view of these matters.

In view of all these influences we may perhaps rather admire the sanity of Christian teaching and wonder at its limitations. For instance in commenting on the Jewish law of divorce Christ makes it perfectly clear that in his view marriage should be indissoluble and that in no event should either of two divorced spouses remarry. His own ascetic tendency to treat such desires as of no great moment is shown in the counsel of perfection denying divorce altogether, and the contemptuous admission that Moses granted it for the hardness of their hearts—not, that is, as a thing just in itself but as a concession to weak and incontinent fools. The extreme view as to the merit of renouncing natural functions is given at the end of one of these discussions: 'There are eunuchs which have made themselves eunuchs for the kingdom of heaven's sake',[3] and of course this is the logical conclusion. Paul admitting no shilly shally and driving straight ahead as usual seems to suggest that this view meets with his endorsement in saying, 'Yet I would that all men were even as I myself. Howbeit each man hath his own gift from God, one after this manner, and another after that.'[4] If then we are to accept the Biblical account it may be said to regard complete continence as more estimable than marriage, and marriage as indissoluble under all conditions. Though the word sacrament be not used there is ample support here for the Catholic view and ample cause for the blight thrown by the Church on the relations of the sexes. It is true that here within the last fifty years we have advanced slightly: we have allowed the marriage to be a civil contract and have made it dissoluble. But to the present day wherever the influence of the Church penetrates the discussion of these questions is clouded by an ecclesiastical haze and embittered by priestly prejudice.

In the question of the Sadducees (where it is as well for those who think all necessary precepts can be found in the Scriptures to note that incidentally no objection is made to a marriage with the deceased husband's brother) Christ slips lightly out of a difficulty which after all was a mere quibble of no importance. The story of the woman taken in adultery which we now have to abandon as not authentic is touching but does not carry us much further. It is not to be supposed that Christ felt or could feel much sympathy with a crime of that character or much understanding of one so alien to his nature and all he does in effect is to suggest that her crime was not much worse than others and no more to be considered hopeless. 'Go thy way': he had no wish to talk with her, but let her not suppose there was no sin: 'from henceforth sin no more'.[5]

Paul does not do much more than emphasise what seems to be the general view of Christ. He, as has been said before, carries the view of continence so far as to consider a eunuch nearer to God than a whole man and allows marriage as a sort of concession: 'it is better to marry than to burn.' It is the more strange, for in one passage he seems to recognise clearly the rights and duties of married persons, and that not from the man's point of view only, but, as clearly as Sarah Grand herself could desire, from the woman's also.[6] He extends the doctrine to virgins in a rather confused sort of way and apparently to widows: marriage to Paul, as indeed in places in the Prayer Book, is only a sort of legalised alternative to fornication.

From these ideas have sprung a celibate priesthood, monasteries and nunneries and all other religious devices for curbing nature and turning her lawful demands into hidden impurities and sterile horrors.

In heaven it may be they are as the angels and there is neither marrying nor giving in marriage: on earth however the union of the sexes is necessary for the continuation of the race, and nature has implanted the strongest instincts and desires to ensure that it shall take place. What then are the ideal conditions of such a union and what are the limits to be imposed on carnal appetites? The natural feelings of clean men and women in a state of perfect health free from artificial restraints upon those feelings will supply the answer. Where the man desires with a full sense of responsibility and respect to embrace the woman, and where she with a lift of her whole being yields herself without fear and without shame, there you get the true union which makes for morality and produces healthy offspring. But these ideal conditions are very seldom attained; questions of money or of social status often unconsciously blur the woman's natural emotion till she fails to clearly read it signs. Early dissipation and immoralities leave the man's finer feelings blunted; social success and selfishness cause the women's to die of atrophy. Worldly counsel of parents ousts the true guide of nature; excited and selfish physical passion is mistaken for the call of love.

... A marriage to be perfect must be between persons of approximately the same age, of sound minds and healthy bodies, filled with a natural love of one another: that is the physical requisite. It must be a public ceremony announcing in the form of the locality that couple's intention to the world and so removing all element of intrigue and concealment: that is the social requisite. The physical desire must never be the object but the triumphant glorious love of two happy and devoted souls must feel that its fitting crown and perfection, the symbol of its existence, is to be found in the union of their bodies: that is the moral requisite. Wherever this last condition is absent the union is adulterous and contrary to the law of God and no social pretexts can cure the fatal defect....

Of divorce, this alone need be said. It is of course an institution not required where all marriages are perfect. But their judgement obscured by passion, vanity, poverty; their hearts mistaken through immaturity or through bad training and the choking overgrowth of social weeds; and their senses blunted by squalor or by vice; young men and women have made, and always will make, occasional mistakes in choosing their mates. To remedy these mistakes and to advance in a lawful manner under the protection of society to a higher union is the object of divorce. When this is more truly appreciated the Church will cease its endeavour to cause unloving couples to live together in sin, or to compel them to change moral for legal adultery.

... Not till the squeamishness which gives vice its opportunity is put away: not till a knowledge of the dignity of sex is substituted for a cruel ignorance responsible for lewd imaginings and whispered innuendo; not till honesty in speech and thought replaces a morbid hiding of truth and a dirty-minded delicacy; not till the admiration for a clean and healthy body has ousted the cult of suggestiveness and drapery, can we hope that true marriage will finally take the place of adulterous unions. Religion and the church have helped little in this but have rather by the suggestion of uncleanness in the body greatly hindered; but every man and woman can help and help mightily by the simple expedient of beginning to be honest with their spouses, their friends, their children, and above all, with themselves, in their thoughts and speech about the relations of men and women.

Vicarious Atonement
'Being justified freely by his grace through the redemption that is in Christ Jesus.' –
Romans 3:24

The idea of a sacrifice to a justly offended deity, to be accepted as a vicarious atonement of sin, was of course natural to the Jews, and one might fairly expect to find it recur in a religion founded by a Jew and modified on all hands by the influence of Jewish tradition. Chapters 4 to 7 of Leviticus are concerned with minute details of these sin offerings, of what nature they should be and in what manner sacrificed, and in the sixteenth chapter we find the idea of the scapegoat, who by means of one sacrifice should bear upon him and take away all the iniquities of the children of Israel, and all their transgressions in all their sins. No wonder that to minds filled with these ideas the death of Christ upon the Cross appeared to have the character of a stupendous sacrifice for the sins of the whole world.

Christ himself in the speeches attributed to him is not held up as giving much countenance to the idea. 'He that believeth and is baptised shall be saved,' at the very end of St Mark, after the resurrection, is about the nearest approach to it, and apart from the doubtful authenticity of the text, the speech is quite unlike the manner and the mind of Christ, who shows elsewhere no indication of considering a mere ceremony, such as baptism, of any importance one way or another.

Paul, however, whose conversion could not alter his characteristic materialism, but only turned its exercise into a different channel, may safely be relied on to remove the ambiguities. As his energy founded and held together distant churches, so his burning desire to make Christianity clear, to drive it into his followers, led him in each case to degrade, to materialise and crystallize into formulae the nebulous outpourings of his Master, with whose mysticism he had nothing in common. So in the Epistle to the Romans we find, 'By the deeds of the law there shall no flesh be justified... for all have sinned... *being justified freely by his grace through the redemption* that is Christ Jesus.'[7] '*Being now justified by his blood* we shall be saved from wrath through him.'[8] And in the First Epistle to the Thessalonians, 'God hath appointed us to attain salvation by our Lord Jesus Christ *who died for us.*'[9] More definitely in the Epistle to the Hebrews, 'Christ was once *offered to bear the sins* of many.'[10] 'But this man after he had *offered one sacrifice for the sins* for ever.'[11] Here we have justification by faith, and salvation by the vicarious sacrifice of Christ fully developed. Let us see how the Church interprets these sentences, and let us turn first to the Articles of Religion. In the second we find, 'Christ was crucified to *reconcile his Father* to us, and to be a sacrifice not only for original guilt, but also for all the actual sins of men.' And in Article 31, 'the Offering of Christ once made is that perfect redemption, propitiation, and satisfaction for all the sins of the whole world, both original and actual; but there is *none other satisfaction for sin*, but that alone.' Again throughout the Communion Service runs this central idea, 'the *redemption* of the world *by the death* and passion of our Saviour Christ' 'by his one *oblation of himself once offered.*' In the Catechism, 'I learn to believe in God the Son *who hath redeemed me and all mankind.*' These expressions are so clear and unequivocal that it becomes unnecessary to multiply further instances, but it is well to study them so that it may not be said any inferences are drawn from them which they will not bear.

What then does the doctrine of Vicarious Atonement, as taught and believed by the Church today, amount to? It may be divided into three parts–first the Deity after the Jewish conception of Him, justly offended with His people's sins and waiting some sacrifice–secondly the sacrifice of Christ upon the Cross appeasing the wrath of this Deity by his agony and bloody sweat–thirdly, the redemption of all mankind by virtue of that sacrifice, and that alone, apart altogether from Works. I may be wrong, but this doctrine has always seemed to me the most blasphemous and paralyzing conception that has ever been invented by any religion. It is of course generally glossed over and concealed, but the quotations I have given show that it is definitely accepted by the Church, and the street preacher, or the Salvation Army ranter, may be heard any day enunciating it in its baldest and crudest form. And as so expounded it has one merit, and one alone–and that only incidental and not necessary to it. I mean the insistence on the fact that the way of penitence is always open, and that it is never too late to turn from sin.

But the blasphemy of attributing anger to a God, who by definition is all foreseeing, and must have known of, and allowed, the sin which now rouses his vengeance; and the crude Jewish materialism which represents Him as satiating a lust for vengeance by causing the lingering death of the Crucifixion, and accepting that is a suitable sacrifice, are astounding in this year of grace. Truly men are ready to ascribe to the Almighty a process of reasoning, and a course of conduct which they would indignantly resent if ascribed to themselves! I cannot but think that many when they come upon this problem satisfy their minds by postulating a sort of Fate or Necessity of the Greek tragedians, which sits behind Zeus, and has immutable laws that must be followed. They probably did not see that in doing this they are deposing their God from omnipotence, and leaving Him only a limited sovereignty. It is very greatly to be feared that all the books of the New Testament, and particularly the life of Christ, cannot, with most minds, outweigh the picture of Heaven and its rulers presented in the Old Testament. What has become of the truer interpretation of God? 'I will have mercy and not sacrifice.'[12] 'A broken and contrite heart thou wilt not despise.'[13] Unfortunately the lower and more material view of a religious truth is easier understood, and therefore more readily finds acceptance in the average mind.

… Why do I say this great scientific truth, which has been lost sight of, is so important? Because without it morality is a mere artificial code, while with its realization it becomes vivid and dominating. A child may burn itself with a hot iron and run for comfort to its mother. But all her love and comfort cannot destroy the fact that he has been burnt, still less can they protect him from being burnt again if he does the same thing. Later in life he eats poisonous berries and again the inevitable retribution follows, though not so swiftly as in the case of the burn. Now he has learnt that the doing of certain acts entails certain unpleasant consequences, and he believes it, so that he acts on his belief. In the domain of morals he must, partly by experiment and partly by conviction, arrive at the same certainty of belief. The punishments are slower, the effects more complex, and less easy to unravel and look at than a burn on the finger. But it is essential for the soul's health that he should learn to regard them as equally certain, and equally inevitable. Then, and then only, will the tendency to avoid wrong acts be always and necessarily, stronger than the tendency to do them. Then only will he realize how, and in what way, virtue is her own reward. And while he thinks these consequences and these results can be escaped altogether by some formula or some hocus pocus, call it a Profession of Faith, a Doctrine of Atonement, or what you will, so long will he remain in a path of error with no certain incentive to virtue.

Speculations

'I beheld all the work of God, that man cannot find out the work that is done under the sun: because however much a man labour to seek it out, yet he shall not find it: yea moreover though a wise man think to know it, yet shall he not be able to find it.'
– Ecclesiastes 8:17.

… In face of all this uncertainty about all these possible subjects of dispute, is not Agnosticism the most modest and wisest attitude? It is idle for theologians to make definite assertions and claim a knowledge of the schemes of the Almighty in an age where folk begin increasingly to ask for proof or at least for logical probability. It is as idle and no less presumptuous for persons whose mental horizon is limited by the things they can see and touch, to try and limit the views of others by the same boundaries, more especially when these limits are constantly overpassed by emotional experiences. An open mind, a willingness to learn, and a readiness to accept such experience as comes our way, is most fitly coupled with a proper humility as to things about which we can only surmise and where certain knowledge is of necessity lacking. This is all that Agnosticism means, and it appears to allow very wide margins of interpretation in these speculative fields, it may nevertheless be united to extreme certainty in the rules of conduct required for daily life. And it may be safely predicted that a serious attempt to live up to the standard of Christian conduct will take us all our time and all our energies, and cause the apparent importance of speculative controversy about things we know nothing of, to grow less and less. 'Be not rash with thy mouth, and let not thine heart be hasty to utter anything before God; for God is in Heaven, and thou upon earth: therefore let thy words be few. For a dream cometh with a multitude of business; and a fool's voice with a multitude of words.'[14]

Priestly Intolerance

'It pertaineth not unto thee, Uzziah, to burn incense unto the Lord, but to the priests the sons of Asaron, that are consecrated to burn incense: go out of the sanctuary; for thou has trespassed.' – 2 Chronicles 26:18.

… Priests rule by terror of the supernatural, by delusions and by ignorance on the part of their victims. Wherever a strong coherent body of priests have exercised great power over the common people, it will be found that the priests had knowledge while the populace was ignorant, and that they frightened the laity with superstitious terrors or deluded them with hopes, in neither of which they had any great belief themselves. But all men and all organizations love power, and a strong priesthood is nothing in the world but a well-organized political secret society with immense power and far-reaching influence. It can never then cause surprise to find that such a class naturally looks upon free-thought of all kinds as an abomination, and education of the populace as the beginning of the end. If the superstitious weapons of their armoury are to be taken to pieces in the presence of the public and shown to be only trick daggers and stage thunders, what have they left to control the masses? If a consecrated priest is shown to be only a very ordinary man, and if the words of his sacred book are to be looked into and criticised as if it were a mere classic, what becomes of mystery, reverence and awe? To Christ it would have been the realization of an ideal that all men should be as clever, as well-informed, and as good as himself—he wished to draw them up to his level—but can our parsons who talk about over-education, proper stations and subjection of the poor, say as much?

No one need suppose that even in this country or in this century, priestly intolerance is dead. Consider the absurd view of marriage taken by the Church, which expressly denies that it is a Sacrament and yet cannot admit that it is a civil contract with peculiar incidents. As a direct consequence of priestly influence we get absurd divorce laws here and even endeavour to impose similar ones on our self-governing colonies. Another matter which also seems capable of always provoking a fine outburst of bigotry is the burial of the dead. When a man has reached that stage of his journey it might be hoped that intolerance need pursue him no longer, but priests seem to fear that a spiritual weapon might be lost if their vigour were relaxed. ...

... When unbaptised children are brought for burial, or Dissenters who have the right to the parish churchyard, the opportunity is often taken to harrow the feelings of the mourners by graveside scandals showing the most the brutal bigotry, and the strangest indifference to that loving and gentle Master whose teachings his ministers so belie.

... We have in this country a State Church technically subject it is true to the civil power, but with ample freedom to work out its own salvation. Its officers have their ordered grades and received their official stipends free from all necessity to conciliate their congregations: its wealth is enormous and its buildings stand in every parish. What a magnificent opportunity for a national Church which might be the centre of the religious life of every soul in the community! Everyone knows how gloriously this opportunity has been neglected: how internecine strife uses energy wanted elsewhere: how doctrinal barriers keep out a vast proportion of the laity and exclude many who would make earnest ministers: how every little difference of opinion is accentuated and magnified: and how in some parishes a mere perfunctory ministration has to serve for the active spirit of Christ. At the head stands a group of Bishops, true princes of the Church, drawing salaries proportioned to the importance of their higher offices. Here we have men of high character, of long service, of absolutely independent position, able

69

one would suppose without fear to break a lance for Christ. It would seem to be their special function to keep the nation in the path of righteousness and to rebuke sin and licentiousness among the great ones of the earth. But the courage of the Hebrew prophet Nathan does not belong to these days, and his mantle seems not to have fallen on our Archbishops. And how do we find these great princes, these prelates of the Church, helping in the national life? They acknowledge drunkenness to be one of our curses: they sit on committees and sign reports: but do we find them coming down into the arena of a parliamentary election, making speeches on platforms and instructing their clergy to use their pulpits in the cause of temperance? Do they warn wealthy brewers of their acquaintance of the sinful nature of tied-house contracts which make for drunkenness? Do they exhort magistrates to make a reality of the licensing laws? Do they instruct their clergy to give evidence against disorderly public houses? When the country is at war do they pray for peace, or do they pray for victory? Do they searched their hearts, or do they stop the ears? Do they preach brotherly love, or do they echo extermination? Did they seek first the Kingdom of God and his righteousness, giving no heed to dignity, office or popularity but trusting these things shall be added unto them?

Alas, we know that Bishops do none of these things: and a look at their record will show that they never have done them. Every political reform, every social advance, even such matters as the abolition of the death penalty for trivial offences, has been stoutly and ferociously resisted by the Bishops in the House of Lords. Did we depend on them to lead us, we should not have advanced in morals or in freedom from the days of the Stuarts. In what way do we hear of their activities being exercised? One publishes a circular about the yards of stair-carpet in his palace, another tells an interviewer how many letters he receives daily, another spends months touring the Churches of his diocese to look for illegal ornaments. We never hear of them as showing a whole hearted desire to reform the Church and make it a business organization: rather from time-to-time some scandal comes to light where a vicar with a large stipend has lived for years away from his cure, and paid some curate a starvation wage to run the parish, while the Ordinary has done nothing. They must believe in a Day of Judgement and yet the number of confirmations, communions, letters, visits, stair-carpets, journey's, etc., will avail nothing there, when they are asked for their tale of souls saved to Christ. One is bound to assume that there is much work of which one knows nothing, much real work in secret, for judging by what can be seen, one finds the state-aided religious organization beaten in earnestness and zeal on every hand by the voluntary ones which support themselves: and one fails to find in the public utterances of the heads of the Church that clear stand for righteousness and improvement which one is justified in expecting. Are the warnings of the great prophet not applicable even in these days? 'Bring no vain oblations; incense is an abomination unto me; new moon and sabbath, the calling of assemblies,–I cannot away with iniquity and the solemn meeting.'[15] 'Woe unto them that call evil good, and good evil; that put darkness for light, and light for darkness; that put bitter for sweet, and sweet for bitter! Woe unto them that are wise in their own eyes, and prudent in their own sight!'[16]

Miracles
'An evil and adulterous generation seeketh after a sign.' – Matthew 12:39.

… It is hard to have patience with those who, taking the words of the New Testament as a direct and complete revelation of God, ask one to accept such stories as evidential facts comparable in character to facts proved at a trial in a court of law. That coarse old writer, Tom Paine, is the best answer to such: if you will treat these things literally as evidence, very well, only apply the ordinary rules of evidence to them, and see the vulgar absurdity to which you reduce the clashing imagery of the Resurrection.[17]

Literalists deserve to be met with literal criticism and if they will read this writer carefully they will be forced to acknowledge that from that standpoint, some accounts are meaningless and others inconsistent, and so they must abandon their verbal inspiration.

Can we wonder that Christ inveighs so forcibly against this seeking for a sign? In a teacher it is the resort of the charlatan, in his followers the craving of materialists. It can add no force to moral maxims, which, if they are worth anything will stand of their own strength. Christ was the last man to encourage so foolish a superstition, to pander to so depraved a taste. He had no wish for a crowd of terrified worshippers running to him because they were frightened by some supernatural trick, or attracted by conjuring performances. He called for inward conversion, a new heart, a changed spirit–miracles greater than those recorded.

How is it then that we find the narrative interspersed with these accounts of miraculous occurrences? The answer is that that kind of embellishment belonged to that age. The births and deaths of all the great persons for a thousand years either way are generally recorded to have been accompanied by portents. Miracles are found freely in the works of profane writers of that period. No great teacher was unaccompanied by a trick or two to be played with the forces of nature when desirable. It was as much part of a prophet's equipment as his mantle or his staff, and of course the greater the prophet, the larger his selection. The physical marvels, such as the loaves and the fishes, the water into wine and so on, were intended to show his control over nature, from which you were to infer his authority in spiritual matters. Great events in his life threw themselves poetically and pictorially into a dramatic and miraculous setting, as the dove at baptism or the tongues of the fire. Healing the sick was an absolute invariable accompaniment: you might as well portray Minerva without her owl, as a prophet without his cures.

It may further be objected that, given the credulity of the age, and the tendency to ascribe miraculous powers it is still impossible that these events should have been inserted into a contemporary life of Christ if they did not in fact happen. To this there is a two-fold answer, namely, that they might very well be recorded even so, and further that we have nothing approaching a contemporary record. To confine ourselves for the moment to the synoptic gospels, it is of course known to everyone that these are translated from the Greek. But it is not so well known that the earliest record in writing known to exist is no less than 350 years after the events it professes to record, and that it is almost certain that the three gospels in their present form were not reduced to writing at all till 100 years after the death of Christ. So that for 100 years you have nothing but the inaccurate verbal recollections of a set of ignorant and credulous persons to rely on for the manufacture of your history. It is as if our only account of the Battle of the Nile were to be obtained and put together from the gossip picked up at Portsmouth today from the sailors who had learnt the traditions extant in the Navy.

Nor, unfortunately, can it be supposed that the story was cast into a final form when it was at last written on paper. There was no printing press to strike off several thousand identical copies: but each reproduction was the work of some copyist writing it out word by word from his original. Literary fidelity as we understand it did not exist in those days and no man thought it a crime to embellish or add to a story he was copying. For many hundreds of years the work was done by religious houses or collections of priests who had a direct interest in enforcing the truth of the narrative and strengthening its support of the doctrines on which their Church was founded. An honest pious and learned man as he worked would be struck with a resemblance to something in the Old Testament and would make a marginal note of the fulfilment of a prophecy: some dull, mechanical monk copying his manuscript a hundred years later would incorporate the note into the text. Some ecclesiastic thinking Christ's remarks on divorce insufficient and inconclusive would add the church's deduction in an explanatory word or two, and a century later, you would find his note put into the mouth of Christ. An ignorant and superstitious monastery would have some tradition of a miracle and would insert it into their copy of the gospels in what seemed a convenient place. When they believed that very similar miracles were taking place every day, it would seem only natural and right that the gospel narrative should have its share. A modern newspaper reporter does not transmit miraculous occurrences through Reuter because neither he nor his readers would believe them: but of his readiness to vouch anything as a fact when his public wish to believe it, we have had recent demonstration from the atrocity-mongers of South Africa. The gospels fared even worse: there was little inter-communication and little check on inaccuracies: and so each copyist, according to his fancy and moved by ignorance, by a desire to elucidate, or even by actually dishonest motives added to, expanded and altered the story before him, and for many of those alterations we are suffering today.

There is no want of modern counterparts to any miracle. It is not long since witches were supposed to work miracles, and suffered death for it. Pepys mentions in his diary how the touch of Charles II cured the King's Evil. To come to our own times, the cures effected at Lourdes are as wonderful, and supported by far better evidence than any in the New Testament. Yet hardly anyone in this country considers them miraculous. Many people are certain that they saw Mrs Guppy fly over London on a broomstick, but if she had charged a shilling a head for the exhibition she would certainly have been punished for obtaining money by fraud. Madame Blavatsky performed all kinds of miracles in India, and when her tricks were exposed, her dupes continued to believe, and reviled, not her, but her accusers. The money-fraud called Christian Science counts its imbecile followers by thousands in America. Even table-turning and spirit-rapping have their devotees. There is a large class of weak-minded persons who like to be thrilled and do their best to assist in deceiving themselves. Of all these modern miracles evidence can be obtained, contemporary, on oath, from numerous persons, many of them above suspicion of corrupt or pecuniary motives. But not one of them would stand the clear, steady examination of a court of law, and no sane person thinks of believing in them. Why then give credence to the far less well authenticated miracles of the New Testament? Why in this instance alone does the use of the critical faculty become a sin?

There are really only two scientific explanations of alleged miraculous events: either that they did not take place, or that they are not miraculous. What, after all, is the meaning of the word miraculous? Does it mean the suspension of the laws of nature? To turn water in to wine, to make bread and fishes out of nothing, to defy the laws of gravity by walking on water, requires no less than this. The question, of course, appeals differently to different minds, but to a person of scientific faith, of believe in law and order, and of any experimental experience or practice in inductive reasoning it is easier to think any human testimony mistaken and worthless, than to conceive of the suspension of the laws of nature. All science is based on the supposed uniformity of nature's working and in no domain of science can experiment discover a single infraction of that law, while we have daily evidence of the fallibility of human testimony. On this head scientific investigation has lately accumulated some striking facts making a subjective hallucination to three people at the same time of such a miracle as the Transfiguration quite possible, though, to the outward eye, nothing did in fact occur. Nor can science admit that there was any age of miracles which has now passed away: it requires uniformity in the past no less than in the present. Moreover such a suggestion does no credit to those who put it forward: for they would not wish us to think that the miracle worker had lost his power, or was afraid of modern accuracy.[18]

The second explanation viz: that the occurrences are not miraculous is also often true. When due allowance has been made for human error in observing phenomena, and for subjective hallucinations, there may still remain something difficult of explanation. The answer of science is that the true explanation will be found to be in accordance with the laws of nature, even if these are sometimes imperfectly understood. The difference between that and a miracle is that the same causes can be depended on to produce the same results: all is uniform and not capricious. Thus the operations of the Electric Telegraph, the performances of Maskelyne and Cooke, the development of a bird from an egg, the effect on the body of states of mind are all sufficient to cause wonder, and are all difficult of explanation, but no one believes them to be supernatural, or thinks them other than the necessary consequences of some well-ordered law of science. So, often, that which is miraculous means only that which is not understood.

Why, it may be asked, attack miracles? Why disturb people who like to believe in the supernatural? The scornful language of our text is sufficient reply: 'It is an evil and adulterous generation that seeketh for a sign.' The mind that wants to bolster its faith with portents and miraculous happening is in a very low stage of development and must shake off this hankering before it can begin to learn to worship God in spirit and in truth. And that literal interpretation of the Scriptures which goes with a belief in miracles, is a danger to faith, and a clog to true religion and progress. Consider only for a moment the material views of the sacrament, of the resurrection, or marriage and divorce, of heaven and hell and the devil, which have resulted from this attitude of mind and the pitiful squabbles founded on these literal views, and you will see how these superstitious beliefs have hung over Christianity like a pall, blinding poor deluded men to that Heaven which is about them on every hand, turning God's truth into a lie, and closing the eye of faith to far nobler miracles of daily occurrence. That is why we should shake free of these delusions of an evil generation, and remember always that the letter killeth, but the spirit maketh alive.

Divorce Reform

The suggestion that Frank was considering a rational assault on the ecclesiastical divorce laws that had put him in prison appears in the various references to the Christian view of the indissolubility of marriage scattered throughout *Lay Sermons*. His first definite step in this direction quickly followed with a radical proposal for an entirely new divorce law presented to the House of Lords on 1 May 1902. In England and Wales at the time there was provision only for divorce on the ground of adultery for a man and aggravated adultery – that is, adultery compounded by two years' desertion, incest or cruelty – for a woman; or the single grounds of bigamy, rape or sodomy.[19] This being Frank's first major speech in the Lords made it all the more audacious. Its reception reflected the size of the mountain he was attempting to climb against the thunder of convention. Undeterred, he followed it with three further proposals across six years. Extracts from his speeches and a 1912 article for *English Review* follow.

House of Lords Debate 1 May 1902: Divorce Bill

Frank first summarised the 17 clauses in his Bill which provided for divorce for men and women equally on the grounds of adultery, bigamy, sodomy, rape, cruelty, three years' living apart or one by mutual consent. It enabled a wife to sue a co-respondent for damages (as a husband already could), abolished judicial separation and restitution of conjugal rights, gave county courts jurisdiction over low-income cases and decreased the time in which a decree *nisi* was made absolute from six months to one.[20] In justification he said–

> The mind of everyone who considers the question of divorce turns naturally to the religious view upon the subject–to the Scriptural warrant for divorce or the Scriptural prohibition of divorce, as the case may be. That occupied a very large portion of the discussions in your Lordships' House in 1856 and 1857, and I find that very divergent views were taken on that subject. In July 1856, the Bishop of Salisbury said– He thought that no teaching could be more plain than this, and he could come to only one conclusion, viz., that our Lord had annulled the provisions of the *libellum repudii* and that divorce and remarriage were, according to the law of Christ, impossible.[21] He, however, admitted that there was one exception allowed for divorce–not for divorce and remarriage, but for separation without the power of remarrying–and that was the case of adultery.[22]
>
> The Bishop of Oxford, whose view appeared to vary somewhat from time to time, said on July 3rd, 1856– He thought that it would be in the

recollection of the House that he had never alleged that any canon of the Church laid down the law upon the matter, nor had he denied that marriage in its essence was other than a civil contract.

On June 25th, 1857, the Bishop of Oxford said– There were many of their Lordships who believed that whatever doubts there might be as to the general power of remarriage after divorce, there was no doubt that the words of our Lord forbade the adulterous woman remarrying in the lifetime of her husband.

Finally, in uttering a last protest against the passing of the measure, the Bishop said–He believed it was contrary to the law of God, contrary to the law of the Church of England, and, as he believed, fruitful in future crime and misery to the people of England. He believed that in passing it they were dealing a more fatal blow to family purity than they could by any other Act.

Whereas the Bishop of Oxford held that divorce and remarriage were impossible, other Members of the Episcopal Bench seemed to think that divorce was permitted in the case of adultery, and that remarriage–in the case, at any rate, of the innocent party–could take place. I have done what I could to arrive at a conclusion on the subject, and my own mind is that Christ, in answering the questions that were put to Him, did not contemplate what we understand by a divorce *a vinculo*. That being so, I do not think it is necessary for your Lordships at this date further to deal with the question whether or not there is a Scriptural permission for divorce *a vinculo*, because that has been settled by the passing of the Act of 1857. I need not, therefore, trouble your Lordships further with regard to the Scriptural argument, which seems to me not to be conclusive one way or the other; and I do not know that your Lordships would feel bound, in legislating at the present day, by some dictum laid down in the New Testament, and variously interpreted. The question was felt to be so difficult in 1857 that the appointment of a Select Committee was moved to consider it, but the proposal was rejected, it being felt that the decision of a Select Committee could have no authority which would be binding on a theological question of this character.

What is our present practice with regard to divorce? A divorce *a vinculo* is granted to a husband for adultery on the part of his wife, and to a wife for adultery on the part of her husband when coupled with cruelty or other aggravating circumstances. It was felt at the time when the Act was passed that that difference between the sexes was an unfair difference, and one which could not be maintained; and, owing to the growth of that feeling, the practice in the Divorce Court has been to find the husband guilty of cruelty, when adultery has been proved, on evidence which is continually decreasing in strength. The other remedy that the present law provides is that of judicial separation, which is a divorce for all practical purposes, but does not dissolve the legal bond of marriage or enable either of the parties to marry again. Such a separation as that is granted for cruelty and desertion. It is a sort of *via media* that has been discovered in this country, and is, I believe, peculiar to this country, between absolute divorce and refusal of divorce; and it is supposed to afford sufficient relief to those who suffer through unhappy marriages. Desertion, according to the ruling of the Courts, cannot commence if the parties have once separated by mutual consent. I speak subject to correction, but I have been advised that where a desertion takes place in the first instance by consent, even for a time limited, that cannot be converted into a wilful desertion by the refusal of one party to return to cohabitation. Your Lordships are, of course, aware of the provisions against collusion and connivance, and for damages against the adulterer. In addition, there is the special provision that a decree when made shall not become absolute for six months, and there is an official known as the King's Proctor whose duty it is to spend the interval in ascertaining whether anything material has been kept from the Court, and whether the petitioner came to the Court, as the expression is, 'with clean hands'. The law as it exists at present in this country is that where one party to the marriage has committed adultery a divorce can be granted, but where both parties have committed adultery a divorce is refused. In accordance with the present practice of the Court, if both parties desire a divorce they are almost certain to be found guilty of collusion. The provision with regard to collusion was originally intended, I presume, to prevent one party committing adultery by agreement with the other; but it has come to mean in practice that one of the parties must be supposed not to desire the divorce which the other party is seeking. An action for divorce has only to be undefended for collusion to be at once suspected.

Then, my Lords, there is a curious claim as to territorial jurisdiction made by the Divorce Court, which makes the law bear harder on many people than might otherwise be the case; for if persons were able to obtain divorces in other places the severity of the divorce law in this country would not affect them so seriously. But, as the law stands, a divorce obtained in another country is not recognised unless the person who obtains it is domiciled there, and the admission of such foreign domicile is practically never made by the Court. ...

We have very close at hand a divorce law which differs materially from ours, and which agrees to a large extent with the proposals I am laying before your Lordships. We have to go no further than Scotland to find a country where divorce *a vinculo* is permitted for desertion for three years and upwards, and that law has not, so far as I am aware, led to scandal or abuse. In America, divorce is allowed for a great many reasons, some of which might appear almost frivolous. The practice is so varied in the different independent sovereign States of the Union, that it is difficult to lay down any general law; but your Lordships are, no doubt, aware of what are the general grounds on which a divorce is granted in America, and that desertion and cruelty provide grounds for divorce in a large majority of the States. The question arises, is there any need for an Amendment of the divorce law? Although not one of your Lordships may be prepared to support this Bill, I still think there is not one noble Lord who can say that the divorce law is in a satisfactory or logical position, or who will not admit that some Amendment is urgently called for. Cases of hardship arise perpetually. There are cases in which persons have been, to all intents and purposes, divorced for years and years, but, notwithstanding, severance of the legal bond is refused to them, and they are condemned to live a mutilated life, without a home, a spouse, or a family, or the chance of obtaining any.

The illusory remedy of judicial separation stands, I think, as the worst ever presented as a settlement of matrimonial differences. That I am not alone in that opinion your Lordships will find from the debates that took place in 1857. I am glad to find that even a Bishop—the Bishop of Exeter— took the view that the remedy was not a suitable one. He said— With regard to the doctrine of divorce *a mensa et thoro*, he thought that it was wholly inapplicable to the nature of the offence, and to the circumstances of the law. It was unknown by the Church of Christ at any period, except under the dominion of Rome; but they were now asked permanently to inflict the corrupt system of that Church upon the Church and the nation of England.

On July 3rd, 1856, the Earl of Donoughmore said— What was the law of the Church? It was a remnant of old Catholic times—a remnant of those laws which were made by the priesthood for the purpose of obtaining complete control over the people, and an invention to raise quibbles with the object of levying taxes for dispensations on the marriages of the whole population of Europe. It was confessedly by mere accident that this part of the ecclesiastical law was retained in our jurisprudence. ... He hoped the day was not far distant when Parliament would adopt a general law dealing with this subject in the plain common-sense view which had prevailed in Scotland for years without having inflicted any injury to the morals of the people—that we should recognise the fact that a wife had the same right of divorce as the husband...

I have another opinion, which I regard as a very valuable one, to quote. On August 6th, 1857, during the passage of the Bill through the House of Commons, Viscount Palmerston said— The position in which man and wife were placed by these judicial separations was a most objectionable one, and if marriage were dissolved at all, he thought that it should be dissolved altogether, that the parties should be entirely set free, and that they should be able to contract other engagements. He thought that parting man and wife by these judicial separations placed both of them in situations of great temptation, where they were liable to form connections which it was not desirable to encourage.

I must apologise for reading so many quotations to the House, but I feel that the words of other speakers in support of my argument must carry far more weight than any words of mine can. There can, I think, be no question that the religious view taken of marriage is a survival of that taken by the Roman Catholic Church. In the days when the Church was first allied with the Roman Empire divorce went on very much in accordance with the principles of Roman law, and with a freedom which nobody wishes to re-establish; but the Church gradually came to obtain control over human relations, and the Council of Trent, I believe, finally settled that marriage could not be dissolved for any reason at all. That survival came near being abolished in this country as long ago as the sixteenth century. Archbishop Cranmer, with the assistance of numerous other eminent divines and jurists, drew up a code of Protestant reforms considered desirable, dealing among other things with the law of marriage and known as the *Reformatio legum.* It may be a surprise to those who have not studied this subject to know that this code provided for divorce *a vinculo* not only on the ground of adultery, but on the ground of cruelty and desertion. At that time, therefore, the country came near obtaining that for which I fear I shall ask your Lordships in vain today. What is it that happens when a marriage is dissolved by a sentence of separation *a mensa et thoro*? Both parties are deprived of the opportunity of making fresh ties; both are left neither husband nor wife, nor is either capable of marrying again. They have no home and no power of re-establishing one, they are deprived of mutual help and comfort, of family life and of home. I submit that increased facilities for divorce do not, as is too generally assumed, tend to immorality, but where divorce is justified, tend rather to morality, happiness, and family life.

There has been a change also in the facts of married life in the present day. Your Lordships are all acquainted with the play *The Taming of the Shrew*, in which a somewhat violent man marries a rather violent and rebellious wife. The methods which the husband adopts to reduce his wife to order would in the present day expose him to a successful petition for cruelty and the wife would get a judicial separation. An argument often used against divorce is that where there is an opportunity of separating, the bond of marriage will be less kept to than when it is known that the bond is indissoluble. But no husband is bound at the present day to live with his wife and no wife is bound to live with her husband. The Ecclesiastical Courts took at any rate a logical view of the matter, and recognised that you must either have a real marriage by which the party who refused to live with the other party should be compelled to do so or to go to prison (and for that purpose gave the action for restitution of conjugal rights), or give up the argument of indissolubility. But what is now the effect of that action? The effect of a successful action for restitution of conjugal rights is not to restore the parties to the married state. The order used to be enforced by the painful process in the last degree of imprisonment for contempt, but since the Weldon Act[23] that is no longer the case, and a refusal to obey the order for restitution is now taken as an equivalent for wilful desertion for two years and upwards, and gives the right to a judicial separation. In this way the action effects the exact contrary of its nominal object.

Since the Jackson case was decided it is no longer the law that a husband may put duress on his wife to remain in his house longer than she wishes.[24] If she chooses she may leave him at the church door, and the marriage which has been effected in the church may be broken at that moment by the wife walking away, and there is no power which can bring them back to a state of marriage. I say that if the state of marriage has in fact been abolished it is no longer an advantage to say that the marriage bond shall be indissoluble. Under these circumstances we are not justified now in saying–though I admit that this was an argument which had force in its day–that persons are bound to live together and will somehow endeavour to make the best of it.

I now turn to the provisions of this Bill. Adultery is already admitted by the law to be a sufficient ground for divorce, and I submit that cruelty should also be a reason for obtaining a divorce. At present it is the means of obtaining a divorce *a mensa et thoro*–a partial divorce–but it would be better for the morality and the happiness of the parties were it recognised that cruelty is inconsistent with the marriage vows that bind husband and wife together. Desertion is also entirely inconsistent with the vows they have taken to comfort and assist each other. I have the support in this view of Mr Gladstone. Mr Gladstone was a strenuous opponent of the Bill of 1857, and he made many observations against it, among them the following– We have many causes far more fatal to the great obligations of marriage, as disease, idiocy, crime involving imprisonment for life, and which is, if the bond is dissoluble, might be urged as a reason for divorce; but that is not what I wish to dwell upon at present. My honourable and learned friend said by the fact of the adultery the marriage bond is destroyed, and then he asked the House to pass a Bill under which nineteen out of every twenty adulterers in the land would be covered with perfect immunity.

Mr Gladstone was, of course, referring to the provision that a husband could not be divorced for adultery only. He proceeded– I repeat, the enormous majority of adulteries are adulteries of men; and having shown that adultery destroyed the marriage bond, my honourable and learned friend immediately demanded a licence to destroy nineteen-twentieths of the propositions he laid down.

On the same point Lord Lyndhurst said in March, 1857– I find that in Scotland adultery on the part of the husband gives the wife a right to a divorce, just as the adultery of the woman gives the man a similar right. The remedy extends alike to the lower as to the higher classes; and yet I believe that the state of the law has had no demoralising effect in that country. Why, then, should we assume that a similar provision would be prejudicial to morality in this portion of the United Kingdom? In my opinion there is no reason why the law of Scotland upon this subject should not be extended to England; and I do not think that one arrangement ought to prevail upon such a point in the north and a different one in the south of the island...

On the question of desertion, Lord Lyndhurst said– There is another alteration which I am most anxious to see introduced into this Bill. I think that when a husband breaks his marriage vow, and, after abandoning his wife for a certain number of years, goes to a distant country with the view of deserting her, divorce *a vinculo* ought to be granted to a wife so deserted. In pressing that point on your Lordships' notice, I would ask you to reflect for a moment on the objects of marriage. Look at the marriage ceremony of our Church. Three objects are there stated–first, the procreation of children, and their nurture in the fear of God; secondly, the prevention of sin; and thirdly, the love, comfort, and protection, in sickness and in health, between the husband and the wife. What is the vow taken by the husband in the ceremony of marriage? Nothing can be more stringent. He vows he will love, comfort, keep, and protect his wife, in sickness and in health, and, forsaking all other women, keep only to her until death do them part. That was the obligation which he voluntarily contracted. It was as strong an obligation as any into which it would be possible for him to enter, and it was one which must exercise the most powerful influence over any man possessing the least degree of feeling. When he disregards that obligation, when he defeats all the objects for which marriage had been instituted– when he passes into a distant country with a view to cut off all communication between him and his wife, is it right or just that she should still be bound to him by our marriage law? ...

... Those remarks were made forty-five years ago, and since that time there has been no material alteration in the divorce law of this country. At a later date, in June 1859, a protest was lodged by Lords Lyndhurst and Hutchinson which cited reasons for granting divorce on the ground of desertion. They stated– It is well known that at the Reformation the subject was anxiously and carefully considered by prelates and divines eminent for learning and piety, and that they came to the conclusion that wilful desertion was a scriptural ground for divorce. We find the names of Archbishop Cranmer, of the Bishops of London, Winchester, Ely, Exeter, and others; of Latimer, Parker, etc., of Peter Martyr, Martin Bucer, Beza, Luther, Melancthon, Calvin, etc., among those who maintained this opinion, and which was adopted by the whole body of Protestants on the continent of Europe.

I think it is, therefore, clear that I was justified in stating that proposals contained in this Bill are not so novel as they may at first sight appear.

I now come to the sub-sections of Clause 1, which provide that either party to a marriage may petition for a dissolution on the ground that the other party is undergoing penal servitude for a term of not less than three years, or has been certified to be of unsound mind under the Lunacy Act; and I submit that lunacy and imprisonment break the marriage tie as much as desertion. Where a wife is devoted to a husband who is sentenced to five years imprisonment, she will wait till he comes out; but there are cases in which that may not be so, and in those cases it does not seem to be unreasonable that the party who is deprived of the society of the other spouse should have an opportunity of dissolving the marriage. The same contention applies with regard to lunacy; and your Lordships will recollect that in the extract which I read from a speech by Mr Gladstone both lunacy and imprisonment were mentioned as justifying a divorce *a vinculo*.

The most novel clause in the Bill is that which provides for divorce after one year's separation where both parties concur in the petition. As I have already explained, the theory of the present law is that one of the parties must desire a divorce and the other not. It often happens that both spouses earnestly desire divorce, though neither is willing to enter into collusion or to take the dirty and obnoxious road prescribed by the present law. At present the only persons who can obtain divorce are those who commit adultery; and, as was predicted by speakers in both Houses of Parliament in 1857, the Act of that year has put a premium on adultery. There are many cases where it is quite impossible for husband and wife ever to live together again, and for those cases this Bill will provide a remedy. The argument frequently used against divorce is that it impairs the sanctity of the home. But in the cases contemplated by the Bill the home has already gone. The effect of these proposals would be to increase, not loose living, but the number of happy homes, and to diminish adultery. There would be fewer scandals and less evidence of a repulsive kind, which neither party would care to produce if a more decent method of breaking the marriage tie were provided. On the subject of the equality of the sexes, I would quote from two or three of the speeches on the Bill of 1857. The Bishop of Oxford said—
He could find no shadow of a foundation in the Gospel for the extension of the right of divorce to a wife. It was distinctly stated that a husband might put away his wife, but no general principle was asserted in the Gospel which would equally entitle a wife to put away her husband. It seemed to recognise an equality in the sexes; but the truth was, that though the sin might be equal in each, yet the social crime was different in magnitude as committed by the one or the other; and our blessed Master, while allowing a husband to put away his wife for adultery, because all the highest

purposes for which marriage was instituted by God would be defeated by the infidelity of the wife, never extended the same right to the other side.

I am afraid that nowadays that will appear rather a Mosaic view to take of the relations of the sexes. Mr Drummond, in the House of Commons, said— His object was to have perfect equality between the two sexes. The laws of England were more severe against the woman than were those of any other country in Europe. That House was a body of men legislating for women, and they had by a code of their own invention, and for their own purposes, contrived to establish the general notion that unchastity in a man was a much less evil than unchastity in a woman.

Mr Gladstone made a long speech, arguing most strenuously in favour of equal rights for both sexes, in the course of which he said— I believe that the evil of introducing this principle of inequality between men and women is far greater than the evil which would arise from additional cases of divorce *a vinculo*; and I take my stand in the first place on this: that if it be assumed that the indissolubility of marriage has been the result of the operation of the Christian religion on earth, still more emphatically I believe it may be assumed that the principle of the equality of the sexes has been the consequence of that religion.

A protest on the same subject was lodged by Lords Hutchinson, Harrington, Lyndhurst, Talbot de Malahide, and Belmore, after the passing of the Bill of 1857, in which they stated in emphatic words their reasons for countenancing equality between the sexes…

It often happens that persons make mistakes in their marriages. If we were all omniscient, no doubt we should all contract happy and successful marriages; but as it is, persons sometimes make mistakes, and in such contracts the Legislature ought, as far as possible, to enable the contracting parties to place themselves in the position they occupied before they made their mistake. I hold that the object of a well-thought-out system of divorce should be to provide a lawful method by which persons who contract such unfortunate alliances might free themselves.

As to damages against a co-respondent, Clause 2 of this Bill leaves the law as it stands; though it is with reluctance that I admit the necessity of doing so. I agree entirely with the observations of Lord St Leonards on that subject, when he said :— He trusted that actions to recover damages, to which a party suing for a divorce must now resort, would be abolished, for he perfectly agreed with the right reverend prelate that if there was anything more disgraceful than another in our legal procedure it was this action for damages. He should like to know what a man was to do with the money so recovered. He could scarcely mix it up with his common funds, or consent to use it for his own benefit in any of the ordinary transactions of life. He would no more touch it than he would touch scorpions.

There are, I suppose, persons to whom it is a satisfaction and a gratification to recover damages for the loss of their wives, and so I presume some such provision must remain. Clauses 3 (Maintenance and Settlements), 4 (Custody, Maintenance, and Education of Children), and 5 (Nullity of Marriage) leave the law as it at present stands; Clause 8 makes alterations in procedure, and Clause 9 provides that it shall not be necessary for any pleadings to be accompanied by an affidavit. The procedure in the Court at the present time is founded almost entirely on the procedure of the

Ecclesiastical Courts, which is quite out of date, and the practice should be made analogous to the Rules in force in the King's Bench Division. I think all who practice in the Divorce Court will admit the advantage of such an assimilation.

Now, I approach a totally different subject, and that is the proposal to give the jurisdiction of the Divorce Court to County Courts. I cannot resist first reading to your Lordships some observations of Mr Justice Maule in passing sentence on a bigamist—[25]

... It is said that those observations of Mr Justice Maule had some effect in obtaining the passage of the Divorce Bill of 1857. That Bill was held out as intended to provide a cheaper remedy for the poor man; but as regards poor persons the Act of 1857 is as much a farce today as the procedure by means of a private Act of Parliament was before that date. The cost of obtaining a divorce, even in an undefended case, varies from £50 to £150, and labourers and other working men cannot afford to spend £50 for the luxury of a legal divorce. Speaker after speaker in 1857 said these powers should be given to County Courts. The Marquess of Lansdowne said– I believe that the evils arising from the want of the power of divorce are as great among the lower orders of this country as among the higher classes– nay, I believe them to be greater. It is possible that if the House will go into the inquiry, some means may be found of extending the tribunal having cognisance of these cases to every part of the country.

The Bishop of Exeter said– The great object of such a measure ought to be to establish the same law for the poor as for the rich. The only way to make justice cheap in this matter, and easily obtainable, was to establish throughout the country district Courts, which would administer justice in each particular locality.

Lord Wensleydale said– His fear was that if such a jurisdiction as that contemplated in this Bill were created no answer could be given to any future demand for an extension of the power of deciding these questions; and no one could then say why it should not be brought home to the door of every poor man, and why the County Court should not have authority to dissolve the marriage tie.

The Earl of Malmesbury expressed the opinion that– A single Court in London might no doubt be rendered useful to all classes residing within the Metropolis; but the people in the provinces would not receive, so far as he could understand, any greater benefit from the measure then they possessed under the existing law.

Lord Lovaine said– Even if this Bill passed divorces would still be restricted to the wealthy. The Government, in fact, proposed to still leave marriage indissoluble to nine-tenths of the people.

In the House of Commons, Mr Collins said– The County Courts were the only Courts to which the poor man could apply for relief in the circumstances supposed by the Bill, but if they were to be closed against him the measure was a mere farce.

Mr Butt inquired, where was the inconvenience of a County Court determining whether a wife had committed adultery or not, and added– A County Court at this moment tried the very issue to which the Attorney General objected. Any tradesman who supplied necessaries to the deserted wife might sue the husband for the cost. The husband might answer that he had a good cause for deserting her, and then the Judge must decide.

Another speaker thought they ought to make some attempt not to destroy all the existing local Courts without providing some equivalent. I do not think that any words of mine are needed to commend to your Lordship a provision for extending justice to the poor. Whatever might have been thought of County Courts at that date, when they existed for the recovery of small debts and nothing else, County Court Judges have now to deal with cases involving some of the nicest legal points that can be imagined, such as the Workmen's Compensation Act, and there can be no objection to their trying such a simple issue of fact as whether there had been adultery or not. The Bill does not propose that cases in which damages are claimed shall be tried in County Courts. Petitioners who wish to indulge in the luxury of damages may well be left to another Court.

There is one other matter and that is Clause 17, which relates to legitimation by subsequent marriage. The practice in this country in this matter differs from that of all civilised nations. I will read to the House a statement by Mr Henry Goudy, DCL, on this subject in a lecture on the survival of Roman Law. He said– In England a son who is born out of lawful wedlock must remain a bastard all his life. The subsequent marriage of his parents, quite lawful in itself, can have no effect on his status; his younger brothers and sisters, born after the legal marriage, will wholly exclude him from the legal succession to his parents or natural kinsmen. He can neither be heir nor himself have heirs on intestacy, except those of his own body. In Scotland the law on this matter is exactly the reverse. The subsequent marriage of the parents of an illegitimate child makes it legitimate. By a convenient legal fiction the marriage is presumed to have existed at the date of the birth, so as to confer the status of legitimacy as from that date. But I venture to think that in any future codification of the law of the family relations, England must be prepared to follow the lead of Christendom and accept the Scottish law on the subject. It seems just that the parents of an illegitimate child should have the opportunity of atoning for their offence by marriage, and saving their offspring from unmerited disgrace.

I think the proposal in the Bill will appeal to everyone as a matter of common sense. In conclusion I have to thank your Lordships for the patient hearing you have given me, and to assure you that I should not have brought this Bill forward had I not been convinced of the urgent need for an Amendment of the divorce law of this country.

THE LORD CHANCELLOR (Earl of Halsbury): My Lords, I very much regret that such a Bill as this has been introduced into your Lordships' House. I cannot help thinking that if the custom which obtains in the House of Commons, requiring leave to be given to introduce a Bill, prevailed in this House, no leave ever would have been given for the introduction of this Bill. In the noble Lord's voluminous observations we have heard a great many things which might be the subject of debate; but the main provision of the Bill, the first clause, shows that practically this Bill is one for the abolition of the institution of marriage. That in itself is enough–at least, I hope it is enough–to prevent the discussion of the Bill. ... I take that alone– I decline to discuss a great many of the other topics which might fairly be the subject of discussion—I take that alone, and I say that the introduction of such a provision as that is an outrage upon your Lordships' House, something in the nature of an insult to your Lordships, and it is a thing which I, for one, deprecate most strongly. I, therefore, propose to take this personally. Of later years it has been the custom that what is, in effect, a postponement of a Bill should be moved, and not its rejection. In an earlier period of your Lordships' history it was very common to move the rejection of a Bill, and I propose to move the rejection of this Bill.

House of Lords Debate 23 June 1903: Divorce Bill

My Lords, when I last had the honour of submitting to your Lordships' House a Bill containing somewhat similar provisions to the Bill which is now before you, I commended it to your attention in a speech which I endeavoured to make reasonable, temperate, logical, and respectful to this House. Some comments which reached me after that occasion might have led me to suppose that I might have succeeded in that endeavour were it not for the remarkable observations which fell on that occasion from the noble and learned Earl on the Woolsack. The usual Motion that the Bill be read a second time that day six months appeared upon the Order Paper, futhered, as might have been expected, by the noble Lord who represents the High Church Party in the Protestant Church, and who endorses the sacramental view of marriage. But that noble Lord and his Amendment were contemptuously brushed aside by the Lord Chancellor, who, in a state of apparent fury, fell upon the remarks I had ventured to make to the House and declared more than once that both my Bill and the observations with which I had endeavoured to support it were an insult to your Lordships. He then proceeded, with the courage of a large majority behind him, to move that the Bill be rejected, a Motion which, so far as I am able to ascertain, has been unknown in the recent history of this House. But that is not perhaps to be wondered at from a member of a Government which has revived several archaic and rusty weapons of the Constitution. Everyone in this House must recognise the conspicuous talent and ability which has raised the noble and learned Earl to the high position he today occupies, but many, especially on this side of the House, also regret that he should not yet have acquired that courtesy in debate which we are wont to expect from other noble Lords more imbued with the traditions of this assembly. It has not hitherto been held to be an insult to the House to propose in a reasonable manner, and to support by arguments, a measure for the amendment of the law where such may seem desirable. But I must not for a moment appear to wish to alienate the sympathies of the noble and learned Earl on the Woolsack on this occasion, for I hope I may claim him with some confidence as a supporter. In that very small fraction of his observations which dealt with the merits of my proposals, the noble and learned Earl called attention to a clause in my Bill permitting a divorce after one year's separation on the joint petition of the parties. That clause is not in the Bill now before your Lordships, and as it was the only one to which the noble and learned Earl specifically objected I hope that to-day I shall not be mistaken in looking for his support.

... I do not know whether any noble Lord supposes that there is no ground for an amendment, and that there are no grievous cases of injustice and hardship under the present divorce law, which differs in its stringency from the divorce law of every other Protestant country. I have received a vast mass of correspondence, with some few extracts from which I am compelled to trouble your Lordships. One gentleman writes and says– 'My wife left me to return to her father after I lost my money more than eleven years ago. There is no deed of separation and no ground for divorce, and yet by the law of England I am married and condemned to lead a celibate life with no possibility of relief. Had I committed forgery, burglary, or any other serious crime, I could long ago have expiated my offence, but from an unfortunate marriage there is no release, unless there is cruelty or adultery, which are absent in the case under notice. This state of things I contend is contrary to every law, divine or human, and demands a remedy.' A woman writes:– 'Your Bill would be a blessing to many poor women. I married at twenty-one a man who turned out to be a great scamp, thief, and forger. My home was sold up, my belongings seized by creditors. When my son was thirteen months old my husband deserted me and went to Canada fourteen years ago. I have never heard of nor seen him since. My wrist was injured for life through my husband's brutality. I have proof of desertion and cruelty, but what chance have I to obtain a divorce?' Another writes and says:– 'Where the parties have for a number of years been separated and positively refuse to live together again they are, in my humble opinion, *ipso facto* divorced; why then should measures be refused to make such definite estrangement legal? ... Where mutual love exists the man and woman never part; it is the absence of it that brings about the evil. The sooner there is some law permitting the deserted husband or wife to marry again after a lapse of years, the sooner will immorality and dissipation be reduced.' Another writes:– 'Are two people grievously unhappy together and without fault or intention, to be literally killed and worn to death, being held together in an unnatural and useless bond, to be made useless to each other and even to their children, while those who live riotously and break all marriage laws are content with them and are often the loudest voiced in upholding them? That is an easy way of carrying out a law impossible often to keep.' Another writes and says:– 'Realising the impossibility of obtaining legislative relief in this country, I am forced to consider the expediency of settling in America with a view to obtaining there that relief denied me here.' Another writes and says: 'It is remarkable how perverted Christianity is trotted out on every possible occasion to bar real progress. To say that reasonable release would destroy Christian matrimony is simply the dictum of a person very ignorant, and very much of a bigot. The Founder never recommended, and certainly would never have enforced, for it would be abhorrent to all his teaching, that two who had got utterly to dislike each other, and whose presence with each other brought out and acerbated all the evil in the nature of both, should drag on a tortured existence together, degrading to both, and leading to all kinds of evils and a strong temptation to murder even.' A young woman writes that four days after her marriage her husband had to leave on the duties of his vocation as officer in the Royal Navy. For nine years he has not been near her. She has not the money to pursue the evidence for adultery.

A man who occupies a responsible position writes: 'I have been married twenty years to a most unsuitable woman, who has never been any help to me, who has persistently got into debt, falsified accounts, confiscated letters, deceived and lied to me so much that it has produced an utter alienation. For seven years we have occupied separate rooms.' Another writes:– 'Oh this dull, stupid English law, with Scotland's bright example shining so near. You have to go no farther than Scotland to find divorce *a vinculo* granted for three years' desertion.'

I submit this Bill to the House as an honest attempt to remedy an intolerable state of things. I ask whether among all the Members of this House there are none who recognise that the present marriage laws do inflict upon a vast number of men and women in this country great hardship; that the present marriage laws lead in many cases to the contracting of immoral alliances between separated men and women, and that the granting of a judicial separation is really to throw upon the world two potential adulterers. It is easy to legislate for human nature, but it is less easy to control it after your legislation. The present law offers a divorce as a reward for immoral conduct. It can be obtained where immorality has taken place, but where both parties are unwilling to be guilty of immorality, the present law denies divorce; and where, as so often happens, women have been deserted by their husbands for an indefinite number of years, they are precluded from ever contracting a fresh alliance, and are compelled to remain for the rest of their lives neither married nor unmarried, with no possibility of establishing a home and all that is dear to the heart of a woman. Is there no one in this House who feels that this state of things needs a remedy? Are your Lordships satisfied, because in your individual cases the law may not bear hardly upon you, to leave such a blot upon the social legislation of this country? The proposals which I have put before you, and I say this unhesitatingly, make for the increase of social purity and for the absence of adultery. They make for a legitimate dissolution of unions that have long since become impossible, and their adoption would tend to purify the marriage relation, to make marriage a more real thing than it is at present, and to make adultery looked upon, as it is not often looked upon now, as a disgraceful, a discreditable, and an unnecessary crime. I beg to move the Second Reading of this Bill.

THE LORD CHANCELLOR (Earl of Halsbury): My Lords, the noble Lord, in the course of a great many observations, has referred to some remarks which I made on a former occasion when a Bill of this character was before your Lordships. I do not propose to repeat what I said then, but I adhere to every word of it. When I made that speech I believe it met with the entire approval of your Lordships then present. I gathered that from the course you then pursued. No one intervened in the debate. The Bill was at once rejected. At present I will only call attention to one aspect of the Bill. The noble Lord does not appear to me to understand the gravity of what he is doing. If your Lordships will be good enough to turn to the schedule of the Bill you will find that he has gone through every one of the Divorce Acts and has swept them all away. ... I do not think myself that I used language too strong when I said that the abolition of the marriage tie, which in one sense the noble Lord has admitted that his Bill would procure, proposed in such a way to a Christian assembly, was an insult, and I repeat the observation. All I have to add at present, I think, is that I invite your

Lordships to reject this Bill, and I hope that we may not have the same proposal repeated over and over again, for the noble Lord and everybody else must know that it is only in the nature of a protest by himself against the marriage law as it exists, but even he has not the faintest notion that any such Bill will be sanctioned by your Lordships.

House of Lords Debate 1 August 1905: Divorce Bill

My Lords, the Bill which I have presented to your Lordships this year, and the Second Reading of which I am now about to move, is a very considerable modification of those measures which I have submitted previously. The Bill is an extremely short Bill, consisting practically of one clause.[26] I have modified the provisions of the Bill which I introduced before in deference to the feelings of the House and to the remarks of the noble and learned Lord on the Woolsack. The noble and learned Lord, speaking, I think, with his tongue in his cheek, referred me on the previous occasion to the wisdom of Parliament which my attempts at legislation were hurling themselves against. I think an historical examination of the circumstances of 1856 and 1857, and of the conditions under which the Matrimonial Causes Act of 1857 became law, will show that the wisdom of Parliament ultimately expressed itself, as it generally does in our legislation, in a compromise between two opposing factions; and that the Bill which was then passed, while opposed on account of its latitude by one section of opinion, was opposed by another section because it did not go far enough.

… I wish to quote to your Lordships an article in *The Times*. *The Times*, I think, will not be accused of being a revolutionary newspaper; yet in a leading article on the Jackson case (March 20th, 1891) *The Times* is to be found recognising the absurdity of a legal fetter when all moral bonds are broken. This is what *The Times* said– 'It has been laid down that a man and woman cannot be compelled to live together against the will of either. Very well. We have not a word to say against it. The principle is in harmony with modern feeling and with modern legislation. But if this is so, if Mr Jackson or anyone else is thus deprived of his wife's society for good and all, why should he be in any way bound to her? Is it not a flagrant injustice that he should in future be compelled to regard himself as her husband, more or less responsible for her actions, certainly responsible for her debts, she bearing his name, and he bearing the burden of her claims upon him? Freedom is a very fine thing, but let it not be one-sided. If a woman for no fault of the man is entitled to desert him, he ought in common justice to be free to have nothing more to do with her and to marry again.' I have another quotation from a recently-published work which contains the reminiscences of one of the most experienced of our stipendiary magistrates, Mr Plowden–who has been driven by his daily Police Court experience to write as follows– 'I cannot help observing that I have often found myself wishing in the course of my duties that magistrates were clothed with the power to grant divorces as well as judicial separations. These latter are only in the nature of compromises, and often fall short of the full measure of relief which the circumstances demand, and which is not less deserved than ardently desired. To stretch a chain is something, but it is not the same thing as to break it. And there must be many and many a matrimonial link which galls and chafes so cruelly that to sever it in twain effectively and once for all offers the only hope of happiness.' Mr Plowden goes on to say– 'With regard to the far larger question of amending the grounds for divorce, whatever may be the objections to such a course it can hardly be contended that the existing condition of things is wholly satisfactory. I say nothing of what some consider to be the transparent unfairness which puts the husband who seeks relief in such a much better position than his wife. What presses on the minds of some people who recognise the propriety of granting divorces is the un-wisdom of limiting relief practically to cases of infidelity. To tell a wretched married couple leading a cat-and-dog life, with no particular blame on either side, that the law will not help them unless one or the other is secretly unfaithful, is really almost an invitation to sin.' These, my Lords, are the deliberate expressions of opinion of Mr Plowden, and you will see that on his experience there has weighed the necessity–the imperative necessity–for some change in a law, which has remained practically unaltered for fifty years.

... I was accused by the noble and learned Earl on the Woolsack on the last occasion when I brought this subject forward of doing so because I had a personal interest in the matter. I confess I did not quite understand the charge. If the noble and learned Lord meant that I was thirsting to avail myself of some remedy I can assure him he is mistaken. But if he meant that I have had experience of the injustice of our present law, I agree with him; but I do not see that that is any reason why I should refrain from doing all I can to prevent other people undergoing unnecessary suffering. It is also said very often that it is not for a private Member to bring in a measure of this character, but it should be left to His Majesty's Government. There are, no doubt, a great many measures that should be brought in by the Government, but I think all practical legislators know that the Government never bring in a Bill until they are forced to do so by the pressure of public opinion. It requires the pressure of public opinion, and very often a pressure extending over a long series of years, before the Government will take in hand a reform, however much it may be required.

I daresay that after many years some measure of this sort or some more comprehensive measure may be brought in by the Government, but at the present time I feel compelled to bring this subject before your Lordships, and I can assure you that some extension of the grounds for divorce, however it may be supported in this House, has already the support of a very large body of public opinion among thinking men and others who have been brought in contact with the necessity of the case and who have felt that the present divorce law does not provide an adequate remedy, more especially in so far as the poorer classes are concerned. This is a subject which your Lordships should be willing to discuss and consider impartially, and exercise your judgment upon as to whether any remedy is needed and what remedy. It is for the purpose of giving your Lordships that opportunity that I have brought in this measure, and I beg to move that it be now read a second time.

THE LORD CHANCELLOR (Earl of Halsbury): My Lords, the noble Earl is entirely mistaken in his reference regarding myself. I certainly had no intention of saying a word which could be supposed to have any personal application to the noble Earl. This is a matter which can only be dealt with by the Government when it is shown that there is a large body of feeling in favour of the change. The relation of marriage has so many consequences attached to it that it would be very rash indeed to make experiments in the law of marriage, and I am sure your Lordships are not disposed to think that any case has been made out at present for an alteration of the law. I therefore feel it my duty to move that the Bill be read a second time this day three months.[27]

House of Lords Debate 22 July 1908:
Matrimonial Causes Bill

Frank opened his speech, written with E. S. P. Haynes, with reference to the discussion 'Marriage in Christendom' at the Pan-Anglican Congress, highlighting the vast differences of opinion. He then continued:

Since I last presented this measure to your Lordships I have received support from a quarter which, from the point of view of legislation and of knowledge of the subject, is, I think, entitled to carry much more weight than the Pan-Anglican Congress. I refer to some observations which were made by Sir Gorell Barnes, the President of the Divorce Court, in the case of *Dodd* v. *Dodd.* Sir Gorell Barnes is eminently fitted to know the hardships and difficulties which occur in the present marriage law, and the great disadvantages that are inseparable from a condition of things where we allow very freely judicial separation, while limiting strictly the right to re-marry and complete freedom from the marriage tie; and he made these observations on a case which arose from a magistrate's order. By recent legislation more and more powers have been given to magistrates to make orders for judicial separation which cause a husband and a wife to live apart, and which have practically all the effect of an order for judicial separation made by the Divorce Court. After pointing out the large extent to which these judicial separations are being obtained—some 7,000 a year— the President went on to say— 'Applied first in an age remote and in a state of society different from the present, the remedy of permanent separation for matrimonial grievances would always seem to have been injudicious, even in days when persons could not escape from their surroundings as they can now, and when they were more amenable to the pressure and censures of the Church, and is now probably to be regarded as more unsatisfactory still and as tending to demoralisation and providing inadequate justice to the innocent. ... Moreover these orders really impose a more serious penalty in the cases to which they apply than a decree of divorce would; for the result of a decree of judicial separation against a man is more severe to him, and in certain cases even to a woman, than a decree of divorce. The consequences of each are, in most cases, very much the same, except that the former imposes the disability of re-marriage while the latter does not; so that, for instance, a man may be more severely punished for the offence of adultery than for the same offence coupled with cruelty or desertion for two years or upwards; and, further in the latter case, the wife has the option of choosing whether she shall apply for separation or divorce. ... I am anxious not to travel out of my province, which is *jus dicere non jus dare*, but ... it is desirable, in my judgment, as bearing on the subject under consideration, to express the conviction, which has forced itself upon me, that permanent separation without divorce has a distinct tendency to encourage immorality and is an unsatisfactory remedy to apply to the evils which it is supposed to prevent. That the present state of the English law of divorce and separation is not satisfactory can hardly be doubted. The law is full of inconsistencies, anomalies, and inequalities amounting almost to absurdities; and it does not produce desirable results in certain important respects. Whether any, and what, remedy should be applied raises extremely difficult questions... but the consideration of what I have found it necessary to deal with in this judgment brings prominently forward the question whether, assuming that divorce is to be allowed at all, as it has been in England by judicial decree for the past fifty years and for a long time before that by Act of Parliament, any reform would be effective and adequate which did not abolish permanent separation, as distinguished from divorce, place the sexes on an equality as regards offence and relief, and permit a decree being obtained for such definite grave causes of offence as render future cohabitation impracticable and frustrate the object of marriage; and whether such reform would not largely tend to greater propriety and enhance that respect for the sanctity of the marriage tie which is so essential in the best interests of society and the State. ...The petition for divorce in this case must be dismissed, for the wife has only proved adultery, and that is not sufficient to enable her to obtain a decree of divorce; and it will not be any satisfaction to her to know that if her case had arisen and her suit could have been brought in Scotland or most other civilised countries she would have succeeded.'[28] The learned President of the Divorce Court, in that judgment, expressed in words far better than any that I could use, the evils which arise from the present state of things; and the concluding sentence of that judgment, I venture to say, should suggest to your Lordships that the subject of my Bill is worthy of your consideration.

... It has been said before, and may be said again, that this is a subject which ought to be taken up by the Government and considered by a Commission or Committee and that no private member ought to attempt to legislate upon it. I quite agree that this is a matter which ought to be taken up by the Government and considered by a Commission or Committee; but it is not taken up, and meanwhile many thousands of people every year suffer great hardship from the existing law. That is my only excuse for again calling attention to the subject. The matter is one which is of great importance and can only be fitly dealt with by the Government of the day; and it is, I venture to think, a matter not so difficult as it is sometimes represented to be. I think a conclave of lawyers would find a remedy for the existing state of things without very much difficulty. But the present Bill has one merit, which was insisted upon by the noble and learned Lord on the Woolsack in the discussions on the Deceased Wife's Sister Bill. That is that it only deals with one point. At any rate it has that merit. I submit the subject to your Lordships for discussion because some settlement ought to be arrived at in the matter, and your Lordships, I think, must realise that when a man in the position of the President of the Divorce Court, holding high judicial office, feels it necessary to make so explicit and so clear a statement as to the disadvantages, the inequalities, and the evil effects of the

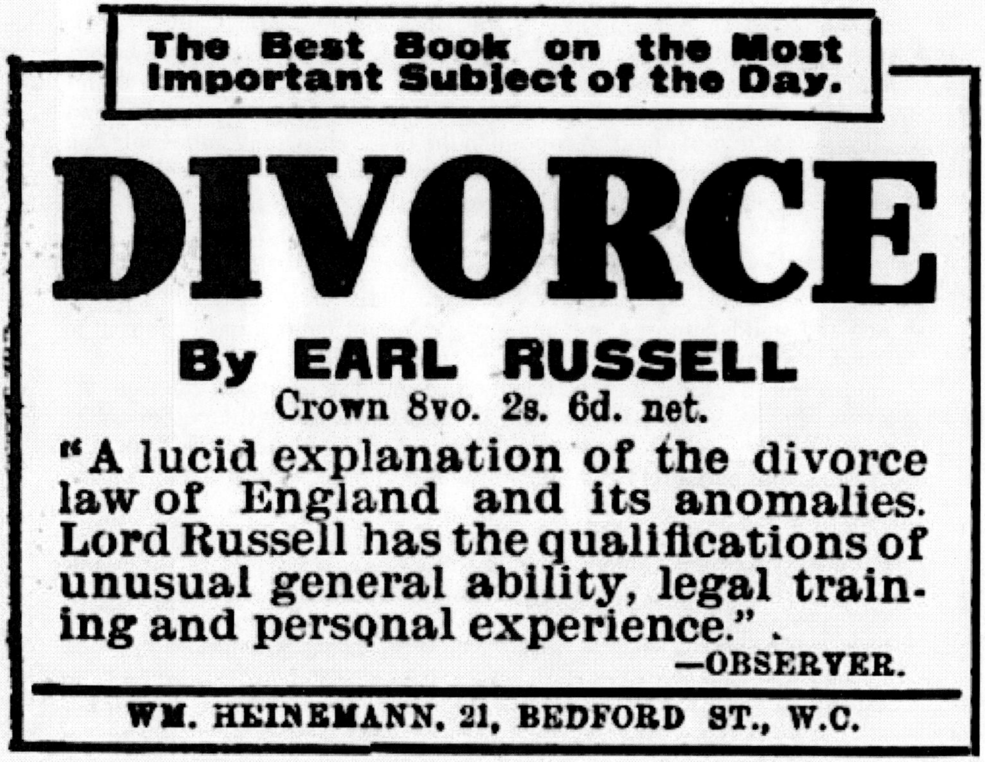

4.4 Advertisement for *Divorce*, 1912.

present law, there must be some grievance which calls for a remedy. I, therefore, beg to move the Second Reading of the Bill.

THE LORD CHANCELLOR (Earl Loreburn): This Bill undoubtedly has the merit claimed for it by the noble Earl that it deals with only one question at a time. I am afraid that is the only merit I can see in the Bill. The proposal, if I rightly understand the Bill, is that a man or woman may be divorced on the ground of desertion without cause for two years and upwards. That is the proposal which is made in the Bill. I will say nothing at all about the sanctions of other kinds affecting marriage, I would simply point out that the noble Earl's Bill amounts to this, that divorces practically may be obtained at discretion or almost at discretion by the parties to the marriage. The woman being the weaker of the two, the man might very easily by his conduct cause his wife to desert him for two years and then get rid of her. I must say for myself that the proposal in the Bill is absolutely impossible and is one to which I will not at any time consent. Therefore, when the question of the Second Reading is put I shall vote in the negative.[29]

'When Should Marriage Be Dissolved?', *English Review*, 1912

England stands almost alone amongst Protestant nations in her refusal to recognise any cause for divorce other an adultery. This attitude is a mediaeval one, as a brief examination of the history of the question will show. In more barbarous ages the wife was the chattel of the husband. She had no rights except through him – she had no duties except to him. Wrongs committed by her were, and are to the present day deemed to be committed by the husband, and wrongs inflicted upon her were wrongs against the husband as her owner. It is not necessary to enlarge upon this, but merely to point to the Roman doctrine of *patria potestas*, the full rigour of which died away as Rome became more civilised, and in English Law to the doctrine of Petty Treason, if a wife murdered or conspired against her husband. So also by the English Law until the Married Woman's Property Act, all her personal possessions became his absolutely, and he had the enjoyment of her land during coverture. The liability of the husband for her torts still exists, and another survival of this view is to be found in the doctrine of felonies committed by a wife in the presence of her husband. If a wife suffered an injury, it was the husband who sought redress, either with his sword or through the Courts of Law. Given this mediaeval conception in full force, adultery became merely a special case of a wrong done to the husband, which entitled him not only to punish the adulterer without the assistance of the law, or by an action for *crim. con.*, but also to put away and get rid of the damaged goods in the shape of the faithless wife. As until 1857 the marriage law of the land was ecclesiastical, and as the Church had retained the Roman Catholic doctrine of the indissolubility of marriage, the husband was not able to put her away so effectually as to leave him free to marry another woman, but only to separate her from bed and board. When divorce *a vinculo* was introduced in 1857 women had begun to have some sort of individual status, and some kind of feeble sense of justice towards women influenced the public mind, so that the remedy which had only been the husband's had to be grudgingly and partially extended to the wronged wife also. The offence, however, which made the remedy possible remained unchanged, and in spite of various attempts in both Houses of Parliament, the historical sense of continuity was too strong for those reformers who strove to introduce other causes for divorce.

In the year 1857 the proportion of legislators and persons in authority subject to the influence of ecclesiastical tradition and to archaic views of woman as chattel was probably of the order of nine-tenths, whereas it is to be hoped in the year 1912 they do not perhaps exceed one-half, except in the House of Lords, always a store-house of outlived traditions. It may therefore be worthwhile to examine merely with the eye of a jurist or social reformer the reasons which make or mar a successful marriage, without going so far as to introduce the indelicacies of that reluctant celibate Paul, who apparently regarded marriage as merely providing a legitimate outlet for carnal lust, or the frankness of the Prayer Book on the subject; though undoubtedly one of the objects of marriage, and a very important one, is to provide a legitimate sex relation. From the point of view of the race, the most important object is, of course, the procreation of children, while from the point of view of either man or woman of a certain age, probably its chief essential is intimate companionship. To the eye of the sane maker of laws it would seem that the special contract of partnership known as marriage should be dissolved altogether when it has failed in its object, and when the partners are no longer carrying on business together, but living separate (subject always to the one special difficulty of the partnership assets which have been created in the shape of children), and it is on this basis that I propose to deal with the grounds other than adultery which should properly give rise to divorce.

Adultery itself may well be retained as a legitimate ground for divorce, since both husband and wife object from a sort of possessive feeling to sharing the peculiar relations of married life with others, and although these objections are stronger in some cases than in others, there is hardly any case where a state of polygamy or polyandry can co-exist with mutual goodwill and respect. In the cases which do exist, the relations between lawful husband and wife have generally become platonic or practically so. Moreover, in the case of the woman, there is a special objection to adultery, owing to doubts to the paternity of the children, since few people are sufficiently altruistic to wish to bring up other men's offspring. Where, however, the situation is not complicated with strong religious views, or strong sentimental views about chastity, it may well be that an isolated act of adultery is far less disruptive of the home life than some of the other causes we shall have to consider.

Let us take next desertion. Where either husband or wife leaves the joint establishment, deserts the home, abandons the children, and is never seen or heard of again, there is a complete destruction of the partnership of marriage as could be caused by death itself. None of the reasons urged either by the Prayer Book or by more modern writers in favour of the sanctity of the home and the sanctity of the marriage tie remain. There is no possibility of the legitimate sanction of carnal appetites, on which Paul and the Prayer Book lay such great stress: there is not mutual help or comfort, and no cherishing: and finally there is no question of the influence of the deserting parent upon the children or their upbringing, and no question of keeping together the home, nor is there any legitimate opportunity for being fruitful and multiplying. Yet in these circumstances England almost alone among the nations denies all redress. Across the border in Scotland, four years' desertion is a ground for divorce; in all the Protestant countries of Europe it is a ground, and in nearly all the States of America and our Colonies. Instance after instance has been brought before my notice in which a husband has emigrated to Canada or to the United States or to South Africa, with the intention of deserting his wife and family, and has never been seen or heard of again. Since the Jackson case it has been established as the law of the land that a wife may desert her husband at the church door, before the marriage between the parties has ever emerged from the mere state of a religious ceremony and a legal tie, without his having the power to do anything to make it a reality. I have never been able to understand the state of mind of those worthy and pious people who in connection with the facts of this nature continue to prate about the sanctity of the home and the terrible effect of allowing marriages to be rashly dissolved. Marriages which have been terminated by desertion are dissolved so far as every single point of the contract is concerned, and for the law to refuse to recognise this is to shut its eyes to obvious and patent facts incapable of denial. As well might it be said that if two young men had adventured jointly on a business enterprise and one of them after a year or two fled to America and disappeared from human ken, his partner should never be allowed to wind up the partnership or to take another partner.

Consider next the question of lunacy. If one of the spouses becomes insane and is confined for years in an asylum, what essential of married life remains for the other spouse? It is often argued that there is something noble and touching in the sorrowing spouse waiting patiently some ten or twenty years for the other partner to recover his or her reason. No doubt there is, but these acts of exalted sentimentality should be voluntary, if they are to have any moral value, and should not be enforced by a species of sexual suttee. From the eugenic point of view, moreover, it is not particularly desirable that breeding from a feeble-minded or insane stock should be encouraged. I heard the Archbishop of York at the Divorce Commission put a poser to a witness something in this form. 'Do you say that divorce should be granted for serious physical ill-health? If not, why should it be granted for mental ill-health?' The only logical answer to his question is that divorce should also be granted for physical ill-health of such a character as to make married life impossible, if the other spouse desires it. This may seem somewhat brutal and unfeeling towards the afflicted person, but I think the converse is apt to be equally brutal to the healthy person, and I am not sure that persons in good health have not, from the race point of view, the first right to be considered. At any rate, while human nature remains what it is, it is exceedingly probable that they would consider themselves and take out in lovers or concubines what the law refuses to allow them as husband or wife.

Long terms of imprisonment may well be treated as analogous to long confinement in an asylum. Habitual drunkenness, cruelty, or other similar grounds sometimes urged may well be put to the test of the separation, by which I mean that if they are so serious that the one spouse prefers definitely and finally to leave the other, rather than to endure them, the case may be treated as one of desertion, although while women remain economically dependent the interposition of any long period of delay may leave them penniless, or put the remedy out of the question for them because their children will be starving.

The thesis with which I am now dealing is that if divorce is allowed for adultery it may, and as a matter of logical necessity and simple justice ought, to be allowed for other causes also. I am not dealing with the advantages and disadvantages of divorce itself, and it will be found that on this specific point there are authorities who could not be regarded as anxious to encourage divorce in itself. For example, Mr Gladstone said in 1857, 'We have many causes far more fatal to the great obligations of marriage, such as disease, idiocy, crime involving imprisonment for life, which, if the bond is dissoluble, might be urged as a reason for divorce.' At the same date, Lord Lyndhurst said, after referring to the obligations of marriage, 'When he disregards that obligation, when he defeats all the objects for which marriage has been instituted, when he passes into a distant country with a view to cutting off all communication between him and his wife, is it right or just that she should still be bound to him by our marriage law?' Associating himself a few days later with Lord Hutchinson in a written protest, he repeats, 'By wilful desertion not only is this sacred promise impiously violated, but all the purposes for which this ordinance of God was instituted are wholly frustrated. Even in the most ordinary contract, the breach of it on the one side puts an end to the obligation on the other, and we see no reason why a different rule should be applied to the contract of marriage, and more especially in a case destructive of the entire objects of the union.'

Lord Shand wrote in *The Times* on the 23rd of April 1891, 'It seems to me that it must be a question of time only when divorce for deliberate and persistent desertion must become the right of a deserted spouse by the law of England as it has already for centuries been by the law of Scotland, where the results have been certainly beneficial... Desertion is as truly a violation of the conjugal obligations as adultery.'

The Times itself made the same suggestion in a leading article on March 20th, 1891. Even a Roman Catholic organ, viz., *The Catholic Herald*, on May 25th of this year says: 'The Catholic Church is perfectly well aware that if for one cause marriage may be dissolved why not for another.'

Let us now consider the question generally apart from specific cases. It is often assumed that these relaxations of the legal tie and extensions of divorce will lead to loose conduct on the part of the community. This line of argument is based on a profound misapprehension, viz., that individuals are guided in their conduct by the law, and not by their own feelings and dispositions. In the case of a person of definite religious beliefs or a person in whom unformulated aspirations and ideals take the place of religious beliefs, conduct is regulated by an individual ethical standard and the law is conformed to either because it falls far short of the requirements of the ethical standard, or in matters of no moral importance for the sake of convenience. The law does not forbid a man to sell a broken-down horse for the best price he can get for it, provided he indulges in no active deception, but a gentleman does not do it. The law does not punish many business dealings which fall far short of high ethical standards as they do of legal fraud. The finer feelings, the nobler sentiments, the most admired actions do not derive in any way from law, but from individual impulses and ideals and rules of conduct. Widows and widowers are not forbidden by our law to marry again, but many of them remain faithful to their memories of the lost and do not marry again because they do not desire it. The law must not, however, set up these standards for other people, but in a just and sound system must confine itself to legislating so as not to inflict unnecessary suffering upon individuals or to impose restrictions beyond what is necessary for the protection of others. It may well be that a faithful spouse is willing to wait during a long term of imprisonment or during confinement in an asylum for the release of the husband or wife, but where this is not so the law has no right to require it. It may be that deserted wives prefer waiting indefinitely the return of their husbands to contracting fresh alliances, but the law has no right to place this obligation upon them. The original excuse (apart from the religious one) which the law had for interfering with the status of marriage was the necessity for protecting the material interest of wives and children and to a considerable extent this excuse is still a valid one. It is necessary, therefore, to have regard in any modification of the harshness of the marriage tie to these interests and to see that they are protected as part of the grant of freedom. In this respect, practically no change is necessary in the present provisions of the Divorce Act.

When, however, the law endeavours to go beyond these material questions and to go beyond what is required in the interests of society, it necessarily fails. The evidence of its failure is the formation of extra-legal and anti-moral relations between man and woman. The deserted wife takes another man who is not her husband for her protector; the man whose wife is in an asylum may and does have children, but illegitimate ones; the husband and wife who live apart, either voluntarily or after a judicial separation, contract relationships which it is not desirable to encourage. This truth was recognised by speaker after speaker in the House of Lords and the House of Commons in 1857, and men so diverse as Archbishop Cranmer, the Bishop of Exeter in 1857, Lord Palmerston, Mr Plowden, and finally Lord Gorell in 1908, have expressed this view in the strongest possible manner.

Seeing then, as we have, that the law conflicts with common sense and ordinary human instincts, by what is our present system of theoretically monogamic and practically indissoluble marriage maintained? It is partly based upon illicit semi-permanent relations not differing greatly from those of marriage itself, but it is still more broadly based upon the provision of an outlet in the shape of wide-spread prostitution, almost universal in the monogamic countries. Lecky, in his *History of European Morals*, sums up the position in this flaming passage: 'That unhappy being whose very name is a shame to speak: who counterfeits with a cold heart the transports of affection, and submits herself as the passive instrument of lust: who is scorned and insulted as the vilest of her sex, and doomed, for the most part, to disease and abject wretchedness and an early death, appears in every age as the perpetual symbol of the degradation and sinfulness of man. Herself the supreme type of vice, she is ultimately the most efficient guardian of virtue. But for her, the unchallenged purity of countless happy homes would be polluted, and not a few who, in the pride of their untempted chastity, think of her with an indignant shudder, would have known the agony of remorse and of despair. On that one degraded and ignoble form are concentrated the passions that might have filled the world with shame. She remains, while creeds and civilisations rise and fall, the eternal priestess of humanity, blasted for the sins of the people.'

This is no picture to be contemplated unmoved by sane and upright men and women, yet nearly every man knows in his heart that it is true. That fair-seeming edifice based largely upon fraud, the sanctity of the home, often encloses an inconstant husband and a subdued and hopeless wife. Such homes as these and such morals as these are not the ideal of a free people in a free country, and it is the blighting influence of ecclesiasticism that we have to thank for this wide-spread curse of artificial and degrading sex relations. For if the edifice is outwardly fair-seeming, those who inhabit it suffer an atrophy of the finer and keener feelings, suffer a lowering of their moral self-respect and a deadening of their life which does harm to them and does harm in turn to the community of which they are members. The influence of this blight is reflected in legislation and in the general social outlook upon questions of the utmost importance, and the young and growing generation suffer most of all until they are moulded into some sort of conformity with the world of moral make-believe.

The witch-doctor and the medicine-man, the curse of every savage tribe, evolve themselves in due course into the priest and the church, who have been for centuries the curse of civilisation, and whose perversions and dogmas are responsible for giving vice all the attractiveness it has, instead of making the healthy path of virtue the natural attractive one. Their hand is not seen only in sex matters, but also in matters of education and in our smug self-satisfaction with the condition of the poor in a country that is called civilised. The root of the evil that is to be attacked lies here; for it remains as true as in the time of Lucretius—*Tantum religio potuit suadere malorum.*[30]

Notes

1. *Scotsman*, 7 Nov 1902, p.7.
2. *St James's Gazette*, 14 Nov 1902, p.17.
3. Matthew 19:12.
4. 1 Corinthians 7:7.
5. John 8:11.
6. 1 Corinthians 7:3.
7. Romans 20:20-24.
8. Romans 5:9.
9. I Thessalonians 5:9-10.
10. Hebrews 9:28.
11. Hebrews 10:12.
12. Matthew 9:13.
13. Psalms 51:17.
14. Ecclesiastes 5:2.
15. Isaiah 1:13.
16. Isaiah 5:20.
17. In the original publication, Frank here quotes at length from *Age of Reason*, beginning, 'The book ascribed to Matthew says…' (p.120) and concluding at end para. 2 on p.121.
18. Here, Frank refers the reader to three paragraphs from *Age of Reason*, beginning, 'Of all the modes of evidence that ever were invented…' (pp. 49-50).
19. Rape had to be of another woman: legally a man could not rape his wife, her consent being inferred from her marriage vows. Charges of sodomy were so rare as to be immaterial: in my research for *Decadent Divorce* (due 2023) I found no allegations of homosexual activity in a sample of every twentieth case from 1881-1901. Gail Savage's study of cases 1857-1900 concurred (email to author 7 Jul 2021) and there are no reported cases. Frank's is therefore the only known instance.
20. The Bill also sought to legitimise children born before their parents' marriage and to legalise marriage to a deceased wife's sister. Though nothing to do with divorce, Frank considered these also irrational and so added them for good measure.
21. In Deuteronomy 24:1-5 Moses ruled that a *libellum repudii* (Bill of Divorcement) can be given by husband to wife if 'he hath found some uncleanness in her' leaving both free to remarry. Christ's explanation and apparent reversal of this is found in Mark 10:2-12. However, Matthew's account of the same teaching has Christ saying a wife *can* be divorced for fornication (Matthews 19:9).
22. Matthew's version is repeated again in chapter 5:31-32.
23. The Matrimonial Causes Act 1884 – the 'Weldon Act' – was rushed through parliament when Mr Weldon – who refused to live with his wife on the ground of incompatibility, but instead provided her with an income of £500 per month, a house to live in and two servants to attend her – was, despite this, destined to be sent to prison for his refusal. The law was changed to provide that refusal to obey an order for restitution became 'desertion' if not complied with within a fortnight and therefore a fast-tracked ground for judicial separation.
24. In *R.* v. *Jackson* [1891] the husband's abduction and detaining of his wife against her wishes after she refused to comply with a restitution order was held to be unlawful.
25. Here Frank quotes in full Justice Maule's famous judgment of Thomas Hall, labourer, found guilty of bigamy in 1845.
26. Divorce for two years' desertion.
27. On division, only three others supported Frank's motion for an immediate second

reading: Lords Gordon and Tweedmouth and Frank's uncle Lyulph Stanley of Alderley.
28. Gorell Barnes' full statement reported at [1906] P 189.
29. On this occasion, only Lord Pirrie voted with Frank.
30. 'Such are the crimes to which Religion leads' (Leonard trans., 1916).

5. Frank on his car, *Motoring Illustrated*

Chapter 5

Automobilism

Many grievances associated with the advent of the motorcar and its growing prevalence on British roads bring to mind the adage 'The past is a foreign country'. Some of Frank's advice to motorists in his *Graphic* column – on size and fabric of roadmaps, recommended optional gadgets (headlights and a speedometer!) and how to respond when a policeman stops your vehicle – now appear rather quaint. Others, however, such as traffic volume and speed in towns, remain relevant. Registration, now taken for granted, was once a particularly contentious issue. It came to a head in 1903 and the influential RAC found itself divided. Those in favour thought accepting registration would enable them to bargain for the abolition of speed limits which had become anachronistic. Those against (Frank included) considered they were relinquishing too much for a concession that would never be granted. The following memorandum was published ahead of a membership-wide postal vote. Frank *et al* lost the argument, but were proved right as regards concessions. Frank would eventually see his proposals legislated when he became Undersecretary for Transport in the second Labour government, 1929.

'Reasons Against the Numbering Proposals: Memorandum Prepared by Lord Russell, Captain H. H. Deasy, and Mr Robert Todd', *Automobile Club Journal*, 14 May 1903.

At a meeting held at the Club on March 6th, at which the question was fully and exhaustively discussed by the members, the resolution against numbering was unanimously carried. A full report of the proceedings will be found in the *Journal* of Mar 12th, 1903, pages 278-289. Three gentlemen were nominated by that meeting to represent their views on the Legislative Committee, and this Memorandum is prepared by them.

It is submitted that numbering is too high a price to pay even for the abolition of the speed limit; that it is no part of the duty of the Club to put forward proposals objectionable to the great body of automobilists; that the concessions in the Scott Montagu Bill would probably be struck out in its passage through Parliament; that delay is expedient, as with the increase of motoring, especially among the governing classes, there is a growing tendency to relax the present restrictions.

There is no reason why a gentleman's private carriage should be disfigured by a label suitable for an omnibus or a hackney carriage, or why a private individual should be subjected to the annoyance of being ticketed and labelled wherever he goes. The reason alleged for this request is to enable offending cars to be identified with less trouble to the police. It would, no doubt be a convenience to the police if all offenders, or possible offenders, against the law were to be conspicuously labelled; but this plan has not yet been adopted in regard to persons convicted of crime, or even to convicts at large upon ticket-of-leave, and there would seem no reason to introduce such an innovation in the special case of gentlemen, who, as a whole, are considerate drivers and law-abiding citizens.

It is said that these proposals are made necessary by the conduct of a small section who have occasionally driven on after causing an accident or being summoned by a police constable in uniform to stop. The principle of English legislation is, however, not to put the large majority of law-abiding citizens to annoyance and inconvenience in order to facilitate the dealings of the police with a small minority of law-breakers. Moreover, it is obvious that persons without a sense of responsibility would not hesitate to cover over their number, to hide it in a cloud of dust, or to smear it with vaseline so that dust might adhere to it. The suggested remedy would therefore be futile as regards the very class which it is proposed to catch, and operative only to cause annoyance to those persons who would stop their car and give their correct name and address under any circumstances, whether numbered or not.

It has not yet been proved that the police are in fact unable to trace motor car offenders, and before that proposition can be regarded as established, it would be necessary to have a return of the number of cases in which a car had been responsible for serious damage to any other user of the road, and the police had not succeeded in either stopping it at the time or identifying it afterwards. Cases of giving false names and addresses after the car has been stopped are not relevant, as they are provided for by a later proposal. As a matter of fact, with the general appearance of a car known and the direction in which it is going, the police are almost invariably able either by telephone or telegraph to arrest it at the next town, and this more particularly, as a fast car will generally be keeping to a well-known main road.

The last suggestion made by the advocates of numbering is that the speed restriction cannot be removed without the offer of a *quid pro quo*. This may be admitted, but the Government are not pledged to large and conspicuous numbers as the only concession, and it need not necessarily be assumed that a Government Department is too obtuse to understand the reasons adduced in Paragraph [3], which would make such a proposal futile for catching worst offenders. If it were asked what other offer can be made, the proposals contained in Question 3[1] are put forward, none of which, it is thought, would be resented by automobilists, and all or any of which might be offered to the Government as concessions.

The combined effect of these three proposals would be to eliminate the probability of bad conduct, first, by requiring drivers to hold a revocable licence, and, in the second place, by making the penalty for such misconduct more than they would care to face. The first proposal for name plates, which might be accompanied by a local registration number, practically eliminates the chances of a false name and address, and provides a ready and final means of identification once the car is at rest.

Those who approve of these views are quested to vote 'No' to the first question,[2] and 'Yes' to Question 3.

'Motor-Cars', *Times*, 24 Sep 1904.

To the Editor of the *Times*:

Sir,- I have read with great interest the correspondence and the leading article in your columns on the subject of motor cars. I must confess that I read the original letter of Dr Jex-Blake with some amazement on account of its misrepresentation of facts, its total ignorance of the subject, and its extraordinary intolerance.[3] The suggestion that deaf persons are properly to be expected in the centre of the highway, reminds me of the suggestion made at Beverley that a 60 ft road was not fit for fast traffic because the school children used it as a playground. We do not pay rates for our highways as playgrounds for children, exercise-yards for invalids, or places of conversation and social gatherings for the loitering public.

May I remind Dr Jex-Blake that, before coming to hasty conclusions, 'we must acknowledge the absolute obligation of inquiring on what grounds the popular opinions rest, and how far they are the result of habit, custom, and prejudice'? Surely, too, 'no thinking man will pretend that no further upward progress is possible; on the contrary, we must surely believe that each year will bring with it its new lessons.' I endorse most heartily the admirable sentiments which I have quoted in inverted commas, and which I have abstracted from a work on 'Medical Women' written by Miss Sophia Jex-Blake in 1872. Has the passage of 32 years caused these admirable sentiments to lose their force?

Now, to take the objections to motor-cars seriously, as far as they can be extracted from the mere abuse in the letters:–

(1) Dr Jex-Blake and many others still assume that motor-cars are used only by the rich, and only for purposes of pleasure. If she will look at a recent number of the *Autocar*, she will find experience from dozens of country doctors, brother practitioners of hers, to whose daily work the motor-car has become a necessity. We all know well enough that the country general practitioner does not roll in wealth or drive about in all weathers for pleasure, and what is true of him is true of thousands of other users. Personally, I use my car to get from one place to another in the most convenient, quickest, and healthiest way, and very seldom make a drive without object for pure pleasure. On the other hand, the very same people often have the impertinence to tell us that we pay nothing for the roads, as if we alone in the community escaped rates.

(2) I admit at once that the annoyance caused to other road-users is sometimes quite unjustifiable, but the new Act provides ample remedies for dealing with inconsiderate drivers. Much of the annoyance, however, which persons profess to suffer from considerate drivers is not justified, and arises from one or other of the following causes:– (a) Prejudice, (b) taking untamed, wild animals on the high road, (c) nervousness on the part of horse drivers, (d) carelessness in observing the rules of the road and giving room to pass,

(e) leaving horses unattended by the side of the road—an offence in itself. I may say, from my own personal experience, that on any ordinary main road not one horse in 200 is frightened by a motor-car. Nor is it the fact that many drivers pass vehicles at 40 miles per hour.

(3) As to noise, it must be admitted that most modern motor-cars make very little noise. The blowing of the horn is imposed by Act of Parliament or by the regulations of the Local Government Board, and those who object to that must get the law changed. As it is now, persecuting police and magistrates have fined many cars for not sounding their horn sufficiently.

(4) As to dust, I agree with all your correspondents that this is an intolerable nuisance both to other road-users and to motorists themselves. But is it not a most singular idea to find the remedy in suppressing motor-cars? Surely, the obvious method is to make roads of dustless material, and I can hardly believe that the resources of modern engineering and modern science are unequal to this. To cry 'Down with motor-cars!' reminds me of one of the witnesses before the Royal Commission on London Traffic, who continued to complain bitterly of the London streets being worn out by the traffic over them, until at last the chairman was obliged to remind him that the object of a street was to carry traffic and to be worn out by it!

(5) As to speed, the opposition to speed in itself is based entirely on ignorance. A modern motor at 30 miles per hour on a main road is safer and more under control that the ordinary horse and trap going eight miles per hour. The speed of a passing car is also very frequently exaggerated.

I fear, Sir, this letter has already extended to an unreasonable length, and I do not want it to be thought that I in any way support or advocate tolerance for those who drive without regard to the comfort of convenience of other road-users. In fact, the Automobile Club, backed by the support of all decent motorists, is ready to do everything in its power to stamp out genuine cases of hooliganism or scorching. But it must be recognised that drivers of horses have a reciprocal duty to other users of the road, which they have too long been allowed to neglect with impunity. The police must prosecute impartially all offenders against highway laws, and horse drivers must learn not to leave their horses unattended, not to drive on the wrong side of the road, not to shoot from a by-road on to a main road at an excessive speed, not to leave too little room at corners, and not to consider that they have by custom a monopoly of the whole width of the road. All vehicles must be lighted, and all horses allowed on the public roads must be properly trained. The use of motor-cars is increasing, and will increase, not because they are the sport of the rich, but because they afford to everyone a convenient and pleasing means of getting from one place to another at any time, irrespective of trains, and of seeing the country *en route*. Ignorance and prejudice have had too much to say in the past. What is now required is to adapt our obsolete highways to the new traffic, and to encourage the building and the maintenance of good roads, and the return prosperity to country inns and country towns.

I am, Sir, your obedient servant,
Russell.
Gray's Inn, London. September 21.

Extracts from 'Motor Notes' *Graphic*, 1908.[4]

Inconsiderate Driving

Probably the most definite advance that has been in the direction of enforcing considerate driving upon motorists is to be found in the latest move by the Automobile Association. Experienced patrols, reinforced by the actual assistance of members of the Committee who are prepared to give up their time to it, will be stationed at various points on the Brighton Road or elsewhere where inconsiderate driving is believed to be prevalent. Motorists will be timed over measured distances, the way in which other traffic on the road is passed or incommoded will be noticed, and offenders will be cautioned. Persistent offenders will be expelled from membership of the Association, and the RAC and the Motor Union will be invited to support this action so far as their members are concerned. This is the first genuine attempt that has been made by any automobile body to purify its ranks.

The Inconsiderate Driving Committee of the RAC, which has been in existence for some years, has never yet brought a case up before the Club Committee for suspension or expulsion. One of the difficulties of the matter is that the police in some of the home counties, notably Surrey and Sussex, do everything in their power to make it difficult to stop inconsiderate driving by setting their futile speed-limit traps and inducing their local Benches to fine motorists heavily for technical breaches of the law on open stretches of road, while the towns and villages are left unprotected. Two deaths have recently occurred in the village of Esher because the policeman who ought to have been on duty there was behind a hedge on an open stretch of road, not to protect the public, but merely to rake in fines. This conduct on the part of some notorious Chief Constables brings the law into disrepute, and turns into enemies of the police those law-abiding motorists who would naturally be their friends.

The Rolls-Royce Works

A large and representative gathering of motorists travelled down to Derby in great luxury last Thursday to take part in the opening of the new works of Messrs Rolls-Royce Ltd. On arrival the guests were conveyed to the works in powerful and silent Rolls-Royce cars, and when the Mayor of Derby and other local celebrities had assembled, a move was made to the works themselves. Here the guests were welcomed in a felicitous and interesting speech by Mr Rolls. Lord Montagu responded in a no less happy vein, and the works were duly declared to be opened. The machinery was then started, and the guests were personally conducted round the shops in parties of convenient size. The works themselves are not large as modern ideas go, but Mr Rolls explained that the chief object which the company kept before it was rather the making of a high-class car than a record output in point of numbers. In view of the feeling that one or two manufacturers of motor-cars have recently rather over-built themselves, there was no disposition to quarrel with this view. Mr Claude Johnson,[5] so long known in the motor world, was much in evidence, but Mr Royce was almost as retiring as his laboratory, which bore the alluring legend, 'Strictly private'.

The Brooklands Fatality

A good deal of nonsense has been written about the tragic occurrence at Brooklands, and even the Coroner permitted himself a lament and a warning. It is, of course, most regrettable that a man should be killed, and another seriously injured, but it is as much one of the obvious risks of motor-racing as it is of steeplechasing or yachting, and a far smaller risk than that regularly taken by aeronauts. A friend of my own, quite a young man, broke his neck teaching a hunter to jump, and was, I believe, sat on by the same Coroner, who, however, made no suggestion then that hunting should be put down or that it was a degenerate sport. I have seen a man's leg snapped in two at football, but no one hinted at suppressing the game. If a man is swept overboard by a boom and drowned, in the course of a yacht race, the incident is scarcely thought worth mentioning. I speak the more freely as I take no interest in racing myself, and have never seen a motor-race at Brooklands, but I recognise that the object of one's life is to live it, and not to preserve existence like some giant pumpkin carefully tended and protected from all harm. When a man comes to die he does not want to say, I have kept on eating and breathing for ninety years, but, *Vixi.*

Motorphobia

It is said that persons who drive motors lose their decent feelings, their sense of responsibility, and even their reason. At the risk of being accused of a *tu quoque*, I must say that I think the charge of losing their reason can be supported against those who attack motors. Mr Cathcart Wason[6] spends nights and days thinking out new ways of harassing motorists. A farmer at Orpington fires a gun at a car and escapes without punishment. A rustic at Slough stretches a wire across the Bath Road and nearly decapitates a driver. An East End crowd mobs innocent motor-buses and is not reproved by the Government or the Press. Lord Queensberry threatens to shoot at sight, and is still at large. Mr Harold Cox[7] wants some fearsome device to stop the car and hurl the driver over the hedge if he goes twenty one miles an hour on Salisbury Plain. I came across a case the other day where a neighbour's dog was accidentally run over, but not much hurt. The car stopped, and names and addresses were given. These things have happened before with horsed vehicles in the country, and between neighbours an apology has been offered and accepted. But the owner of the dog was a victim of this disease, so he took out three separate summonses, all of which, I am glad to say, were dismissed.

Nearly ten years ago, in the early days, when my little Benz was, as was her wont, standing lifeless by the roadside, a gentleman and his daughter came by on horseback. He said, 'I wish all these infernal machines would blow up and kill their owners.' I relied, 'My dear sir, what would you think of me if I expressed a wish that your daughter's pony should run away and kick her brains out? And yet of the two it is the more likely to happen.' It may be that this unfortunate disease is only the bacillus of British conservative in a new form, as the same sort of thing appears to have been said at the inception of railway travel. The poisoned atmosphere the foul stenches, no man safe, all crops ruined, even the supreme assertion of the Highways Protection League that the motor-car pursues you on to the footpath and into your house; they are not new, they have been said before, not a hundred years ago, of the now familiar railway train. Perhaps that memory is our best consolation.

The Boycott of Surrey

Agitation and protest against the powers that be has been brought to a fine art in Ireland, and among other valuable weapons they have taught us the use of the boycott. The AA now proposes to turn this powerful mode of persuasion on Surrey. Stung by the monstrous and unreasonable fines inflicted on their members for speeds which were moderate, having regard to the straight and deserted roads on which they were attained, and by the ceaseless persecution to which their scouts have been subjected, they have turned at bay at last. No doubt every kind of insult and contumely will be heaped on them for their action – variants on the theme of the naively indignant Frenchman, '*Cet animal est tres mechant; quand on 'l'attaque, il se defend.*' The Portsmouth Road, from Kingston Vale to Liphook, has been the scene of almost continuous speed limit traps, particularly on the open slopes of Hindhead, the Cobham Fairmile, and other similar stretches; and the AA has, therefore, appropriately scheduled this section for the commencement of the attack. Since the professed object of the Surrey authorities is the enforcement of the law, the AA will see that it is enforced on those other users of the highway whom the police neglect. Since a speed of twenty-one miles an hour is a breach of the law, the AA will see that the twenty-mile limit is enforced on resident owners of cars as well as on visitors. Since visitors to Surrey are persecuted by the police and fined by the magistrates, they will be advised to retaliate by spending no money in the boycotted district, either with hotels and repairers, or by taking out their motor and establishment licences in the county. By these means it is intended to bring home to the people of Surrey that considerate drivers suffer injustices to which they will no longer tamely submit, and that they do not intend to be treated without protest as cyclists were treated some fifteen years ago.

How to Meet the Inevitable

While the present persecution of motorists goes on there is no driver who does not stand a very good chance of being stopped and spoken to by the police at some time or other. My experience leads me to the conclusion that these interviews are not always conducted in the wisest way by the motorist, and a word of caution may be useful. The policeman who stops you may be at the end of a short distance or a long distance trap, he may think your number irregular, or he may that you are driving to the common danger. For any of these reasons, or for no reason at all, a policeman in uniform is entitled to hold up his hand to stop your car, and to require to see your licence. A driver should, therefore, always stop at once, and, if possible, before reaching the policeman, as if a summons results the evidence is generally to the effect that 'he ran so many yards past me before he could stop'. The licence should be produced, and, in addition to this, the name and address should be given if asked for. The initiative should always be left with the policeman, and the wise man will make no statement or comment on what is going on, nor allow the passengers on his car to do so. If he does he will find to his surprise the truth of the old legal adage, 'Anything you say will be taken down, altered, and used in evidence against you.' Unless the motorist is quite sure of the law, of his temper and of available corroborative evidence from his passengers, he will be well advised not to raise quibbles as to handing over his licence instead of showing the face of it, or as to the sergeant who works a police-trap being in uniform. When the police have finished all the inquiries they desire to make and all the writing down, it will be time enough for the motorist to begin to speak. If he has not already learnt it in the course of the proceedings he should now ask in the hearing of his passengers to see the stop-watches, to know the length of the measured distance, to see the beginning and end of the measured distance, to know what particular offence is alleged against him, and should make any other inquiries that should be pertinent to the matter at issue. It should be carefully noted that these should be questions and not statements. The only statements he would be well advised to make are to call attention to the horse-power of his car, if it is small, to the fact of its possessing a speedometer, if this is so, and to the reading of the maximum hand, if he has one. Finally, he should insist courteously but firmly on any police constable who has written anything down in his notebook reading the entry over to him so that it may be checked then and there, and he should also ask to be allowed to look at the entry, and should require the constable to supplement the entry by writing down any material statement that he, the driver, wishes to make.

Mistakes that are Made

The foregoing precautions may seem elementary, but I have come across more than one case where people have been summoned and convicted because they refused to hand over their licence for the endorsements to be inspected. In the police court it has become a refusal to hand it over at all or to allow it to be seen. In other cases people have been summoned for refusing to give their name and address, and because they describe themselves by their official title instead of complying with the provisions of the statute. Again, I have heard casual remarks by passengers attributed by the policeman to the driver, exculpatory statements treated as admissions, and the policeman's notebook omitting something that the driver did say. The driver and his passengers should be as cool as the police, and should make their own joint memorandum of the circumstances at the time, remembering that when it comes to the fight exaggeration and untruth must tell against either side that employs it.

What a Policeman May Not Do

It may not be supposed from what I have said that a policeman can do exactly as he likes. For example if the car is standing by the roadside during a meal or a puncture repair, and nobody is at the wheel, he cannot, under the Motor-Car Act, demand to see the licence, nor need he be answered if he inquires who is the driver. If he seems likely to give trouble, it will be wise for a different driver to start taking the car away to the one who was driving before, provided he has his licence upon him. When a car is stopped by a police constable he cannot ask for the name and address of any person in the car except the driver, and he cannot ask the driver to give the name of the owner. Nor can the driver of the car be arrested without a warrant if he gives his name and address and produces his licence. By way of exception, in the case of an accident, the car is bound to stop, and any person may ask the driver both for his name and address and for that of the owner. No constable has power to stop a car for more than a reasonable time for making his inquiries; he cannot detain it, nor can he board it, or require it to be driven to any particular place. Finally, when in court no driver is bound to produce his licence either before or at the hearing, but only within a reasonable time after the endorsement, and to protect himself he would be wise to hand the licence to a friend during the hearing so that he can say he has not got it with him.

Impartial Justice

Bitter is the cry that rises from many motorists of the injustice from which they suffer and the ferocious sentences which are inflicted on them by the great unpaid. In Surrey ten labourers can kick their wives for a smaller sum than it will cost one motorist to exceed the speed limit on the open slopes of Hindhead. A carter who deliberately obstructs a car will be fined 10s; a motorist whose tail lamp accidently sparks out, or whose number-plate gets dirty, pays £2. It is, of course, too much to expect motorists to adopt the heroic remedy, but I do not hesitate to say that if every convicted defendant elected to go to prison, and so cost the country money instead of enriching it, we should have many fewer prosecutions. Meanwhile the game continues. A man who denied being there, and was not identified, has been fined and deprived of his licence for three months for frightening a magistrate's daughter. The East Sussex police have found their long-distance timing not sufficiently profitable, and have reverted to the short trap. The official reason is driving too fast in villages, but, oddly enough, the villages are left unprotected, and the traps are set on straight roads. Brighton, which has thus become too risky a journey from London for any self-respecting man to take, has just held an indignation meeting to protest.

Accessories

There is one accessory which no car should be without, and that is a speed indicator. The best of drivers, even upon cars that they know, cannot help under-estimating their speed after they have been running comfortably on a wide and straight road, while on the other hand there is no doubt that speeds in excess of thirty-five miles an hour are almost certain to be over-estimated by the passengers in a car. There are lessons to be learnt when watching a speed indicator which will surprise those who have not been in the habit of using one. A mileometer attached to the hub is also useful to check the distance if anything goes wrong with the dashboard indicator.

The next most important item is acetylene lamps, and it is worthwhile spending some time in adjusting the brackets to get the light thrown forward in a level beam above the road and straight in front. When driving through a lane it is not of very much use to the driver to have the green hedge brilliantly illuminated and the centre of the road in comparative darkness. personally, I always feed my lamps now with dissolved acetylene instead of using carbide. The plant is rather large and rather heavy, but after the first cost I doubt if it is more expensive in view of the amount of carbide that is wasted if the lamps are used intermittently. The advantages in the absence of smell and mess, and in the power to light up or extinguish the lamps instantly by turning a gas tap are so great that no one who has tried it would revert to the carbide generator.

Maps and Routes

Those who have occasion to motor far and wide about the country, and not always on main arteries, know the importance of good maps. Of course, the 1 inch Ordnance come first for accuracy of detail and clearness. Though essential for locating small roads and individual houses, they are too bulky to carry on tour, and for this purpose the coloured half-inch are almost universal. The best I know are the seven-guinea roller map, and the £5 folding map in leather case. I prefer the first on account of the convenience of looking at it in wind or rain, and the small chance of tearing it. Either of them gives you all England and Wales in one case, so that you don't find after starting that you have left behind just the one map you wanted. Among road-books the C.T.C. stand first, but are almost too detailed for the motorist. The *Contour Road Book* is almost perfection, except when it hasn't got the road you want, or when it disguises a ferry as if it were dry land. For Scotland the *Contour Book* and Bartholomew's half-inch folded sheets are sufficient equipment. All these aids must be used judiciously. For instance, if is too late to look out an intricate by-road in the car with the wind blowing. Routes should be carefully written out overnight, with distances, and the map learnt so as to do without referring to it if possible. Finally there is Newnes' shilling *Touring Atlas*, most interesting for the passengers and most useful for the tourist to get the general lie of the land before working out details.

Notes

1. Q3. [Added at the request of Lord Russell, Captain Deasy and Mr Robert Todd, but against the views of the majority of the Legislative committee as being 'a mere waste of time'] Are you willing in exchange for the removal of the specific speed limit to consent to the following additional restrictions? (*a*) Small and inconspicuous identification plates, (*b*) Certification of drivers, (*c*) An increase of the penalty for automobilists guilty of serious offences, such as giving false names and addresses, or endeavouring to avoid identification after causing an accident.

2. Q1. Provided that the three following concessions are obtained:– (*a*) Abolition of the specific speed limit, (*b*) Alteration of the law as laid down in Sutton *v.* Mayhew, (*c*) Raising of the tare limit,– Are you in favour of identification of motor cars by means of numbers of names conspicuous when the cars are in motion?

3. Sophia Louisa Jex-Blake (1940-1912), physician and campaigner for women's education. Her letter entitled 'The Motor Tyranny' appeared in the *Times* on 6 Sep 1904, p.5.

4. Frank's column appeared weekly from 13 Jun – 26 Dec 1908.

5. Claude Goodman Johnson (1864-1926), then managing director of Rolls-Royce, good-humouredly nicknamed himself 'the hyphen' (https://www.gracesguide.co.uk/Claude_Goodman_Johnson, accessed 18 Aug 2021).

6. Liberal MP for Orkney and Shetland.

7. Liberal MP for Preston.

6. Frank, *c.* 1901

Chapter 6

Rights and Freedoms:
Suffrage, Workers' Rights,
Liberty and War

The ten-year period from 1908 saw a marked expansion in the range of causes Frank put his name to. Where previously Frank had spoken for causes that affected him personally, he now turned his attention to wider issues.

First there was women's suffrage. Frank had been converted to the cause by second wife Mollie who had been an active campaigner for women's rights from the mid-1890s. She and Frank met in 1898 when, as a member of the Women's Liberal Association, she supported Frank's campaign to represent Hammersmith on the LCC. This chapter begins with a report of Frank's first major speech for women's suffrage at the 'Great Demonstration' on 17 December 1907.

In December 1912, Frank joined the Fabian Society – the first peer to do so. In a public statement he said his reasons for so doing were 'general agreement with the Socialist idea of placing the control of industry, and the means of production, in the hands of society for the benefit of the masses, and in this connection I attach special importance to the nationalisation of the land.'[1] Despite speculation, he did not immediately join the Labour Party but announced himself its 'candid friend', maintaining an independent line on Labour politics and trade unionism until after the First World War.

The war raised other injustices Frank could not ignore. Though he supported the war he abhorred conscription and the inhumane treatment of conscientious objectors.

'Men's League for Women's Suffrage: The Queen's Hall Meeting', *Women's Franchise*, 26 December 1907.

[The first speaker, Willoughby Hyett Dickinson MP, had moved the resolution 'That in the opinion of this meeting the Parliamentary Franchise should be granted to women on the same terms as it is, or may be, granted to men']:

The Earl Russell, who followed, having paid a tribute to the work of Mr Dickinson in introducing Women's Franchise Bills to the House of Commons, explained that he himself believed in Women's Franchise not only as a matter of justice, but also – and in greater degree – as likely to produce benefit to both men and women. The noble lord proceeded to criticize the attitudes of various classes of persons, showing how partial and narrow-minded were many of the lukewarm advocates, and how fatuous were the arguments of many opponents. Some men seemed to think that all women must perpetually be looking after the comfort of men or the welfare of children; others were apparently inclined to compare unfavourably the capacity of the ordinary woman with that of the individuals who 'prop up public-houses', the sanity of a mother with that of a man in love. No examination is necessary for a man who claims the vote; why should a woman be deprived of it because some men doubt her intelligence? All such objections were beside the point. The fundamental reason for granting the vote is that the voters' wishes may be ascertained. (Applause.) They may be foolish, but time alone could show their folly. Economically women were at a disadvantage – in the factory, in the wages market generally, 'they have to be happy with what they can get.' Women's Trades Unions had some effect, but the Parliamentary franchise would give them still greater power; candidates would be compelled to listen to their needs. (Loud applause.) Women had worked hard in political matters, but the promises made to them in regard to the Franchise were always made to them with an infinity of mental reservations.

The noble lord then dealt with the results of the recent policy of the militant societies, and enthusiastically admitted that it could claim the credit of changing the movement from an academic into a practical question. No one really liked to be 'lectured by a complacent magistrate', but so illogical, and so uninfluenced by anything except violence and rowdyism is the English political mind, that until you adopt these rowdy tactics you remain a mere jest, a mere pious wish. (Great applause.) Women have been fooled long enough. They do not intend to be fooled any longer (Renewed applause.) At the same time, while conceding to women the fullest freedom of judgment as regards their policy, and as an enthusiastic Suffragist, the speaker regretted the breaking-up of meetings. 'Where there is a set meeting, and a set number of speakers, who have certain speeches to make, and a large audience that wishes to hear them, to prevent that meeting taking place, and prevent it being held, is, to some extent, an interference with the right of free speech.' (Applause.) 'What would your own feelings be if your meeting tonight were broken up in that way?' (Applause.) Lord Russell then concluded his speech by expressing the opinion that the responsibility and power which women will acquire with the Franchise will make them better women and better citizens. He welcomed the work of the Men's League.

Letter to Bertie[2]

57 Gordon Square, London W.C.
3 March 1908

My dear Bertie

I see in the papers that you are to be made F.R.S! What an honour! at your age too. Ever since I saw it I have been strutting about swelling with reflected glory. It's the first sensible thing I have ever heard of philosophy doing. One can understand that if one can't your books.

Seriously though I do congratulate you most heartily: I have always

looked on an F.R.S. as superior to any position on earth, even Archbishop
or Prime Minister, & the feeling still survives though I know a good many
personally.
Yours affly
Russell

The Suffragettes: Earl Russell's Support of By-Election Policy, *Daily News*, 3 Apr 1908

To the Editor of *The Daily News*:
Sir,–I have been amazed at the letters which have appeared in your columns
concerning the action of the Suffragettes at Peckham.[3] Still more strange are
the letters, which are not mere angry expressions of a party man, but which
accuse the Suffragettes of having no sense of right or of proportion, of lacking
logic, and of showing themselves unfit for political power.

The policy of the Suffragettes is a perfectly clear and an easily intelligible
policy. They are women who say that to them the grant of the franchise is a
matter of more immediate political importance than any other political issue.
Personally, of course, I do not think so, but then I am not a woman. But in
what way does their position differ from that of a Roman Catholic who thinks
that the maintenance of his religion is of more importance than any political
issue, or from that of an Independent Labour man who thinks that the
various Labour questions are of more importance than any party issue? Are
those who now advance these wild arguments against the line of policy
adopted by the women prepared to say that those who agitated for franchise
reform before 1832 ought to have discontinued their agitation if the
Government of the day had brought in a measure on some totally different
subject, which was in itself desirable? If not, why do they apply a different
standard to the tactics of the women?

A zealous and an extreme temperance reformer may put the cause of
temperance reform before all other causes, and he may therefore find himself
supporting a Liberal candidate, although his traditions and his opinions in
all other political matters are Tory. Well-known Tories have put the cause of
Free Trade before allegiance to their party on other political questions. High
Churchmen, although in other respects Liberals, have put their particular
solution of the education question above the claims of the Liberal Party on
other political issues. Why is it suggested that what is reasonable, natural,
and recognised in the case of men holding these various opinions strongly,
becomes abnormal, illogical, and discreditable when adopted by women?
...

The women say, and are fully entitled to say, that they at any rate put the
possession of political power in the shape of the vote above and before all
other political questions, and that until this concession is made to them they
decline to consider any political question upon its merits. The answer of the
Government might well be to give effect to the majority of three to one in
favour of this course, and thereby instantly to turn every one of these women
into a supporter of the Government. While their answer remains the brutal
and senseless one of imprisoning women and treating them as ordinary
criminals in prison, they need not whine at the antagonism they provoke,

nor need their supporters make themselves ridiculous by their hysterical outbursts and their childish suggestions that the Suffragette movement is engineered and financed by the Tories.

Yours, etc.

Russell

57 Gordon Square, W.C. March 31, 1908.

What the Militants Have Done:
Earl Russell's Defence of a Principle,
Daily News, 8 Mar 1912

To the Editor of *The Daily News*:

Sir,—I do not think I have ever read a letter more deplorably lacking in logic than that of Sir William Byles,[4] which you publish in your column today. It shows that hysteria and want of logic are not confined to the militant women. In order that I may not be misunderstood, let me begin by saying that I deplore and condemn the recent tactics of the WSPU, and that I am thoroughly convinced that they have done great harm to the prospects of Women's Suffrage this Session, because many persons and many members of Parliament are only anxious for an excuse not to support the enfranchisement of women.

But what does Sir William Byles say? He says that he believes as strongly as ever in the enfranchisement of women, and in the next paragraph he says that he will stand aloof and not vote for it. If Sir William Byles had adopted this attitude with regard to the enfranchisement of men in 1832, does he think he would have been counted as in favour of the Reform Bill of that year? Or, to take another instance, if Sir William Byles were to say that he believed as strongly as ever in the sanctity of human life, but that he would not raise a finger to prevent murder being committed, would he expect to be believed? Is Sir William Byles prepared to carry these principles into other political matters, and to refuse to support the principle of trade unionism because there have been riots in Tonypandy?

He surely cannot be ignorant that there are other Suffragettes and Suffragists in the world besides Mrs Pankhurst and her followers, and he ought also to know that in opposing the Conciliation Bill[5] he is doing exactly and precisely what Mrs Pankhurst desires, and playing into her hands.

I will conclude as I began by saying that his statements are illogically incompatible, and that I should not care to have to fight a cause with strong supporters who are not prepared to do anything to support it.

Russell

March 7.

'Lord Russell Protests' in *The Syndicalist*, March 1912

The *Syndicalist* was established in January 1912. In their first edition, there had been an 'Open Letter to British Soldiers' in which was said: 'When we go on strike to better our lot... you are called upon by your officers to murder us. Don't do it...' The attorney general had authorised prosecution of the authors and printers for incitement to riot, for which the *Syndicalist* editor was sentenced to nine months' hard labour and the printers to six months. Frank was among those invited to comment on the sentencing:

I am invited to contribute to a number of the *Syndicalist*, and I feel that I am rather rash in accepting this invitation. I do not know what a Syndicalist is, and I am fairly sure that I am not one myself. I have never read a number of the paper, and indeed, I never heard of it until the Attorney-General thought fit to inform the whole world of its existence and its questions by prosecuting the Editor and the printers. But I have an inherited passion for justice and free speech, and therefore I feel no reluctance in making one or two remarks.

First, as to the actual words for which sentences of hard labour were imposed, and which were published in full in the *Times* without any fear of prosecution. They do not strike me as very terrible, but my Tory friends and the majority of my Liberal friends say that it is due to my having an irresponsible and anarchical mind. The first statement, that soldiers are called upon to murder men who go on strike, is simply untrue, and I don't suppose any soldier or workman would believe it. It is, of course, sometimes true that soldiers are ordered to fire on a riotous mob who are destroying property with violence. Once matters have reached that stage civilised government may fairly be said to be at an end, and the occurrence of such an incident reflects no credit on either the workmen or the Government. It is perfectly true that in the last resort the safety of life and property in a civilised community depends upon force at the moment, but it is quite as true, and more often lost sight of, that if it depends upon force only it is not a civilised community, but a martial tyranny. Force which has not got the moral sense of the community behind it has no real value as an instrument of law and order in a modern State. A policeman who arrests a pickpocket in the Strand and takes him to the police-station, generally without resistance, does not do so by virtue of the fact that he is bigger and stronger than the pickpocket, still less by virtue of the fact that he carries a baton, but because he has the whole moral sense of the community behind him; and the pickpocket is for the moment an outlaw outside the pale of the community's protection. If this were not so every arrest would be a mere fight, and its result would depend upon the preponderance of physical strength on the side of the policemen or the criminals. A mob of riotous workmen intent upon doing physical injury to any workman who is not a unionist, or intent upon wrecking other people's property, are equally outside the pale of the community, and however much justice there may be in the demands of labour which they are seeking in a rough and ready way to enforce, they do as much harm to their cause as the Government that has to use bayonets against them does to the cause of law and order.

All the same, if I were one of the class likely to be shot by soldiers, it would not seem unnatural to me to appeal to them not to shoot me, and I think the prominence given to this appeal by the Government prosecution has done far more harm than ever the appeal itself could do, and has inevitably embittered and hardened class feeling. A wise Government does not assume that people take to extreme measures without extreme provocation, and seeks rather for the cause of the unrest than a mere suppression of its symptoms. The running sores of the body politic are not to be cured by being hidden under sticking-plaster, but by seeking the internal cause that produces them. A certain portion of our population have votes and the opportunity of using them at the ballot-box. I could wish that all adults had them. They have in this way a power to make their grievances felt even in Parliament, and to compel Governments to remedy them. They have also the terrible weapon of the general strike. If the capitalist class remain deaf to argument and obdurate to temperate appeals, these more forcible appeals can be used without breach of law and order. But in the industrial fight that I see coming upon us it would be a fatal thing if it should come to be thought that the police and soldiers are tools of one class, to be used only against another, and are not looked upon, as they should be, as merely the instruments of the community as a whole for preserving the safety of life and property for every individual from the highest to the lowest. It is for this reason above all that I deprecate the recent prosecutions, whatever technical justification there may have been for them, particularly while Sir Edward Carson is allowed to remain at large.[6]

House of Lords Debate 22 January 1913:
The Immunity of Trade Unions

This debate was triggered by *Vacher & Sons* v. *London Society of Compositors.*[7] The action was for libel, which the Society applied to have annulled on the ground that it was protected from a civil action under the terms of the 1906 Trade Disputes Act.[8] The courts found in the Society's favour and the Lords upheld this decision.

THE EARL OF DUNMORE rose to call attention to the recent decision of this House as the Final Court of Appeal respecting the immunity of trade unions from civil liability for wrongful acts; and to ask His Majesty's Government whether it is their intention to propose any alteration in the Trade Disputes Act, 1906.

Frank's response:

... We have been considering tonight a most important subject, and I think it is to be regretted that more members of your Lordships' House have not been present and taken an interest in it, because in my opinion these industrial questions and disputes are the important questions of the future, far more important than our ordinary political and Party divisions, and it is very necessary that as far as we can in the comparatively calm atmosphere of this House we should endeavour to consider how they are to be dealt with... I have always felt that the [Trade Disputes] Bill was an extremely dangerous one. I have never concealed that from myself, and I do not think I concealed it from the House when the Bill came up here.

You adopted, as the noble and learned Viscount on the Woolsack [Lord Haldane] said, one of two methods to remove a grievance, and I think he suggested himself that it was open to question whether the Bill was ideally desirable in the abstract, but that it was, perhaps, the lesser of two evils and the best way out of a difficulty. That, I think, was the only apology he was able to make for the Act. It is very easy always to raise a suggestion that it is necessary to protect the sick and benefit funds of the trade unions. That is less necessary in a sense now that we have the National Insurance Act, but it is very easy to raise sympathy in the case of any raid on these funds. It has been pointed out, however, that the trade unions themselves have always reserved the right to use these funds for the purpose of industrial warfare. No one denies them that right. What you have said is that they shall have all the rights of combatants but suffer none of the penalties of combatants, and by this Act you have set up, I will not say a class of individuals, but an organisation which is above and outside the law. That, I venture to think and always have thought, is an extremely dangerous thing to do, and may have very far-reaching consequences.

It is perfectly true that the individuals who do these tortious acts remain liable, and it is quite irrelevant to deal with tortious acts which are criminal because criminal acts you can punish under the Criminal Law. There are, however, tortious acts which are not criminal, but which none the less inflict a great deal of pecuniary damage on other people and may inflict a great deal of pain upon them in the case of grave libels. It would be perfectly easy for a great organisation of this kind–and we owe it only to the fact that on the whole workmen have behaved very well and have not used in a wrongful manner the immense power given them that it has not occurred–it would be perfectly easy for a large organisation with a great war fund to do any amount of damage to business concerns and other people for which you would have no remedy whatever against them. They could put forward men of straw to print the libels and issue them, and unless the libels were criminal you could not touch these men of straw except by way of civil action. That would rehabilitate the personal character, no doubt, of the person libelled, but would not recompense him for any pecuniary loss he had suffered. By this Act you allow Organisations to carry on campaigns of this character with impunity, and I think that is an extremely dangerous thing. I ask your Lordships to consider what the position would be if such an organisation as the militant suffragettes were to disguise themselves as a trade union and publish their pamphlets inciting to crime and carry on the mischievous part of their work under that protection. You could punish the individuals, but you could get no injunctions against the organisation or against the persons responsible for publishing the pamphlets. That is one thing which I think your Lordships should have considered.

In dealing with these matters it is, perhaps, necessary to say that I am speaking not only as a friend of Labour but as a friend of trade unions and an admirer of the work that trade unions have done and a believer in their necessity. I think that Labour has many grievances and has still much to ask for, but I am that generally unpopular person in this matter, a candid friend. I think it well that one should not encourage people, as was very well said by Lord Charnwood, to think that they may do those things that are wrong and suffer no penalty, and that one should not put trade unions in a position that they can do wrong things without being punished for it. We have also to consider the principle of individual liberty, and that principle is a great deal infringed by the picketing provisions of the Trade Disputes Act. When that Act was in this House in 1906, I implored the then Lord Chancellor, Lord Loreburn, to modify in some way those provisions. My recollection is that I then pointed out that you made it perfectly possible under that Bill for no fewer than 1,000 men to picket the house of an individual workman. It is perfectly true that such a picket might be peaceful in the sense that they might not break the man's windows with stones or have cudgels in their

119

hands, and might not resort to blows. But your Lordships can perfectly well realise what a workman and his family would feel if there was a raging and infuriated crowd in the road outside his house. That is what my noble friend meant when he spoke of domiciliary visits. I did not understand him to mean that the picket would go into a man's kitchen or his back garden and trample his flower beds. A workman's house is not like a mansion standing in a park. It fronts on the road, and the crowd outside would be as near to him as the noble Lords opposite are to me, and their observations on his conduct during the strike, which would reach the ears of himself and family, might amount to a very considerable invasion of his rights and to very serious intimidation. Those things have been made possible by this Act.

The noble Lord asked whether consideration would be given to this question and to amendments of the Act. In Question No. 1 the noble Lord asks whether His Majesty's Government will watch any further tendency to the employment of libel or other tortious conduct as a weapon in trade disputes with a view to the amendment of the section if necessary. The noble Lord on the Front Bench said that that was a purely legal question. That is the very thing I should have said the question was not. I should have said it was a question of policy. You are not asked to amend a particular section or how to draft another section to replace it. You are asked whether you will watch conduct which arises under that section and which is justified by that section with a view to considering as a matter of political policy whether it is well that the section should be amended. The noble Marquess opposite who intervened early in this debate said that he rather objected to his side being taunted with having assented to the passage of this Bill through this House in 1906, because his Party objected in any way to being saddled with the responsibility of it. … I think they allowed it to pass because they were afraid of arousing the opposition of the working classes and through fear of the working class vote, because they believed that the workmen were as a whole desirous of obtaining immense powers which I think will prove to be really harmful for them.

As regards the other Questions, I think we all agree in the proposition that we wish workmen to have the weapon of the strike at their disposal when they wish to strike, and not in any way to be subject to injunction from the Courts or any other restraint in striking; but I think we ought to feel that we want to give liberty also to other people who take opposite views in the dispute. It is considered nowadays almost an improper thing–I will not say by His Majesty's Government or necessarily by a majority of the other House–to allow a black-leg workman to take work or to encourage him to work during a strike. I can understand the irritation of workmen on strike when other workmen attempt to take their places, but until we change our ideas of individual liberty in this country and change our laws on this subject the duty of the Government is to allow every individual to make up his mind, not subject to coercion, but subject only to argument as to whom he will sell his labour. I have no particular sympathy with the black-leg in any particular trade union, any more than we have in the union to which the noble and learned Viscount on the Woolsack and I belong. We all wish to keep up prices. But I think it is the first duty of the Government, while legislation remains as it is, to consider individual liberty, and I regret that there should be an impression abroad that any Government would look lightly on disturbances that might take place in the course of a strike. We know perfectly well that during any large strike there will be excesses, and the trade unions are not to be blamed for those excesses and the Government is not to be blamed for them. They are apt to take place as part of the natural irritation of the people engaged in the strike. But it is not to be supposed that those excesses are to be looked at as other than sporadic and exceptional, and I think my noble friend is to be congratulated on having raised this question to-day. It is a desirable thing that the working of this Act should be considered. I see no reason why the Government, who are in touch with the representatives of Labour, should not put their heads together and consider whether some means cannot be devised short of this absolute and dangerous immunity which is now given to labour organisations, by which the legitimate aspirations of trade unionists can be satisfied.

Letter to Bertie[9]

6 Bond Court, Walbrook, London
11 Nov 1915

Dear Bertie,

At last I have a chance of returning your manuscript, and writing to you about it. Incidentally, thanks for the little book, which I have not yet read, but will.[10]

With regard to the article, of course I agree with the whole spirit of it, and with nearly every word you say. Something of the same kind was said by Loreburn in the House last night, though I am afraid his object was mischievous.[11]

Leonard Courtney also spoke on the same lines, but rather in the air, with the manner of a nonconformist school master.[12]

I have just been talking to Ernest McKenna,[13] who, although he did not say so in terms, practically adopted your analogy of two dogs fighting in the street, and admitted that we could only hope for an inconclusive peace, and that there could be no smashing; but also feels somewhat as you do the extreme danger to civilisation, and regards revolution as certain, at any rate on the Continent. I wonder if this shows that the Cabinet are alive to that danger.

Generally, I agree with you as to the myths of hatred that arise between the two countries – what Bernard Shaw called the ecstatic condition – but I think you go too far. You talk about atrocities having occurred on both sides, and about our being deluded with lies, but you surely cannot seriously believe, after the Bryce report, that there is not good evidence for definite German brutalities, which are not paralleled on our side. Possibly the murder of prisoners has occurred on both sides, but it has never been official and deliberate on our side, as it undoubtedly has been on theirs. I find it difficult to believe that you would not, at any rate to some extent, in common with the rest of us, shrink from a German and all that he represents, after this war. Surely it is not true that 'moral reprobation is nothing but hatred'.

I am not at all sure that I do not feel that the victory of our side is of enormous importance, but perhaps I would rather put it the other way, and say that the defeat of our own side would be a European disaster. I will perhaps go so far with you as to agree that an inconclusive peace, when both combatants have realised that they cannot gain anything by war, would be better than going on, perhaps even than a victory.

I should only really feel this, however, if Germany became a republic, and threw out the Hohenzollerns, and the Prussian tradition. I cannot the least agree with Shaw as to the desirability of peace in which we are preparing for a fresh war.

Are you really fair in treating the ideals as the same on both sides? Can we parallel the outspoken Bernhardi in England, or do you find the ideals of peace supported in high places in Germany. I quite agree that it is easy to make the rather neat point about Finland and Persia, but it is not true, as you say, that everything else is idle talk; and I rather agree with Gilbert Murray that in your desire to make your case, you go a little beyond that strict assertion of the truth which you preach.[14] I saw some correspondence in the Cambridge Magazine too, from which I gathered you have said rude things about bishops and armaments.

I do not like bishops but I do not think as badly of them as all that, and I doubt if I should say so just now, if I did.

Most of this is really beside the point, because of course I agree that if you have to say it, you must, even now. I could wish that in some ways you would put it a little differently, because in the cold-blooded antagonistic point of view, there is just at the moment something a little jarring, which hurts, much as though J. M. Robertson,[15] contemplating a Christian martyr burnt at the stake, were to spend the time in pointing out that there never was an historical Jesus. Deluded or not, many people have these ideals, and firmly believe in them; and while one would not mind your making them think, I think you do rather unnecessarily affront what to them are great emotions.

Am I going to see you again before Christmas? Let me know if you are in London. I see Christmas is on Saturday, and Boxing Day on Monday, so I hope you will be able to come from Friday to Tuesday.

Yours affectionately,
Russell.

'A National Dishonour', *New Statesman*, 22 Jan 1916

To the Editor of *The New Statesman*:

Sir,–In the House of Commons last week a Liberal Prime Minister made proposals having for their object to compel citizens of this country to fight, whether they desire to do so or not. This is an invasion of our liberties so grave, and a reversal of our recent traditions so serious, as to render it impossible to keep silent; and the situation is not less but more grave because a majority of the House of Commons and perhaps a majority of the country approve of the present proposals. In the relations between a community and its members there must necessarily be restrictions upon individual liberty, and the more complex the organisation of the community the more numerous and detailed must be the restrictions. The growth of these restrictions is not incompatible with an increasing amount of liberty in those matters which make the real individual life. As both a socialist and a strong individualist I realise to the full the pressure of both these considerations. As an instance of the former we may take the growing, detailed and sometimes irksome requirements of the Public Health Acts: as an instance of the latter the growth of individual liberty in matters of religion. The object of political action in a free State should be to restrain as little as possible the freedom of the individual to live his own life, think his own thoughts, and spend his own energies in the way that seems most desirable to him, except in those cases where the public safety or welfare imperatively demands interference with this freedom. This principle is often lost sight of nowadays, and those who are in power frequently seem to welcome coercion for its own sake because it saves them the trouble of thought. Thought is slow, painful, and laborious: coercion is easy, and appears to superficial observers to give the results desired. But the spirit which argues in this way is a spirit of brute force, of violence, and of unreason: it is not the spirit of a free people going rejoicingly and proudly on its way. The nation coerced, dragooned, and regimented is a nation infected with the Prussian spirit: it is no longer that free England of whose traditions we are proud.

In the case of the compulsion now proposed it cannot be unhesitatingly said that there has been on the part of the Ministers great care for the social future of the nation, much judgment in the methods used, or much thought as to the requirements of the situation. It is admitted that the Cabinet has hardly considered, much less made up its mind upon, the two vital questions as to how many able-bodied men can be withdrawn from the service of their country at home, and to what indefinite extent the credit and the capital of the nation can stand the present rate of expenditure. So far as the present measure is not a mere response to the clamour of the capitalist Press, it is more than suspect of being the fruit of political scheming of a not very creditable character. Lord Derby has conducted with magnificent vigour a campaign which he described at its inauguration as a winding up in bankruptcy. In the course of that campaign he and his political associates bound our Prime Minister to a pledge to married men. Whether Mr Asquith ever saw or carefully considered the full implications of his pledge I do not know, but he did in effect leave himself in a position where he was bound to redeem it, though he has admitted that he did not anticipate this necessity. Always in the background in political gossip there is mention of the active and sinister figure of Mr Lloyd George pushing his Chief down the slippery slope of coercion, threatening to resign, and boasting of munitions as though he and the Harmsworth Press alone had ever thought upon the subject. Meanwhile further political pressure is applied by other reactionaries, including the House of Lords, and the threat of an automatic dissolution of parliament this month. This is not the atmosphere of grave and sober consideration in which statesmen with a single eye for their country's good should approach the consideration of so momentous a change in our national life. What has become of the speeches about honour and freedom at stake? What of the glory of a free people rising in its might and voluntarily to resist the Prussian tyranny? Freedom is suffering, it is true, but at the hands of her own professed supporters, and glory departs from commanded battles fought on both sides by men pressed and driven by their masters.

The debate which has taken place has shown that the present figures are so conjectural that no one can assert that the final residue will be other than negligible. On the other hand, there is no doubt of the absence of that general consent for which Mr Asquith also stipulated and a minority of over 100 members is by no means negligible. The decision of the Labour Congress and the withdrawal of official Labour from the Government produce a situation of the gravest danger to the country. Organised Labour, already suspicious and alarmed by alternate threats and cajolery, sees an exclusively capitalist Government in power, and, in view of what the Tory Press has been saying, not unreasonably fears industrial compulsion. And why not? We have been told munitions are as important as men, and as essential to win the war: and compulsion is easier surely in the workshop than on the field of battle. For an unascertained number of unwilling men in khaki the Government is prepared to destroy our unity, to damp our ardour, to split the country transversely into the drivers and the driven, and to run the appalling risk of strikes in munitions, in coal mining, and in transport. On the ground of expediency alone is such action expedient?

The record of the Government, both before and after the Coalition, has been one of indecision and hesitation, and of weakness. For many months they could not screw up their courage to deal with the question of drink: they have not yet screwed up their courage to deal with incompetence in high places. Men have been sacrificed and money has been squandered without careful thought for the resources of the nation, and without a true co-ordination of means to an end. Now the time has come that we are told that more men must be wasted and more muddling through allowed; and the common answer to all I have said is that no efforts must be spared to win the War.

My case is that proper efforts – efforts of mind and efforts of thought – have been too much spared, and my answer is that winning the War is not an end in itself, but only a means to an end. Those of us who support this War, and there are few who do not, consider that, horrible as it is, bloody as it is, ruinous as it is, and destructive as it is of European civilisation, we yet support it because we believed and want still to believe that we are fighting for the right of a man to live his own life in freedom without fear of the highway robber or the armed assassin.

The response to voluntary effort has been magnificent, and has far exceeded all expectation. To abandon so recklessly that great glory, and to admit that our citizens have been driven and compelled to fight for freedom is to my mind a national dishonour and a deep disgrace. It is or should be repulsive to any man to order another man to fight for him. And if the ideals for which we are fighting are to be destroyed, not by our enemies but by ourselves, it were far better to conclude at once any kind of peace, and to begin to take stock of civilisation and rebuild it, rather than as now *propter vitam vivendi perdere causas*.[16]

Yours, etc., Russell.

12 January 1916.

House of Lords Debate 4 May 1916: Treatment of Conscientious Objectors

My Lords, I think it necessary to carry a little further the other portion of the Right Revd Prelate's speech,[17] because the answer to which we have just listened has not really dealt with it. I do not refer to the decisions of the Tribunals themselves. That is a very interesting matter which might be discussed in a legal way and might give rise to various important questions such as were pointed out to the House, because I think most people will admit that many of the Local Tribunals have been very cavalier in their treatment of these questions. But that is only one of the issues. Another of the issues–to my mind perhaps the more important of the two, or quite as important–is the way in which these men are treated after their objections are disposed of, and what is done to them in the military prisons in their confinement, to which the Right Revd Prelate alluded and which has been very shortly dealt with in the answer.

To take, first of all, the correctness of the decisions of the Tribunals, I have no doubt that in many cases great care is given to the decisions. I admit that in many cases it must be a very difficult question to decide, and of course I admit also that it is not desirable that those who are actual shirkers should escape, as it were, under the petticoat of a conscientious objector. But if a man who has been denied exemption by a Tribunal on the ground that he is not a conscientious objector continues to refuse to take off his clothes and to put on khaki and in that intermediate stage remains in a cell, as I understand these men have done, for an unusual period without food, it is obvious that he has some objection at any rate to military service, whatever may be the foundation of it, and it is a strong thing to say that anything short of a conscientious objection will make a man take those extreme steps.

Whenever one portion of the community endeavours to impose its will upon another portion there always will arise conflicts, at any rate where there is any individual freedom of opinion and individual way of thinking. There are many cases in which the community, nevertheless, does impose its will, but it always becomes a question how far it is in the interests of the community itself that this imposition should be continued. You had before the war similar elements of unreason on the part of the Suffragettes. On the whole, I think the conclusion which people came to was that letting them starve was not the method of curing the trouble; at any rate, it was not the method adopted. I do not think I need argue the question as to whether any recognition should be given to these men, because that has been already settled by the Statute. It is therefore not a question which one need now discuss.

But what exactly does the community desire to do with these men? Does it hope with people of inflexible determination, to make good soldiers of them? That seems to be wildly idealistic. Does it desire to shoot them? If so, the simplest thing is to say so at once and shoot them out of hand, which would cause fewer of these disgraceful scenes. I understood that there was in the Military Service Act a clause which it was stated in another place provided that persons who conscientiously objected to and refused to perform any kind of military service were not liable to be shot. I am told that many of these men who have been refused exemption have been drafted into units and sent out to the Front where they will almost automatically be shot for refusing to obey orders in the face of the enemy. Is that desired? Because that is a question which may arise. I would also beg your Lordships to consider what effect it is likely to have on our men at the Front to have forcibly put into their regiments non-soldiers of this kind who will behave in this way. It may make them very indignant, but it certainly will not raise the prestige of any battalion that has these men drafted into it. The noble Lord who spoke last said, What would you think of a battalion a certain number of men in which refused to obey orders? But those men went there voluntarily, or at any rate raised no conscientious objection.

While I am sorry for the conscientious objectors on account of their physical suffering, I do not know that they require one's sympathy in other respects. But what I am more sorry for is a community that puts itself in this position. I think we do a thing which is very unfortunate for our own national character in raising these kind of questions. Presumably when this clause was put into the Military Service Act it was recognised that conscientious objectors would be a difficulty. They have been a difficulty in other walks of life before. We have the instance of the education rate, and vaccination. The general sense of the community, as a whole, has been that the best way to deal with that sort of difficulty is as far as possible to slide over it, to suppress it, and not make it too prominent. But in these cases the action of the Tribunals and of the military authorities afterwards has done everything possible to increase the friction, discontent, excitement, and indignation which these cases have aroused. I am informed—and my information agrees entirely with what the Right Revd Prelate said—that many of these young men who are conscientious objectors are men whom in ordinary times you would say were of the highest character and highest principles, and that they take this stand entirely on the ground of principle. What is done to them at present, I am told, is that they are not allowed food very often, and that, as the Right Revd Prelate said, they are coaxed and bullied—men of education and of great ability.

Is it desirable to treat a class of the community in this way, no matter how strongly you disagree with their opinions? I agree that all persons of strong opinions are a nuisance. It is very tiresome when people will not think the same as you do, and still more tiresome when they will not do what you tell them to. But if they will not, surely the best course is to take the easiest way out of it and make as little friction as possible. If it is true that these men are being bullied and starved and cajoled into taking military service, and if it is true that they are being sent to the Front where they will automatically commit a military offence that must be punished by death, it seems to me that what was said in another place when this clause was inserted in the Military Service Act is not being carried out. To accentuate this position is a thing which does not do any good to us as a country, which does not do any good to the Army, and which does not do any good to the conscientious objectors themselves. Non-combatant service is offered to them. This they will not accept in most cases because they consider that it is very near to combatant service. But there are plenty of other things they can be given to do, such as making roads, such as building ships—a very urgent necessity at the present time—or, as the Right Revd Prelate said, if you desire to punish them you can intern them until the end of the war. But do not treat them in a way in which any noble Lord individually would be ashamed to treat a fellow creature. If they are not to be handed over to the civil authorities and to civil imprisonment, then we should at least have some assurance that they will be treated as human beings ought to be treated.

House of Lords Debate 4 July 1916: Military Service–Conscientious Objectors

EARL RUSSELL rose to call attention to the operation of the Military Service Act with regard to conscientious objectors who have not been so found by the Tribunals, to the case of C. H. Norman, and to complaints of brutal treatment at Wandsworth Detention Barracks and of the commandant, Lieut. Colonel Reginald Brooke, and to move to resolve–

That in the opinion of this House it is undesirable to subject military prisoners to punishments not authorised by law.

My Lords, I have to call your attention this afternoon to some extremely painful matters. We have had in this House one or two small discussions on the question of the conscientious objector, but they have generally dealt rather with legal considerations than with the actual facts. Today, even at the risk of wearying your Lordships, I think it necessary that some of the actual facts should be placed before this House. Your Lordships are familiar, from the discussions we have already had, with the fact that the Act provided that there should be an exemption for conscientious objectors who were so found by the Tribunals. The Question that I have put down relates to objectors who were not found to be conscientious objectors by the Tribunals, and I venture to say that almost every one of these represents a case in which the Tribunal has failed to carry out the duty which Parliament imposed upon it. I know the suggestion has been made, in answer to previous Questions, that the men concerned have been found by a competent authority, sometimes not once but twice, not to be conscientious objectors, and therefore they have to be considered as ordinary soldiers. The noble Marquess opposite (Lord Salisbury), who has experience on the Central Tribunal, knows, I think, that the Tribunals have not always succeeded in adequately distinguishing between them, and that the instances in which they have failed to give that relief which the Act of Parliament contemplated are not mere ones and twos, but are, unfortunately, more numerous than they should be.

When the Tribunal has not been effective in carrying out the duties imposed upon it, you have the result that there is drafted into the Army and into the military machine technically a soldier–merely technically a soldier–a person who is, in fact, a conscientious objector to any form of military service. There then at once arises the inevitable result. There is a conflict with discipline, the discipline of the Army. The persons who administer the military machine cannot be expected to put up with breaches of discipline. The conscientious objector, if he is, in fact, one, whether he can be expected to or not–and apparently by the Army authorities he sometimes is expected to–does not, in fact, submit to the military discipline, and you get the inevitable conflict which has had many unfortunate instances to which I will draw your Lordships' attention.

There are, of course, legal punishments of all kinds provided for refusal to obey discipline, but there has also been in a great number of cases a great deal of illegal pressure and illegal punishments, and it is to those that I desire to draw your Lordships' attention to-day. The object of that punishment is very easy to understand. It is administered by people who are of opinion that a conscience can be formed, or at any rate that the conclusions of a conscience can be modified, by sufficient physical pain and ill-treatment, and they hope, by the ill-treatment of persons who occupy this position, to make them give up their position and to serve in the Army without raising their conscientious objections; and in some cases they have succeeded, as your Lordships will hear.

I now propose to read to your Lordships some of the circumstances that have happened. This is a case from a barracks where several reports have been collected. This writer says– 'It has been a terrible day for them. One of them, S., has given in. They were stripped and scrubbed up and down fiercely several times. "Horrible torture," they said. One fainted. We saw the corporal, and he was nearly insane'–That is the corporal who had been administering this form of illegal punishment–'He had had such a terrible day with C.O.'s that he wanted to chuck the job and go to the cells instead. He was told to go on and he swore horribly, saying he would break our hearts and kill us to-morrow... It is a most terrible ordeal... A military prison seems to be a special place for torturing us.' Another man says– 'When we refused to obey orders we were either kicked in the back or hit in the face, in addition to being dragged round by the ears. ... B. is the biggest brute I have ever seen, read or heard of. There are now only four sticking it, and they have just had a scrub and been badly kicked. K. and R. can hardly walk.' Another report, referring to the same man, runs– 'The greatest bully in the camp, Lance-corporal B. (6 ft. 6 in. in height), after a time kicked us out of the tent and tried to make us march. A. I. got badly kicked on the leg. T. B. and D. C. each got a terrible blow on the side of the head. W. H. got his face badly scratched. J. J. got a thick ear and his nose bursted, while I had a stunning upper-cut breaking a tooth. He put us on our backs and ate his breakfast in front of us as we lay there (we got no breakfast). We were taken to the washhouse, and there–gave in... It was a terribly brutal ordeal.' Another, referring to the same corporal– 'Also I. was kicked terribly; he can only crawl along leaning on me in terrible pain.' In these cases, as your Lordships will notice, the treatment had had the results hoped for. A visitor to this camp writes– 'The four persons are still standing out, and of the five who were sent here on Saturday all have given in except D. and S. ... I saw the fellow, Lance-corporal B., who has been the person to give the brutal treatment... When he learned who I was, he made it in his way to come round by me (while I was waiting to see the commanding officer) to say "I've only seven now!" The commanding officer would not yield. He would not admit that the men were being badly used, and said that so long as they were in the Army they must yield to discipline. I pleaded for a Court-Martial very hard indeed, but he would not promise to give one. He pointed to the fact that so many had given way already! We talked a good deal about the Army, Prussianism, etc., and, after telling us what they would do with such like in Germany, "Yes" he said with pride, "and in Russia", and he would be glad if they could do it here... It is most pathetic to see our boys; they looked so ill, worn, and depressed.' Here is another case– 'The commandant said "Take him to the special room." Four of them then set on me... The sergeant I have mentioned deliberately punched me behind the ear, and all of them set on me again and bruised me more.' A little further on– 'We are getting knocked about in a terrible manner. We have been threatened to be shot–a message from the War Office, I was told. They are trying to stop letters from getting out. We are all getting bashed about. H. and I fainted to-day. F. has a swollen face.' Your Lordships know that persons of ordinary health and of military age do not faint readily from comparatively slight knockings-about.

Here, in this same report, is an illustration of the effect which this unfortunate conduct is having upon discipline, one of the things which I myself most desire to remove– 'To-day they dragged another to church, which struck one as rather blasphemous. The opinion in the ranks is that they deserve what they get, but already I note a slight but very slight change in the demeanour of some of the men, chiefly old soldiers, or men who have knocked about the world. The corporal who beat his man on the face expressed great respect for him in my hearing, but doubted whether he could "hold out against such a mighty big machine." I am not particularly squeamish, having seen and taken part in many curious things.' I believe that the majority of the cases I have been reading to your Lordships refer to Wandsworth Detention Barracks, but there are also several very bad cases which have been supplied to me from the Whitchurch (Salop) Barracks. Some of these cases referring to Lance-Corporal Barker, the man called 'B', are from Whitchurch. This is one of the things this man said– 'You are the damned ring-leader. I'll break your bloody heart. I've tamed the others. I'll scrub you myself; you're my man. I'll scrub you until the blood comes.' 'He scrubbed me cruel,' says this man; 'I was forced to cry out.' Here is the case of a man who was ordered to fall in– 'I refused, explaining that I was a conscientious objector. The commanding officer then called upon Corporal Barker, who had been specially sent for to deal with us.' This is, again, the same man. Apparently that was the way in which he dealt with them. This is from another letter– 'He said, "March." We did not. He kicked me on the ankle. I fell. He then kicked me just below the knee; it is bruised yet. He again said, "March." I staggered along slowly, so he kicked me again on the thigh. I went down again. I thought my leg was broken. I felt some one helping me up. It was Dan. He helped me back to the tent. I could not walk myself. Then we were taken to the baths and scrubbed with a stiff sink brush. Dan practically appealed to be shot. So you can reckon what it was. We were followed by about 4,000 men, a lot of them booing.'

It may be suggested, and it has been suggested, that these stories are not true. I say at once that as far as I am concerned I am not prepared to accept any official denial of these stories, and that I should not be prepared to believe in any inquiry that was not conducted by independent people who were in no way under the domination of any official pressure whatever. These stories–I say at once that I am not acquainted with them myself–come from people who I am assured are reliable; and your Lordships heard the speech which was made by the most Revd Primate the other night in this House.[18] The most Revd Primate is not, I think, too ready to array himself against authority, or to give any support whatever to law breakers. Nor would your Lordships think that he was a man likely readily to believe stories of this kind which were without foundation. But he himself told you that the evidence was such that he was convinced that unfortunate incidents had taken place–incidents of the character which I have been reading to your Lordships. I say, therefore, that official denials will convey no conviction to me, and ought not to convey any conviction to any member of the public. These things have been officially denied in the other House, where they cannot be challenged and where no debate can be raised on a Question. The Government are responsible–every member of the Government is responsible—for allowing anything of this kind to continue, and every one of your Lordships is responsible if you do not protest against this kind of treatment and allow it to continue. It is not a responsibility that can be shelved by professing not to believe the stories, or by thinking that one has not personally ordered it, or by thinking that it is taking place unofficially and unauthorised in barracks. It is a responsibility which every one of us must share, the Government most of all, if it is allowed to continue one moment after attention has been drawn to it.

I now want to call attention to the special case of Mr C. H. Norman.[19] In this instance I know the man myself. I have known him for several years, and can assure your Lordships that I am prepared to accept as absolutely correct any statement that he makes. I have no sympathy with his opinions and am quite willing to admit that he is in many ways a very wrong-headed and very obstinate person. But the point with which I am dealing is merely the question of how he was treated. This is a diary of what happened to him at the Wandsworth Detention Barracks on the 23rd or 24th of May of this year— 'Met with shower of abuse on arrival. Asked for some paper to make will. They asked whether I would put on uniform—refused. Taken to cell and forcibly dressed. Repeated request to make will, as I might not be alive more than three or four days. Officer went to commandant. I was taken to reception room and signed for things. Commandant arrived, and without a word to me ordered me to be taken to hospital and put in strait jacket. Was taken there and put in strait jacket, which was too small and caused me great pain. I told the attendant, but he could do nothing. Commandant and another officer arrived. Commandant mocked at me and spat at me. Other officer asked whether I was all right—a question which amused me in the circumstances. Medical officer came about 8 p.m., but did not explain anything. He said commandant had said I had threatened suicide. I told him I had asked to make my will, and that was all. I could not move myself in strait jacket and suffered a good deal, because I wanted to go to the lavatory but was lying on the floor and could not attract the attendant's attention. I did finally and went, and then was left standing. I had asked in the beginning for a chair, but was refused it... Sergeant-major came in and another officer, and asked how I was. I told him I was feeling ill. Medical officer came at ten, and released me on my giving my word against doing harm whilst under his authority. On the next day I was in hospital. On asking leave to write to my solicitor or friends, commandant swore and spat at me, expressing hope that the medical officer would put me in strait jacket again... On the 26th May the commandant visited me again, cursed me, and said he wished I would cut my throat; that I was a coward who ought to be shot. Also spat at me... June 1st, ordered to parade by commandant, who again cursed me, and said I should be sent to France and that it was a pity I was afraid to kill myself. Commandant again said I should be put in strait jacket. Ordered C.D. 1 and put in darkish cell; bread and water diet; all privileges taken.'

I have also received a letter from Norman's father, a portion of which I propose to read to your Lordships— 'As the father of this young man, I can say without the least hesitation that his strongest convictions for years before the war were entirely anti-pathetic to every form of military influence'—I am quite able to endorse that, and if ever there is or has been a conscientious objector, a person with every possible sign of the crank about him, it is this gentleman, C. H. Norman. The letter from the father goes on– 'It cannot possibly be in the interest of the nation that a young man of talent, imbued with strong intellectual convictions (however mistaken), and who has always had the public interest if anything too much at heart, should be subjected to every form of degradation and physical suffering because he will not abate the full force of his conscientious scruples.' Since these events, of which I have read you the diary, Norman has been court-martialled and sentenced to two years detention. At least I gather it is detention from the fact that he remained in barracks and was subject to military control; at any rate, he has not been removed to a civil prison under the understanding–referred to by the noble and learned Lord, Lord Parmoor, the other day–regarding the operation of the new Army Order, and I saw the other day in the newspapers that there has been a second Court-Martial on this same man. The reason for a second Court-Martial while he is serving one sentence and the effect of it I do not know, but I shall be glad to learn; and I shall also be glad to learn whether it is proposed to remove this man, who has suffered so much under military discipline and control. If he is not to be removed it is a breach of the spirit of the Act and of the Tribunals and of the Army Order, because he is, to my knowledge, a perfectly honest conscientious objector and a person who ought to have whatever relief is to be extended to such.

I have also stated that I desire to call attention to the commandant referred to in the diary which I have read. The commandant is Lieut. Colonel Reginald Brooke, and the facts in some of these cases connected with him cannot be denied, because they are in writing in his own hand and are therefore available to confute anybody who attempts to deny them. This was a case in which a man had written a letter referring to the treatment of somebody else, and the commandant refused to let it out of the camp. Of that, naturally, I make no complaint. But he wrote on it this endorsement– 'Letter returned. Not of the sort I will pass. If your news as to Private Rendal Wyatt is true I am delighted to hear it, and sincerely hope the whole lot of the conscientious objectors will be treated in the same way. (Signed) REGINALD BROOKE, Lt. Col. Commandant, May 19, 1916.' He was also sent an inquiry about another conscientious objector named Forrester, and to this he replied– 'Private Forrester was given sentence by me, and I shall continue to act in my Barracks according to my orders, without any regard to what you and the "so-called public" may think. I do not care one atom for public opinion.' On another occasion he said to the father of two men who were suffering there– 'I mean to make these men soldiers, and I shall continue to give them severe punishment while they disobey military orders. I don't care for Asquith or Parliament. I shall do just as I like with these men.' I am not sure whether it was not, perhaps, the sacrilege committed in his reference to the Prime Minister that has caused him to be removed from his position, rather than his treatment of these men. He said to another conscientious objector– 'I don't care a damn for your conscience. You'll do what you are told, or by God I'll make your life a hell. You will be put in a strait jacket twenty-three hours out of the twenty-four, and don't you think you'll leave this place when your time is up. I have power to bring you before a General Court-Martial and keep you here in my charge.' It may well seem incredible to your Lordships that anybody occupying an official position of this responsibility could act and speak in this way. I should like to inquire why this gentleman has been removed, and whether there is supposed to be any truth in any of the statements that have been made about him, or whether his removal has been in the nature of a promotion. If any of these statements are true I should have thought that the proper course to take would have been to have a Court-Martial upon him, and afford these people the opportunity of giving their evidence and having the matter dealt with on oath. That course has not been taken. And when one remembers that his immediate official superior, or at any rate the person who deals with conscientious objectors at the War Office, is Brigadier-General Childs, to whom I have called your Lordships' attention before, one may, perhaps, not wonder that brutality in a subordinate is excused or winked at.

LORD SANDHURST: Oh, oh!

The noble Lord says 'Oh, oh.' I will give you my reasons why I say that. Brigadier-General Childs was asked whether he knew any Quakers, and he replied that he was glad he did not. Since then he has given evidence and been cross-examined, and I understand he said he thought the best thing to do with conscientious objectors was to have them all shot, although the words he used referred to Army Order IX (a) which I understand has the same meaning. I do not know whether the noble Lord will deny that this has been said by this officer on oath and in public. I came across, in *The Times* on Monday, an interesting address by no less a person than His Majesty to the cadets at Sandhurst on the duty of an officer, in the course of which the King said— 'You must cultivate a high standard of honour and moral conduct... These qualities have always been the distinguishing characteristics of officers in the British Army.' Is it contended, in view of what has been said, and in view of what cannot be denied without an official Inquiry at which these people are given an opportunity of making these charges—is it contended that this gentleman to whom I refer comes within that definition, and that he behaves as one would desire a British officer to behave?

There have been other incidents at other barracks, but I desire today only to call attention to those which I have mentioned. But I would ask what is intended to be done in this matter. There are only two logical courses. I need hardly say that, characteristically, neither has been taken. One course is to regard these people as outlaws entitled to no sympathy and to no consideration, and in that case the best and kindest thing is to shoot them out of hand if you feel justified in doing that. The other course is the one that was contemplated by the Act of Parliament when it contained the clause in question. You may treat these men as lunatics, if you like, but they are people holding opinions so strong that you cannot influence those opinions by argument nor by physical persecution. You can apparently, as I showed in the earlier instances, cow them to the extent of making them, through sheer terror, do that of which their conscience disapproves, but that is a method which I, and I think all of your Lordships, deprecate.

The official answer, no doubt, will be what we have heard before—that these men have had the opportunity of going before the Tribunals, and that the Tribunals have refused their claim. As a matter of fact, in the case of Norman, he did not go before the Tribunal, although of course he had only himself to thank for that. But when it turns out that these men are conscientious objectors in fact, that answer will not do. Since I put this Question on the Paper we have had an important statement by Mr Asquith.

After making it, Mr Asquith said— 'I think, perhaps, I may appeal to my honourable friends to read my statement carefully in print.' I have taken that course, and when this statement was referred to last week I ventured to think that it would have to be read very carefully before we could suppose that it carried out what we understood was the intention—that is, that these men should be civilly imprisoned and dealt with civilly when it was found that they were real conscientious objectors. The Prime Minister's statement began— 'The procedure to be adopted by the War Office in the case of soldiers, under Army Order X, of May 25, 1916, sentenced to imprisonment for refusing to obey orders, is as follows …' The first thing that is not clear is whether this applies to those who were sentenced before Army Order X was issued. The second point is that it is limited to a sentence of imprisonment. You can sentence a man to two years detention in barracks, and so escape sending him into civil custody. This is an evasion which makes the Order unsatisfactory. The only thing that will make it satisfactory is that every one of these unfortunate men—mistaken, if you like, but at any rate very unfortunate in the way in which they are being treated—should be brought under civil custody, and that there should be no technical quibbling differences as to when their sentence was and the form it took. The Prime Minister's statement goes on— 'All Court-Martial proceedings on conscientious objectors will be referred for scrutiny to the War Office.' It is then said that if they supply the information required in the questions it will be examined into. I hope they will all be advised to supply that information and have it examined into. But I have seen some of these people. They are extraordinarily unreasonable, and it may quite well be that some of them will not do that. Then the Prime Minister said— 'If the information is refused … the prisoner will remain under military control, his sentence will at once be commuted to detention, and he will be sent to a detention barrack to undergo his sentence.' What exactly is the meaning of that? Why are they to be sent back to military control unless it is to be assumed that they are shirkers, and then what is to be done with them beyond imprisoning? I think the Prime Minister's statement does not go sufficiently far, and does not make it sufficiently clear that these men are going to be properly dealt with.

This gradual growth, as it has been, of militarism in this country—and militarism, as Mr Bodkin said when prosecuting for the Crown, in a sinister sense—requires to be looked into. It will not be put up with indefinitely by the people of this country, and it will not be got over by denying the facts or by issuing Orders which do not honestly deal with the difficulty. My own impression is that, to begin with, there were very few people indeed who had any sympathy with the conscientious objector, or who were in the least anxious to fight his cause in any way. But I am perfectly certain that the action that has been taken by the Government and the conduct which has been allowed to be meted out to these men has been such as to produce an unfortunate and most undesirable sympathy for them, and has also to a very considerable extent helped to injure discipline in the ranks of the Army. I am as anxious as any member of the Government can be to remove that, and I ask the Government to endeavour to deal with the matter seriously and in a comprehensive spirit.

But all that I have called attention to today are the illegalities which have been committed. I think there is no politician, no statesman, no member of your Lordships' House, who would be prepared to say that he is in favour of a prisoner of any kind, for whatever reason, being subjected to illegal or brutal treatment. These knockings-about to which I have called attention are no part of any official sentence and they are illegal, and I hope that an expression of opinion by your Lordships will lead to those who have to deal with these men realising that if they punish them as, so long as matters go on as they are, they are bound to do, they must punish them in accordance with the law, and not by methods which are extra-legal and which are unfortunate and do a great deal of harm. I do not think any of your Lordships will disagree with the Resolution which I now beg to move.

Moved to resolve, That in the opinion of this House it is undesirable to subject military prisoners to punishments not authorised by law.–(Earl Russell.)

On Question, That in the opinion of this House it is undesirable to subject military prisoners to punishments not authorised by law–

A Division was challenged and the Bar cleared, but there being no Tellers for the Not-contents the said Resolution agreed to.

Letter to Bertie[20]

Telegraph House
16 Jul 1916

My dear Bertie,

I have seen the Trinity announcement in the paper,[21] and whatever you may say, I very much regret it. No doubt these stuffy old dons were very uncongenial to you, and were also unfriendly on account of your views, but still, I always thought you well suited to an academic life, and a personality of great value to the young – in stirring their ideas. I think as time goes on you will miss it more than you realise and possibly regret it.

I can't attempt to shape your career for you – you must be the only guide and only judge of your own actions – but don't finally cut yourself off too rashly and above all beware of popular audiences. The average is such a fool that any able man who can talk can sway him for a time. What the world wants of first class intellects like yours is not action – for which the ordinary politician or demagogue is good enough – but thought, a much more rare quality. Think out our problems, embody the result in writing, and let it slowly percolate through the teachers of the next generation. And don't suppose the people you meet are as earnest, as deep or as sincere as you are.

As mere experience and learning about human beings what you are doing now may have its value, but you see what I am trying to say is that you are *wasting* yourself. You are not making the best use for the world of your talents. As soon as you come to see that you will change your activities.

Well, I don't preach to you often, because as a rule you don't need it, but at the moment I think you are a little (or rather, a great deal) carried away.

It's a long time to Feb 1 – why not go to America sooner? – they ought to be glad to get rid of you!

Come and see us when you are in London and try and spend a few placid days here with us in August.

Yours affectionately,

F.

House of Lords Debate 17 December 1917:
Representation of the People Bill

My Lords, I think it is safe to say that the reform which this Bill makes is the largest since the Parliament Act, if it is not indeed more important, for that was largely a matter of machinery, and this Bill admits to the franchise and therefore to the government of this country an enormous mass of voters, and makes really the greatest change that has been made.

... The noble Marquess who initiated the debate (Lord Salisbury) said that manhood suffrage is now inopportune. I think it may be truly said that there has never been a Reform Bill presented to your Lordships' House without there being a large number, perhaps a majority, of your Lordships ready to say that the extension was inopportune. So much is that the case that the noble Marquess based his argument largely on the fact that it is impossible not to pass this measure now. People expected, and you may say demanded, it, and I think His Majesty's Government will hesitate very much before they prevent the passage of this measure or some measure like it.

Then the noble Marquess finished by saying that the same argument did not apply to women: that in the one case when you add 2,000,000 men to the Register it is really an addition of the same kind, while women voters are a difference in kind in the addition that you make. Well honestly, even after the long and explanatory speech of Lord Bryce in opposition to the proposal to enfranchise women, I do not quite know what that means. Does the noble Marquess mean to take his stand upon the fact that they have a servile sense, that they are an enslaved race, and that therefore they are not to have the possession of free men in the shape of a vote? I can hardly think that he cares to adopt that argument. Still less do I think it likely that in the twentieth century he adopts an argument based upon a very ancient and long since disused culture and religion. Yet if he does not base his argument on one of those two things, what does the noble Marquess mean when he says there is a difference in kind? I recall the speech of Shylock to Antonio—

'If you prick us, do we not bleed? if you tickle us, do we not laugh?'

Does not the same argument apply quite as forcibly to any man or any woman? If a woman is short of food, is she not hungry? If she works hard, is she not tired? If she suffers from unpleasant conditions of labour, is she not equally impoverished and weakened by these conditions? Why cannot the argument for women be based upon the simplest and most straightforward reason—the reason that they are human beings; not that they are a special class, not that they will be able to uplift our politics, but simply that they are human beings; and if the franchise is a weapon that they need for their self-defence and for the protection of their interests and of their labour, women need it just as much as men.

Lord Bryce, when he discussed this matter, talked about the fitness of voters, and admitted that this was a very Victorian argument. What do we mean when we talk about the fitness of voters? Lord Bryce himself mentioned the suggestion to repudiate it, that every male voter understands all the political considerations which should guide his vote. Is it suggested even that every member of your Lordships' House could give an intelligent vote on some question connected with, say, the foreign politics of Persia? I would not undertake to say as much for myself. There are questions of which some people understand more than others. We do not grant the vote for fitness; we grant it—and I venture to suggest that this is the real essence of the vote—for the protection of the voter; and we grant the vote for what is much more important than that—namely, for the protection of the State, in order that through the ballot-box the State may learn, from the organised opinion of those who have grievances and who desire their remedy, what those grievances are. I suggest that the vote is granted nowadays on no kind of fitness, but as a substitute for riot, revolution, and the rifle. We grant the suffrage in order that we may learn in an orderly and civilised manner what the people who are governed want. The noble Marquess who opened the debate admitted that we want the consent of the governed. I know no way in which we can get that except by giving the governed an opportunity of a free expression of their opinions in the ballot box. If those considerations apply to any class they apply to women. The noble Viscount (Lord Bryce) took as his illustration the class of female domestic servants. I wish to say nothing against female domestic servants, particularly nowadays when they are so difficult to get; but is not that, after all a parasitic class? Is that a class which one should take as an illustration of what one means? The noble Viscount seemed to me, when he spoke, as if he had never heard of the working woman, of the woman who has to live, of the widow with her children, of the wife who is supplementing the income of the house, and of the woman working in the factory. She has the same conditions affecting her as has the male worker, and she has just the same right to have her voice in saying how she is to be protected against those conditions.

The noble Viscount said that the law was equally fair for men and women. Many of your Lordships have conducted contested elections, and you know very well—nobody knows better than those who have conducted contested elections—that grievances which have not the pressure of the vote behind them can be, and are, disregarded by candidates. I did not mean to give much time to-night to the question of woman suffrage. I had hoped that this was a question which had almost passed the stage of contest and was accepted. Indeed, the noble Marquess himself said that he would not vote against it. I trust that it may now become law. That it is a momentous change I do not deny. That women will always vote wisely I do not for a moment suggest. Do all men vote wisely? What opportunities of political education have women had in the past? For the noble Viscount to say that women do not meet, and do not talk, and do not agitate—I wonder where he has spent his days. Women, on the other hand, are very persistent, and will be undoubtedly very uproarious if they suffer any longer.

There is another curious distinction drawn in the Bill when we grudgingly give this vote. I have always said and I say it again, that once you give the vote to ten women I am satisfied. You have admitted the principle, and the rest follows. Perhaps the noble Earl opposite, if he speaks, will use that as an argument for not giving the vote at all. But you have been careful to make distinctions. The intelligent women of twenty-seven, say a borough councillor, or an inspector of nuisances, or a woman occupying any of the numerous public offices which women so effectively fill, is not to have a vote because of her sex. The boy of nineteen in the trenches, who probably knows nothing about politics, is fit to vote on political questions according to the Bill. He has very likely never bothered his head about politics; but he is to have the vote simply because he is in the trenches. I say nothing about that distinction, because it is one which will remedy itself. It is unjustifiable by any rule of logic, and that is probably sufficient reason for putting it into British legislation. But the groundwork of the argument, I think, for giving votes to women is not that they will vote this way or that, but simply because they are human beings. If you wish, of course, to give women a real opportunity of protecting themselves in connection with the grievances from which they suffer, the franchise is the proper way of doing it.

I must now mention a matter which I am astonished to have heard no speaker refer to to-night. I trust the reason is that most people in this House are ashamed that it is in the Bill. I refer to the disfranchisement of conscientious objectors. That is a blot on this Bill, and I will tell your Lordships why I think so. It is a blot first of all, in my opinion, on statesmanship to disfranchise a man because you do not agree with his opinions, which is, after all, what it comes to. It is not a very wise thing to do. I know what the argument is. The argument is that these people will not take up arms to defend the State, and therefore they are no part of our civil State, and deserve no civic rights. I admit the logic of that argument, and if logic were to be discovered in the other parts of the Bill I should have nothing to say about it. But from the statesmanlike point of view it is not, I believe, a wise thing to disfranchise a class because you disagree with its opinions, no matter how strongly you disagree. I do not agree with these gentlemen myself. But there are a great many people with whom I do not agree; yet I have no desire to disfranchise them.

Let me point out what would happen if the principle is established for the first time in our legislation that people shall be disfranchised for opinion. It is for opinion, because you can no longer say that it is for refusing to fight. You definitely say in the Bill that they are disfranchised if they have stated that they have a conscientious objection. That is the actual ground of disfranchisement. But suppose that next year a wildly Conservative and loyal and patriotic—as noble Lords would call it—House of Commons decides to disfranchise in this country everyone who believes in Republicanism. Why should you not put those people into a Bill next year; and then the next year put Syndicalists into a Bill? And once you came to this you would get very near to the point where in alternate years the Parties would proscribe each other. The franchise which was sought to be established by Cromwell would have made the Reform Bill of 1832 unnecessary. He gave votes to all sorts of people, but he thought that malignants ought not to vote. I do not think that is a wise precedent to follow from the statesmanlike point of view.

Look at this from what can be said against it as a piece of ordinary common sense. You give the vote to the forger, to the thief, to the pander, to the bawd, to the white slave trafficker—they are all to have the vote; but you deny the vote to a man whose offence is that he has a conscience. You deny the vote to men like Stephen Hobhouse and Clifford Allen simply because they have consciences with which you do not agree; yet you give the vote to every real criminal, you give it to the convicted murderer after he has come out of prison on the expiration of his term. I submit to your Lordships that you are establishing a very dangerous principle, and one which I think this Parliament, and the majority of those who have put this provision into the Bill, will live to look back upon with shame. I am not going to move any Amendment to it in this House. I do not propose to say any more about it, but I submit to your Lordships these considerations, which ought to weigh from a statesmanlike point of view. I think it is to be regretted that His Majesty's Government did not set their faces against the proposal when it was first made. This Bill is a large and very important measure of enfranchisement. I agree that it is revolutionary, and that your Lordships, if you are afraid of revolution, have some reason to fear it. Although it is disfigured by the unfortunate blot to which I have referred, the Bill as it stands has my blessing, and I hope it will soon be on the Statute Book.

Letter to Bertie in Brixton Prison[22]

On 1 May 1918, Bertie was convicted under the Defence Against the Realm Act for making statements in NCF organ *The Tribunal* 'intended or likely … to prejudice His Majesty's relations with foreign powers'. He was sentenced to six months' imprisonment in the second division, commuted to six months in the first on appeal. As Bertie's brother, Frank became his point of contact with the outside world and took over all personal, financial and business matters for him. This first letter gives a flavour of Frank's activities on Bertie's behalf until his early release on 14 September,[23] and references Frank's own 'holiday' in Holloway 17 years previously.

7 May 1918

My dear Bertie,

I was very glad to get your letter[24] and much surprised. I have written to Wrinch,[25] Jourdain,[26] Whitehead,[27] Rinder,[28] Lady Ottoline,[29] Carr,[30] and I have seen Malleson and given him a copy of the letter.[31] The Governor told me that your washing could be done near the prison, and the Warder or the caterer would make the arrangements for you. Writing materials. The Chairman of the Visiting Committee promised me that the prison should be telephoned to say that you should have writing materials for the week-end. I am now going down to the Home Office to see why this promise has not been kept. I hope more books will arrive now. The *Nation* and *Common Sense* shall be sent direct. Miss Rinder writes 'I will see about your notes when we return to London next week, and am collecting more books which shall be sent indirectly they reach me.' Percy[32] sends this message 'Haven't worked since Friday *Phil* being well again. Expect to go Manchester 11th.[33] *Second thoughts* has gone the way of *Black 'Ell*.[34] G.J. hasn't been able to write as yet but wishes to be remembered to you.[35] He has been in the country and looks very fit. Morgan Jones[36] now has a grand official manner, I feel my visits are an intrusion.' I quite agree about the delightfulness of the holiday, and when you are properly furnished with materials for your work I think the time will not pass too slowly. I have made formal applications to the Visiting Committee about various things, but they are not all granted yet. I look with terror on the prospect of your cultivating your mind even further, it is quite unintelligible enough already, but I suppose your philosophical friends will enjoy the horrors that you will produce in Brixton.[37] Elizabeth[38] is in the country hard at work, and grumbling about the weather. As you see the *Times* now you know the news. There is increased grumbling at Mr Asquith.[39] Gardiner[40] has thrown him over definitely. Shortt was wandering about the Club looking for someone to congratulate him and finding none;[41] and French is pitied.[42] The early break up of George is still expected.[43] Meanwhile it is hoped that this bad weather will hamper the German offensive. I go on busily with my Munition work in the intervals of running your errands. More washing shall be despatched to you shortly, also ink for your fountain pen, which I sent last Saturday. There were also two books in the parcel I sent you on Saturday. Good Wishes from some illegible person at the Athenaeum Club, and enquiries from G.M.[44] 82 Woodstock Road, Oxford, as to whether he can come and see you some time? I wish all your correspondents would not sign with initials.

All my good wishes. I am so cross at your having been kept without papers all this time.
Your loving brother
F.

They think Maurice the last straw.[45] Saw Buggles Brice of the Prison Commission this morning and he practically promised you all I asked including your watch and reviews for Massingham.[46] Also arranged that the prison should be telephoned to at once by the Home Office about your writing paper.

Notes

1. *Daily Herald*, 9 Dec 1912, p.1.
2. RA1, Box 6.27, 119590.
3. The WSPU backed conservative candidate Henry Gooch in the by-election in protest against the Liberal government's failure to support women's suffrage. Letters to the *Daily News* questioned their judgment and fitness to vote in light of Gooch's well-publicised pro-liquor stance.
4. Sir William Byles (1839-1917), Liberal MP, pacifist and proponent of worker's rights.
5. The Parliamentary Franchise (Women) Bill, which would have given voting rights to property owning women and became known as the 'Conciliation Bill', was defeated for the third time in the Commons on 28 Mar 1912 by 222 votes to 208 (*Hansard* 36, col.728).
6. As a privy councillor, Sir Edward Carson KC had sworn loyalty to the Crown, but was reported to have been party to a plot to set up a provisional government in Ireland 'in certain probable circumstances' (*Manchester Guardian*, 15 Mar 1912, p.6).
7. [1913] AC 107.
8. By the terms of the Act, a trade union could not be sued for damages incurred during a strike.
9. RA1 Box 6.27, 46902.
10. The 'little book' is most likely *Justice in War-Time* (Nov 1915) and the MS its title essay subtitled 'An Appeal to The Intellectuals of Europe', originally published in *International Review* (Zurich) on 10 Aug 1915 (Blackwell, *Bibliography*, A15; C15.18).
11. On 8 November 1915, Loreburn had deplored the lack of government transparency and warned that 'revolution and anarchy' may be the result of a long war (*Hansard* 20, cols.181-6).
12. *ibid.* cols.194-201.
13. Brother of Reginald McKenna (1863-1943), Chancellor of the Exchequer.
14. Gilbert Murray (1866-1957) took issue with Bertie's comment that the invasion of Belgium was known 'for many years' to strategists as 'an inevitable part of the next Franco-German war' and that his suggestion the Foreign Secretary would 'not promise neutrality' if it did not occur was 'misleading' (Murray, p. 7-8).
15. John Mackinnon Robertson (1856-1933), well-known advocate of the Christ myth theory.
16. 'To destroy the reasons for living for the sake of life' – Juvenal, *Satires*, Satura 3.8, l.84.
17. The Lord Bishop of Oxford had tabled questions asking the government whether they were prepared to remedy apparent inequality by the tribunals and whether those whose claims for exemption had been rejected and therefore remained incarcerated would be transferred from military to civil authorities.
18. The Archbishop of Canterbury stated that the 'harsh and cruel punishment' of COs had been 'adequately substantiated' (*Hansard* 22, c.490).
19. Clarence Henry Norman (1886-1974) sat with Bertie on the National Committee of the No-Conscription Fellowship.
20. RA1 Box 3.29, 007052EU.
21. Bertie was sacked by Trinity College ostensibly for having been convicted under the Defence Against the Realm Act for having written 'an undesirable pamphlet' (Clark, p. 289).
22. RA1 Box 6.27, 079960.
23. Bertie's letters from Brixton, extensively annotated, can be found at https://russell-letters.mcmaster.ca/.

24. Bertie's first personal letter from Brixton was to Frank, 6 May 1918 (RA1, Box 6.27, 079957).

25. Dorothy Maud Wrinch (1894-1976) had studied mathematics under Bertie at Cambridge and followed him to London when he was sacked from Trinity.

26. Philip Edward Bertrand Jourdain (1879-1919), English editor of *The Monist*. Bertie had asked for 'everything published by his firm'

27. Alfred North Whitehead (1861-1947), co-author of *Principia Mathematica* (1910-13).

28. (Winifred) Gladys Rinder (1883-1965), suffragist and prominent NCF member.

29. Lady Ottoline Morrell (1873-1938), intimate friend of Bertie's. Bertie had asked all these friends to send him books.

30. Herbert Wildon Carr (1857-1931), Philosophy professor, King's College, London. Bertie credited him, Murray and others with securing his remove to the first division.

31. Bertie had asked that his letter be forwarded to Lady Constance Malleson ('Colette', 1895-1975), with whom he was then having an affair, and her husband Miles Malleson (1888-1969).

32. Pseudonym for Colette.

33. Colette had been touring with a theatre company, performing *Phyl*.

34. A booklet and play, respectively, by Miles Malleson; both banned under DORA.

35. G.J.: another of Colette's pseudonyms.

36. Morgan Jones (1885-1939), NCF National Committee member.

37. Bertie had written, 'I hope soon to have writing materials: then I shall write first a book called *Introduction to Modern Logic*, and when that is finished I shall start an ambitious work to be called *Analysis of Mind*.

38. Elizabeth von Arnim (1866-1941), Frank's third wife.

39. Herbert Henry Asquith (1852-1928). This concerns the Maurice debate (fn.45).

40. Alfred George Gardiner (1865-1946), editor of *The Daily News*.

41. Edward Shortt MP (1862-1935) had been appointed Chief Secretary for Ireland.

42. Field-Marshall Viscount French (1852-1925), hero of the second Boer War, had been appointed Lord Lieutenant of Ireland.

43. David Lloyd George (1863-1945). See fn.45.

44. Gilbert Murray

45. The very day of Frank's letter, a letter from Major General Sir Frederick Maurice (1871-1951) appeared in *The Times* accusing the government of falsifying information about troop levels on the western front, and directly accusing Lloyd George of misleading the house. Asquith called for a select committee to investigate the charges. Frank predicted the fall of the Lloyd George government as a result. The following day the *Daily News* described the event as 'a grave crisis' which only 'may not' bring down the government. Frank's personal animosity towards Lloyd George following conscription was strong. In a letter of 16 May 1918 to Gilbert Murray he referred to Lloyd George as 'that creature' (RA1, Box 5.33, 053529). Lloyd George successfully defended Maurice's charges in the House on 8 May.

46. Henry William Massingham (1860-1924), editor of *The Nation*, for whom Bertie reviewed a book on Kant during his incarceration.

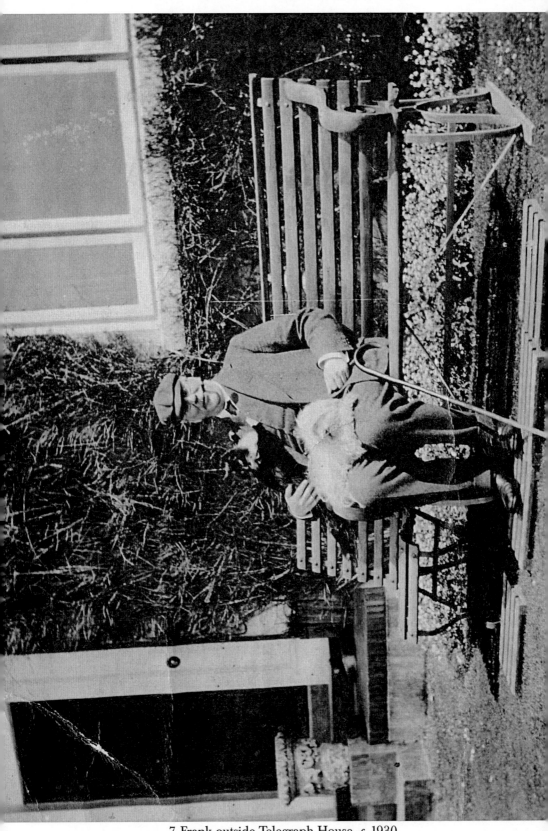

7. Frank outside Telegraph House, *c.* 1930.

Chapter 7

The Post-War World

After the war, Frank continued his pre-war campaigns and assault on the Church and added prison reform and birth control to his agenda. He also wrote with tolerance and humanity on a range of other social issues. In the 1920s he found a new platform for his protests. *John Bull* had been established as a Sunday paper in 1820. In 1906 it was relaunched by Horatio Bottomley MP (1860-1933) under the slogan 'When you read it in *John Bull*, it is so'.[1] In 1922 assistant editor Charles Pilley took the helm after Bottomley's infamous libel trial and subsequent imprisonment for fraud. Frank's direct style suited the journal perfectly. His second contribution was a blatantly frustrated attack on the divorce laws, demonstrating a new style for a popular audience. The first minor reform of the divorce laws passed the following year. In 1927 he was made an honorary associate of the Rational Press Association and in 1929 took office in the second Labour Government becoming their 'maid of all work' in the Lords.[2]

House of Lords Debate 25 February 1919: Industrial Unrest
Debate on the Motion of Lord Buckmaster–viz., 'That there be laid before the House Papers relating to the present industrial and economic conditions–' resumed. Frank's contribution:

> … I propose to deal for a few moments with the causes of labour unrest, and I should like to say, by way of preface, that I associate myself entirely with what was said by Lord Buckmaster in initiating this debate, that labour as a whole is certainly not anarchic or revolutionary… I would deprecate in any of these controversies the use of Bolshevik or Bolshevism as applied to any section of our own community. That word is associated–and rightly associated–with excesses of the most terrible and horrible description, with uncivilised and savage actions, and I should be sorry to think–and I do not think–that any section of my countrymen, however extreme, are anxious to be associated with actions of that kind. …
>
> I think that the cause of labour unrest is not a thing of yesterday, not a thing of last year, not a thing even of the war, but that it dates back for at

143

least a generation. It dates back, my Lords, to the time, really more than a generation ago, when industry as we know it now began in this country, and when employers and capitalists recklessly and thriftlessly took to using and exploiting the manhood of this country for the purpose of making profits, when the old doctrine of industrial competition took no account whatever of the lives and bodies of the working men who made those profits and who carried on those industries. We exploited in those days–it is useless to deny it–the lives of these people, and this has to some extent come to be realised. It is not forgiven, and I do not think it is likely to be forgotten. What was the life of the working man? ... It began perhaps at eighteen, and finished perhaps at forty-five or possibly fifty. And, from the point of view of the employer–and I think we might well say from the point of view of the State also–did anybody care what happened to him either before he began his work or after he had finished it? He was used, and he was then thrown aside on to the scrap heap of society, very often driven to the workhouse to end his days. We all recognise now that that is a state of things which is not good from the purely selfish capitalists' point of view, but much more so is it not good from the ethical or moral point of view. Moreover, what we now recognise as the duty of the State is that it is an immoral proceeding which the State should not countenance, a proceeding which does not make for the well-being and for the prosperity of the country as a whole. Out of these men so employed we made large profits, and to this day large profits are made out of the employment of workmen by the diversion to the employer or capitalist, or whatever you like to call him, of a proportion of the earnings of each man so that the one man at the head of the business draws a large profit from the labour of those employed in the business.

I do not subscribe for a moment to the doctrine of Marx that labour and labour alone is the source of all wealth. I am rather apt to think in these days, or at any rate in this country, that labour itself has begun to recognise that that is not a complete statement of the case, and that many other things besides mere manual labour are required before you can produce wealth in a country. But I think that labour has realised that it is a very important and essential contributing cause to the production of wealth, and it intends to have a fair share of that wealth. Consider the question of conditions. Your Lordships have had some extracts read to you already during this debate on housing conditions as they existed quite recently, and you know something from the Army statistics about the general health of the proletariat of the country. It is not a thing for us to reflect upon with pride that those who have been known as the governing classes of this country for so many years have only been able to produce, or have been content to allow to continue to exist, a state of things in which insanitary hovels are regarded as proper places in which to house a man who is contributing to the nation's wealth, in which his health is neglected, in which a large portion of the population is attacked with tuberculosis and other diseases, and in which the opportunities of the working class for recreation have been unduly limited. These things have happened in the past. To some extent they happen today, and I think it is the culmination of all these things which has produced the present state of labour unrest and the present demand on the part of labour.

We have had sweated industries. Your Lordships quite well remember the example of the chainmakers who before the war, even after all that had been done for them, were still receiving a miserable wage. The labourer has not had that amount of leisure for recreation, that amount of opportunity for advancement, which a wise and paternal Government would have given him. We have put up with the existence of slums in our great cities. We have passed Acts of Parliament about them comparatively recently, but we have done very little more than the passing of these Acts. We have not, each one of us separately and all of us collectively, said that we will not tolerate that state of things any longer, that we will not sit down comfortably under it, that we will not regard it as possible to live our own lives while such things co-exist with our lives.

Look at the conditions before the war of low wages and housing—15s. a week, and I believe in some counties even less, for a man to bring up his wife and family upon, and to support life. Is that a thing on which we can reflect with any degree of pride and satisfaction? But that was not altered voluntarily by the governing class—by the class which had the money. That it was not is something, I think, which redounds to our discredit, and a fact for which I believe we are now suffering. Housing in the country was in most cases inadequate, in many cases quite insanitary; and if I am told—as I may be told by subsequent speakers—that there have been many excellent landlords who have built many good cottages, who have had model villages and things of that sort, I frankly and fully admit it. There have been individuals—I am glad to think a growing class of individuals—whose own conscience has been so shocked by this state of things that they have even been prepared to remedy it at their own expense, regardless of the fact of whether it was profitable to do so or not. But that is not quite my point. My point is rather that the community as a whole has remained selfishly happy and contented with its own enjoyments and with its own leisure, while things of that sort were allowed to go on unchecked. These, I think, are the things for which labour finds it difficult to forgive the capitalist class.

Did capital and did the community ever really wake up to its responsibility, and ever really take these matters in hand except under pressure and under threats? There has been good will, there have been good words and good intentions, but have those who have control of those conditions made serious efforts to alter them until they were forced to do so? Has every pulpit occupied by every parson resounded with denunciations of that sort of thing in every parish Sunday after Sunday until it was remedied? Has every politician, whenever he has spoken, said 'I will not consider that my work is done until those who work for this country are properly treated and properly housed?' No, my Lords, we know that that has not happened; we know that, in spite of philanthropists, and in spite of a good deal that has been done, the general social sense of the community has not really been pricked and stirred to such an extent as would make it take active and definite action. And I think it is for that supine content that we are very largely suffering today.

I do not think that the reason why we did not do these things was due to ill-will on our part; in fact, I think I may say that, with regard to the majority of landowners, certainly with regard to a great many of what may be called capitalists among the industrial classes, it was not due to ill-will. Nor do I think that it was due altogether to mere laziness; but it was due to what we as a nation suffer from a great deal, and that is a want of imagination, a want of picturing to ourselves conditions with which we are not immediately familiar and with which we do not come directly into contact. There is none of your Lordships, on seeing such things as you read about in Reports, but will say 'This must be remedied; I cannot sleep comfortably unless it is corrected.' I think we all feel like that. But when a thing is not before us we do not think about it. We are content to think of labour as of a man who checks his time on by a clock in the morning and checks it off in the evening; and, for the rest, we do not much know, we do not much care; we merely hope he will come back next morning. I think it is things like that, coupled with the increasing independence caused by the war, and coupled with that general sense of upheaval which no doubt is present in the world at large, that has led to the stormy sea of unrest which surrounds us today.

What was the panacea which we were offered on the first night of this debate in the speech by the noble and learned Lord on the Woolsack [Lord Birkenhead], whom we have recently welcomed to this House? So far as I could make out, it consisted shortly in this, 'Trust the Government. We have not had much time, but every remediable wrong will be righted; trust the Government.' That seemed to me a little like an invitation which we used to hear in nursery days, about opening your mouth and shutting your eyes and seeing what would come to you. Labour, I think, has got a little beyond being invited to trust a Government, or to trust a Commission, or to trust anybody of people, however eminent or however well meaning.

The King's Speech contained what seemed to me some very significant words with regard to the spirit in which this has to be met, with regard to the putting aside of vested interests and vested prejudices and really shaking ourselves free of those traditions, meeting it in a new and a broad spirit. When I considered who was responsible for the phraseology I could not help feeling that some of those to whom sentiments of that kind would normally appear to be alien must have been rather terrified and rather frightened before they gave their assent to phrases of that character; and I only hope that the history of this Parliament will succeed in persuading the masses that those phrases are genuine, that they will be lived up to, and that they do express the spirit of this House of Commons. I should not have guessed it. I should not have guessed it from the composition of this House, and I should not have guessed it from the speeches which were made during the Election. Many unfortunate things were said–some of them by the noble and learned Lord on the Woolsack himself; and I think that the people were promised many things which will not be performed, and were led astray in some directions in which that leading astray, will probably cause trouble later. I do not know who in the labour world trusts either the present Prime Minister or the present House of Commons. I think, if they did, there would be a better hope for the future. I wish that they did.

As a symptom of the sort of feeling of unrest and independence of which I spoke, and of the way in which it is growing, I would mention what struck me as rather significant. I purchased the other day on a bookstall one of those illustrated magazines which one gets in order to while away an hour on a railway journey–a magazine which one has never hitherto associated with labour questions, or serious questions of any sort, and in which one certainly has not expected to find any indication of anything resembling a social revolution. In the pages of this normally harmless magazine I found an article

about 'The Black-coated Man', an article which said with great vehemence–
Mr Black-coated Man, we have done with you. You stayed at home; you did
not suffer the risks of the war. You were our master; you made the money
while we sweated and toiled. We have finished with you, Mr Black-coated
Man; we are coming back, and coming into our own. The article was, I think
I may fairly say, revolutionary in sentiment, and it was somewhat significant,
that in an organ of that kind we should find sentiments of that sort expressed.

I think it is not so much labour that wants education (although a great deal
of education is wanted there, too) as it is the class of capitalists and the
governing bodies of this country themselves. Our newspapers do not give–
practically never give–a fair representation of labour conditions or of any
labour dispute. The chief organ of this country, *The Times*, has lately changed
that policy, and has had, I think I am right in saying, more than one leading
article advocating that the cause of labour should be presented quite as
strongly and quite as clearly as the case of the capitalist. That is a sign of the
times, but it is a rare and a novel thing; the ordinary paper that is read by
the man in the train, the ordinary paper that is read by the clerk in the street,
or going home in the evening, has seldom, indeed hardly ever, anything but
a sneer for any demand of labour, or anything but a gibe at the attitude of
labour, or its method of demanding something new. Labour can no longer
be met with sneers and with gibes, and it would be well that these journals,
which belong to and are controlled by the capitalist class, should seriously
give their mind to dealing with these questions as if they were questions at
least equally important with the franchise or something of that kind.

A great deal depends on the point of view with which these things are
approached, and I think one very useful thing about this debate has been
that, so far as I can charge my memory, not one single noble Lord who has
taken part in it has in any way flouted the claims of labour, or has in any
way treated labour as a whole as being an irresponsible and unreasonable
body of men. That, I think, is a very useful feature of this debate, and will
have a good effect. But when I say labour should be educated, how can you
educate a distrustful labour? How can you educate a person who does not
believe a word you say to him? How can you educate a person who sees in
every agreement you make–and not altogether, I am sorry to say, without
reason in the past–some loop-hole, some way in which he thinks he is going
to be done later. Look at the tube strike the other day. There was untold
inconvenience to millions; and why? Because the men understood they were
to have something which the actual written letter, perhaps, did not give them.
That appears to have been, so far as I can make it out–although I share the
difficulty of my noble friend on the Front Bench–the principal reason of that
strike.

And labour feels this. It feels that when new arrangements are made about
piece-work, about hours, about any sort of settlement, it is always running a
risk of being in some way gerrymandered. It suspects your Statutes; it
suspects, I fear, your Commissions. I see that it is divided even against the
Bill which is now before Parliament. Then there is a complaint that the crisis
has come upon us suddenly; that we are taken unprepared; that it has been
unreasonable in the point of view of time. I do not think that this complaint
is well founded. I believe that many of the demands that are now being put
forward have been put forward not only for months but in many cases for

years; that they are not novel; that they are not a surprise; and that the material with which to answer them–be it by granting them, or be it by saying that they are impossible to be granted–could be, ought to have been, should have been, ready in the Government's possession the moment they were challenged.

Let us consider the question of the coal-miners, which is, perhaps, the most urgent of the problems before us. We are all agreed, I think, that work of that character is arduous, unpleasant, and, more than that, dangerous both to life and to limb. So much is that so, that I have been told today that many of those who before the war worked in coal mines, having had an experience above ground, are unwilling and reluctant to return to those conditions. We shall none of us deny that. The noble Earl, Lord Brassey, who spoke from this bench, told your Lordships that he himself knew the conditions. If that is so, we shall all agree that an industry of that character should have as short hours and as adequate remuneration as it is possible to give it. The demands which they made have been made for some time. I do not think that on the whole the Government would be prepared to say that the leaders of the coal-miners have been unreasonable. I read with great care, as no doubt all your Lordships did, that very interesting discussion which took place between the Prime Minister and Mr Smillie;[3] and the effect that it left upon my mind was that Mr Smillie's answer was, 'You ask us now at the last moment to hold our hands, and you say it is unreasonable that we should not hold our hands for a fortnight. But my answer to that is that these demands have been before you for some time; that you have never given any serious attention to them unless you were forced and unless you were pressed to do so; and that if you now ask me to hold my hand I do not feel any confidence that you will give any attention to them in the future, or those behind me do not feel any confidence that you will do so.'

That is how I read the situation. Whether I am right or whether I am wrong, I do not know. But if that is so, if this Commission is unable to report in time–and really on a subject of this character I do not know how any useful Report can be produced in a few days–if those for whom Mr Smillie is responsible, but who, after all, have the control, are not amenable to his advice–for I believe that the leaders of the miners would anxiously advise them to avoid precipitating a conflict–but if they prove not amenable to that advice we shall have upon us a strike of a very serious character, not only a strike of a very serious character to industry itself, not only of a serious character from the actual privations to which it will lead, from the loss of business to which it will lead and the injury it will do to the country, but of a very serious character because we do not know how such a strike may spread and what will be its end. I think that everything that can be done should be done to avert such a calamity. I hope and believe that the Government fully recognise the seriousness of it, and that they will do all they can. But I think they have to be blamed to some extent for supineness and inertia in the past for not foreseeing this situation, for not getting ready to answer demands which are not altogether novel...

Social revolution has come, and it is impossible to meet it with any sort of chicanery or smooth words, and still less is it possible to meet, it with anything in the shape of force. If once we recognise this and then face the facts, I think we shall have some chance of doing better than if we continue to live in a world that is past and to apply remedies that are no longer adequate. The capitalist mind itself must undergo revolution, in order to march with the times. Exploiting has come to an end. The remedy is greater efficiency and increased production...

The economic position of the country is a very serious one. The pre-war budget, roughly speaking, was £200 million; the post-war budget will be, roughly speaking, £800 million. Where is that additional £600 million to come from? It cannot come out of labour, except to a very small extent. It must come from us, the capitalist class, who have the money, and it cannot come out of us, the capitalist class, unless you have a revival of industry– shipping going to-and-fro full, factories and warehouses full, and everything going at full pressure in the industries of this country. For otherwise we shall have no money to pay any taxation, no matter what our nominal possessions may be. We must all work with a new spirit and with a sense of communal responsibility. The thunders of the Defence of the Realm Act have frequently been directed against those who say anything about recruiting. We shall do well to direct, not the official and legal thunder, but the moral thunder against anybody who thinks that labour can be dealt with by lip service, or by any sort of sneer against workmen, upon whom we all have to rely in the last resort for the restoration of this country to a condition of prosperity. If labour problems are dealt with in this way, and if labour once feels it can trust those whom it is entitled to trust and those responsible for the Government of the country, we shall have made a great advance towards the solution of unrest in general.

The Tube – A Complaint, *Times*, 10 Nov 1919

To the Editor of *The Times*:
Sir, – Our tubes have been Americanized, and intimations greet us on every hoarding, that travelling has now become rapid and convenient. Well, I desired to get home last night from the Fabian lecture, and as it was drizzling and the streets were very dirty I thought I would try the tube. I am a slow walker, but it does not take me more than 20 minutes to walk from Covent Garden to my house, and although I didn't expect the tube to be as quick, I thought it would be worth it to escape the dirty streets. I had reckoned without the malignant American ingenuity which has been devoted to the intricacies of tube management. First of all, I just missed the lift; that might happen to anybody: the next lift landed me on the platform just as the train I wanted was running out; that not only might but does happen to everybody on the tube. I was still calm and patient, and calmly and patiently waited for the next, until a notice caught my eye, 'Next train passes this station.' Then a slow smouldering British indignation began to rise, and I asked myself what was the good of a system of urban transit in which at 10 o'clock at night stations were skipped. As a lifelong Conservative I longed for the old Underground. Alas! the American has not done with me yet. When the third train stopped at the station the same malicious notice board said, 'Passes Russell-square', which was where I wanted to go to. I got in, I got out at Holborn, I got in yet a fourth train, and at last reached Russell-square. Total time for the journey of one mile from Covent Garden to Russell-square, 22 minutes. The Americans may argue that I had plenty of fun for my penny –

two lifts, two trains, and the chance of admiring the beauties of Holborn Station. But what my simple British soul wanted was to get home.
I am, Sir, your obedient servant,
Russell.

Letter to Bertie[4]

Telegraph House
29 April 1921

My dear Bertie,
The American Associated Press rang me up about ten days ago to ask if it was true that you had died on 29 March in Japan. I told them that I thought it was very improbable first because you wouldn't do such a thing, secondly because you weren't in Japan, thirdly because I should have heard of it if you had, and fourthly because if the news came from America there was a prima facie presumption that it was untrue. I communicated with Miss Wrinch and she tested these general and simple ideas of mine by the proper formulae in one of your books and said the answer came out right. But in view of the frequency of your letters to me and the way in which you have kept me so well informed of your doings it might well be true!

However you see I am backing my judgment by writing to you.

We have had great fun here with Archdeacon Wakeford, a person hitherto unknown to fame. He stayed at 'The Bull' at Peterborough with a young woman without a nightgown which was appreciated, but also without a wedding ring which was not. He chose a cathedral town not too far from his own Cathedral of Lincoln and in order that there should be no mistake about it took the young woman to Peterborough Cathedral and presented her to the Dean and Chapter. The Consistory Court condemned him: he appealed to the Privy Council and the judgment of F. E. Smith and Buckmaster which occupies a page and a half of *The Times* has affirmed the condemnation. I enclose the judgment which may amuse you.[5] I need hardly say that half the Church folk believe and will continue to believe that he is innocent. The *Weekly Dispatch* invited me to contribute an article on the 'Penalties of Fame' or 'How one of our own young men stayed at The Bull in similar circumstances without any fuss being made about it'. I declined even under the attraction of an alternative title which occurred to me, 'How Publicity embarrasses Peers'.

Since then we have had another stricken field of ecclesiastics in the House of Lords when a Divorce Bill received its Third Reading by 87 to 48 and the Bishop of Durham was seduced into making an impassioned speech in its favour and voting with us.[6] Lord Gorell, an amiable nincompoop, had introduced a Bill to give legislative effect to the Minority Report and the two Archbishops with their white-robed satellites had blessed it although we pointed out to them with tears in our eyes that there was nothing in St Matthew about the equality of the sexes. The wicked Buckmaster in Committee poked in an Amendment giving divorce for three years' desertion, Gorell abandoned his baby and the Bishops tried to wash off the Holy Water with which they had liberally christened it by purging it with hyssop. (By the way what is hyssop? is it a cathartic or an abstergent? and do you administer internally or externally?)

Of private affairs that might interest you I know nothing. Miss Wrinch calls unexpectedly in the afternoons when I am not here and says she will ring up next morning but doesn't. I wrote to Lady Ottoline about the rumour but have not heard from her. Sanger I saw for a moment the other day and he enquired after you. Massingham speaks of you occasionally and appears to receive poems. Miss Anderson[7] whom you no doubt remember has been for weeks in a Nursing Home and parted with the whole of her inside, the doctors now guarantee her to be exclusively stuffed with sawdust. The Bishop of Birmingham whom I think you don't know has put his name to a courageous Report on Venereal Diseases.[8] Ireland remains as hopeless as ever. The Coal Strike is still going on but we were just saved from a revolution by the Triple Alliance: emphatically not by Lloyd George who wanted one. LG's stock is going down: Derby welcomed him enthusiastically to the Unionist Party the other day. The Bank Rate has also gone down a little but taxes haven't. The Aunt Agatha is ill at Bournemouth and says she is too poor to afford *The Nation* – in which by the way I wrote an amusing article about a film the other day.

Now there's a much longer letter than you deserve and if you don't answer it and promptly I shall haunt your dreams disguised in Chinese characters. Yours affly,
Russell.

'The Bible on the Film', *The Nation & The Athenaeum*, 16 Apr 1921

Lord Russell writes us:–

Moved by some rather good notices and by the novelty of the idea, I turned somewhat hesitating steps to the Palace Theatre last night to see the presentation of the 'Dawn of the World.'[9] After the performance perhaps the most dominating impression left on my mind was how any inducement could be sufficiently large to bring Mrs Patrick Campbell (who, after all, is an artist, and one that most of us remember with admiration) to take part in the jejune prologues and to sanction by her assistance some of the scenes that follow. Still, the earlier part of the performance was undoubtedly well done on the whole, and would have been interesting but for its exasperations. The Garden of Eden was quite good, although it did not seem to me sufficiently flowery: so was the Serpent: so were Adam and Eve, who were just sufficiently 'not ashamed' to pass the Censor. We did not have the flaming sword, although I thought this was a trick particularly adapted to the capacities of the Cinema. Cain and Abel were quite good, too: so was the Tower of Babel. Then we had a great deal of Joseph, and the natural irritation of his brethren at his provoking dream was convincing and realistic. Potiphar's wife was all she ought not to be: with the worst Oriental touches. The scenes at Pharaoh's Court were magnificently staged, but entirely failed of their effect because of an extraordinary American Cinema tradition which requires even the most stately personages to walk at seven miles an hour and to waggle their shoulders from side to side like a runner in the last stage of exhaustion at the end of a three-mile race. In spite of the producers, I am convinced that no Pharaoh ever moved in this unseemly manner. Then the 'close-ups' of Potiphar's wife, Joseph, and others, 'registering' emotion in the approved manner, were very painful and irritating. I am afraid I have not a true movie mind, for I thought the quotations of the Bible's own perfect language the best part of it. Even here one was driven to inarticulate fury at times by mistakes which no third-rate proof-reader would have passed, and it is difficult to understand any London management allowing them upon its screen. We then had Moses and Aaron, the brickmaking, the Red Sea, the Tables of the Law, the Striking of the Rock, and Lot, with one of the more unfortunate incidents illustrated but not described. Incidentally it was rather curious to note that apparently not 10 per cent. of the audience knew what the incident was. Two of the very best effects were the fire and brimstone and the turning of Lot's wife to a pillar of salt.

Well so far, so fairly good: subject to the exasperations and annoyances I have mentioned, one had been able to appreciate the display. But after an interval of ten minutes came the second part, and here the producers allowed themselves to break loose. Solomon – one at any rate thinks of him as an opulent and dignified figure, but here he was looking like an Arizona cowboy on the prowl; the Shulamite woman a village hussy. We had many scenes of the pursuit and approach, interspersed with the magnificent words of the Song of Solomon, and defaced with 'close-ups' 'registering' passion. However, the time had come when the American movie spirit could be controlled no longer. It broke all bounds, and after these two had at last met these noble words were flashed up upon the screen: 'Where is your house? I'll come to-night – and we'll be happy.' I could bear no more. I flung myself out of the theatre, and rocked across Cambridge Circus with such unseemly mirth that I barely escaped arrest by the stolid and respectable police on duty. Well, well, as I said before, I fear I am lacking in the true movie spirit.

'Modern Freedom *v.* Past Prudery', *Weekly Dispatch*, 15 May 1921

Horace pathetically begins one of his Odes 'Martiis coelebs' (perhaps I had better put it in English)–'What is a poor bachelor like me to do when Christmas comes?' Or, as I may well ask: What right has a poor old thing like me, approaching my sixties, and old fashioned at that through being brought up entirely by grandmothers and great-uncles, to talk about the young of today?

Not much I admit, yet if I say anything unkind of them, let them be sure it is not set down in malice; for my heart goes out to them, and I love them all, even if that love be tinged with envy.

The outstanding difference between my young days and the present is Freedom. From the nursery to the altar, and, indeed, after, the increase of liberty has been most marked.

Among the public school class the ideals of Miss Edgeworth were the accepted tradition of my youth. Children were to be seen and not heard; they were to make no undue noise which could penetrate to the ears of their parents; they were to be respectful to their elders, and even to submit with a dutiful smirk to being kissed by them: If they were allowed in the drawing room at all they were to sit still and look good on a chair and not to fidget; on no account to speak unless spoken to, and then to answer promptly and with deference. When I had fulfilled this ideal grandmother would give me a sweet out of her comfit-box.

In my earliest youth I had the good fortune to escape this, and was nurtured on Rousseau's *Emile*, which has more modern ideas as to the free play to be given to the individuality of children. This enabled me to appreciate more vividly and remember more acutely the later restrictions when I used to be questioned minutely as to where I had been, whom I had seen and what I had done. Even up to the age of sixteen I was expected to disclose all letters I received and read them aloud at the family breakfast table.

For girls, of course, the supervision and restrictions were much worse and much more minute; a cousin of mine was told at age sixteen to put up her parasol in going up St James's Street, as it would be indelicate to allow the men at the club windows to look at her.

Well, we are frequently told in sermons, particularly by Roman Catholic divines, that liberty has degenerated into licence and that the present state of things is most regrettable; and there is an element of truth in it, but upon my soul I prefer it to the state of mind which regarded all men as lustful ogres and all respectable girls as potential Rahabs.

I know but little personally of the younger generation. I am told that chaperones have almost disappeared; that young men and young women go to the dances unattended and return from them unattended; that they go unattended for motor drives; and that they lunch and dine together with great freedom. There is also a mysterious something called a dancing partner, and a new habit among the perfectly respectable of going to subscription dances, an idea which would have been unthinkable. The frivolous and the well-off are perpetually dancing, even in the day time; they endure and apparently enjoy such horrors as jazz bands and new kinds of dances imported from America; they are perpetually at music-halls, and they are the chief supporters of revues.

All this part of it does appear to me as morally bad because they cease to possess a critical faculty; they can no longer distinguish between good drama and a thing like 'Nighty Night';[10] they cannot read decent books or even well-written novels and would throw aside a Conrad for a Garvice.[11] Moreover, the want of discipline in childhood and the racketing life of youth make their minds frivolous; incapable of appreciating politics or economics and of developing in later life those qualities which have made our ruling class fit to rule. In the majority of cases an incurable levity dominates their soul. Still, in quite an appreciable number of cases a more serious view of life is taken with advancing years, and at any rate in their old age they are more attractive and even more intelligent beings than the old Victorian country squire with no ideas outside turnips and the Church.

There is another class where freedom between the sexes—largely due, I think, to the Suffragette movement—and a fuller enjoyment have now penetrated, and that is the class of men and women who are not the idle rich but who have to spend a portion of each day earning their living. Journalists, artists, writers, and smaller professional people generally enjoy great freedom of conversation and have no conventional limits to their activities.

These are the people who constitute a large proportion of women's and mixed clubs, societies on all sorts of subjects, meetings for discussion and so on, and in their case I am inclined to think the change is almost entirely for the good, for before this they had only the alternative of a musty, limited, paralysing existence or of a deliberate kicking over the traces. I can imagine nothing better for our middle classes than to throw off the curse of being respectable in the Victorian sense of the word.

These people are by no means without ideas, they exude them at every pore—crude and ill-digested often, but at any rate seething with life and movement. In this class it is by no means unusual for the sexes to go freely on expeditions together involving nights away from home, without the results which the Victorian mother would have considered inevitable.

Now, has all this led to a deplorable licence, to a decay of morals, and to a deterioration of the English character? I confess the freedom of the modern young woman's speech and the things she knows terrify and alarm me, and I do not myself think that internal operations or venereal disease are any more fitting for discussion at a dinner table than would be the killing of a pig, but in so far as these things represent a revolt against our former prurient hypocrisy they are good.

It is well to know the world as it is, and for this purpose frank discussion of all matters is necessary and frankness between the sexes. It is said that in America co-education makes for sane relations with the opposite sex, but opinion is not unanimous on this point.

In my adolescence I was brought up in a house where all realities, including money and sex, were taboo; frankness and simplicity are best in these matters; but undue and unnecessary dragging to the front of sex is no more to be commended than would be the constant turning of the conversation to the price of the silver forks, the clocks, the gardener's wages, or the cost of meat.

It is very essential also to remember that a frank facing of reality and an absolutely natural dealing with the material world of facts need not and must not allow itself to fill our horizon to the exclusion of ideals and the life of the spirit. A touch of Puritanism is good for human nature, so far, at any rate, as it means having a definite purpose in life and a certain austerity of view which regards that purpose as essential and facts as comparatively trivial and incidental phenomena.

Let us not forget what Matthew Arnold said about character (the strong point of his father's headmastership) and the Jewish sense of righteousness: If all is frivolous, life will lose its savour; existence will be purposeless; marriage will be without seriousness, and therefore without sanctity; while old age will be trivial and futile.

The ideal of education should be the making us fit for life, and to be fit for life means to be fearless, open, honest, unashamed, and well-informed. The modern freedom is superior to the ancient reticence in all its respects, and, I firmly believe, tends to increase the true respect of man for woman and woman for man. But if there is to be character, a sure footing among the troubles of the world, a fruitful life and a contented old age, this knowledge and this freedom must be guided and controlled by a certain discipline, a certain secret austerity, and a certain self-respect and sense of values to which we used to give the name religion.

The old can best help the young, not by trying to confine the youthful spirit in bonds which it has burst, but by guiding it and directing it aright with their long knowledge and experience so that is many activities may make for happiness and good and not for emptiness and desolation.

'The Difficulties of Bishops',
Rational Press Association Annual (1922)

It is hard not to sympathize with the Bishops in the difficulties in which they frequently find themselves placed by their complete divorce from modern thought and modern feeling. It is true that this divorce is rather official and hierarchical than personal and real, but that if anything enhances their difficulty. They are subscribing members of that corporate body the Church, from which they receive their emoluments, and to which they owe their position; while the dogmas to which they have subscribed are not believed in by the vast majority of the laity, and, if the truth be known, scarcely swallowed even by themselves without a certain amount of jesuitical adaptation. Their Church teaches and their creeds recite that Jesus was born of a Virgin, without human agency, by some miraculous divine propagation; but it is scarcely credible that any one of them believes this in the literal sense. So much for the beginning of his life: at the end of it their creed teaches that he rose from the dead and in his natural body ascended into heaven; this also requires a sturdy digestion. Nor let anyone suppose for a moment that when the Church of England was constituted in its present form there was any dubiety, any subtlety, or any transcendental explanation possible; these things demanded to be believed as literal physical facts. Now add to these the literal inspiration of the Scriptures (Old Testament as well as New), the mass of mediaeval lumber known as Early Fathers and the traditions of the Church, the Church Service, and the Articles of Religion to which they have subscribed, and you can picture to yourself the difficulties of a Bishop, an official and accredited representative of his organization, compelled to face modern problems.

The result is that in questions of the discipline of the clergy, the government of the Church, education, divorce, the Table of Affinity, and marriage generally, we find them taking a definite and concerted line opposed to the trend of public opinion and landing them in conflict with the State – a conflict which they view with terror, for the situation is still further complicated by the Erastian position of the Church in this country. When I ventured to inform the Bishops the other day in the House of Lords that the Church of England as it now exists was a creature of statute, the observation was received with derision and vehemently repudiated by the Episcopal Bench. None the less, it is true. So far as the parent Church of Rome is concerned, the Church of England is a mere dissenting sect of heretics doomed to everlasting fire; so far as its own organization is concerned, it is regulated by Acts of Parliament. The collection of tithes, the position of incumbents, the dignities and powers of Bishops and their emoluments, the area of their dioceses, the causes for which a priest can lose his temporalities or be unfrocked, the right of Bishops to sit in the House of Lords, the King as head of the Church – nay, more, the very Liturgy and Articles of Religion themselves – depend upon statute law, and statute law alone, for their validity. Parliament, if it chooses, can tomorrow take away all such funds of the Church and such buildings and property as it has not already vested in the Ecclesiastical Commissioners, and can decree to what classes of persons the parish churches shall be open for preaching and divine service, can settle the formularies of the Church and compel subscription to them as the price of office, and can prohibit any other body from calling itself the Church of

England. These facts, not realized by the laity and carefully glossed over by the priest, are always acutely present to the minds of the heads of the Church, and always lead them to be careful not to provoke conflict with the State too far.

So far as the Church claims to be allowed to manage its own affairs I have little to say, and am willing to concede to it practical autonomy upon the same terms as Parliament has conceded it to other corporate bodies. This was recognized to some extent by the Enabling Bill of last session, although the Bill as introduced raised many serious constitutional difficulties, due to the arrogant claim of the Church to be superior to Parliament, whose creature it is. When, however, we come to questions which affect the life of the nation as a whole, such as education, divorce, or marriage, any claim of the Church to impose its own sectarian views upon the whole population, believers and unbelievers alike, must be sternly resisted. This attitude was well expressed by Lord James of Hereford fourteen years ago in the debate in the Deceased Wife's Sister Bill. 'Guided by my own conscience and seeking such guidance as will assist me, I protest against this country, blessed with the results of the great Reformation, going back to the opinions of the early bishops and learned men of narrow views for rules as to what is right and wrong for the social life of to-day… There can be no law in this matter but the law of Parliament.'[12] Yet Lord Braye, a Roman Catholic peer who always takes part in these debates, has the incredible audacity to say that 'the House of Commons is not the place, nor is any Parliament the place, to undo the marriage law which has been once committed to the Christian Church'. For this reason, however much I may sympathize with the Bishops in their difficulties, I do not propose to say anything to diminish them.

Take education. The Church's claim was roundly that this was a Christian nation, and that therefore in the national schools the principles of Christianity at least should be taught to the young. That is to say, the Trinity as opposed to Monotheism, the Virgin birth, the Divinity of Christ, the vicarious Atonement, the Resurrection, and the Day of Judgment were to be taught in the public schools during school hours at the public expense to all children. This outrageous claim has been resisted bit by bit by providing that even in Church schools the hours of religious instruction should be no part of the official time-table and should not count against the Government grant, and that the children should be allowed to absent themselves. In schools provided by the public purse there subsisted for many years a thing called the Cowper-Temple compromise, by which undenominational religion was allowed to be taught; and, I believe, this is still the case. The system of allowing the existence of any school receiving public money which was not a State school, first, last, and all the time, is a thoroughly vicious one, and the constant squabbles both in Parliament and in every individual parish have been a great hindrance to the course of education. This lowering of educational efficiency, and this attempt to foist upon all of us doctrines in which only some of us believe, we owe entirely to the bad influence of the Church. The Balfour Act,[13] which remedied some of the more obvious anomalies of the drawbacks to education, was throughout influenced by the sinister shadow of the Church, and suffered in consequence by not being a charter of education pure and simple without regard to vested interests.

Now let us take divorce. Here these unhappy folk are in a worse tangle than ever. The position of the Catholic Church is very simple; divorce for any cause has been firmly disallowed since the Council of Trent, and rich people have had to get over the difficulty by fictitious decrees of nullity granted for a proper consideration. The Catholic Church is a coherent whole, and its rules are binding upon the Catholic laity. It seeks with calm impudence to fasten its rules upon those who are not members, but has always been willing to call upon the civil power for this purpose. Since, however, England is nominally Protestant, the audacity of its attempt is recognized here and repelled without any difficulty. When, therefore, Lord Braye says 'the Catholic Church is opposed in every country in the world to the principle of divorce', and says of so feeble a Bill as Lord Gorell's, 'I am not interested in the details of the Bill, because its whole principle is hostile to my convictions', and that in consequence 'the ultimate result of these Bills, if they be pushed to their logical conclusion, will be polygamy', these observations, although received with respect as expressing his personal opinion, have no effect upon the Legislature. Nor when he says, 'We regard marriage as a sacrament founded by divine ordinance and made indissoluble for ever', is such an utterance regarded as anything but a recognized Catholic point of view. Such expressions do perhaps, however, have two effects on different classes of persons. In me and those who think like me they create a certain impatience, and make us say to ourselves: 'Since we are not compelling you to use the Divorce Court, and since you say that none of your co-religionists ever will use it, why do you seek to interfere with the liberty of the rest of us who consider it a useful institution?' On the other hand, I can readily imagine that to the Archbishop of Canterbury and his followers such words are a cause of embarrassment, for Lord Braye expresses exactly the attitude of the High Church Anglican and an attitude which would so readily support the arguments of the Archbishop of Canterbury, if only the constitution of his Church permitted its adoption, and only if there were not the shadow of so many Erastian compromises in the background.

For what is, so far as it is possible to understand it when it is perpetually shifting and being shifted, the official attitude of the Church of England? I have perused with care a small book published by Dr Chase, the Bishop of Ely, entitled *What Did Christ Teach About Divorce?*[44] Now, in the very forefront of the book – in fact, in its preface – I find, as one might have expected, that there are considerable differences of opinion on this subject even among eminent divines, and that the Bishop of Ely says: 'On several essential matters I am constrained to differ from Dr Charles.'

In order not to complicate the argument, we will accept the Bishop's strangely unwarrantable assumption that there was only an interval of some thirty to fifty years between the time when Christ spoke and the time when his sayings were recorded in the Synoptic Gospels. We note in passing that he admits that other authors have edited the Gospels. And scoffers might suggest that they edited them to suit their own taste; and even to the believer it is an awkward comment on the suggestion of literal inspiration. Indeed, my good Bishop admits in terms that 'we are precluded from supposing that in the first three Gospels we have anything like an exact and verbatim report of what Christ said.' From an authority so limited and so unpromising we are invited to draw conclusions of certainty, and to assume that the words 'What God hath joined together let no man put asunder' apply 'not only to

Christian marriages, or to marriages with religious rites, or to marriages entered into seriously and soberly, but absolutely to all marriages', and that 'every man and woman who marries, however lightly and unworthily', is under this ordinance. Well, well, our good Bishop has *per incuriam* slipped very much into the position of Lord Braye and the Catholics. All marriages without religious rites – e.g., those of savages according to their tribal customs – are to be subject to the particular God in which the Bishop believes, and to the particular ordinance contained with the Scriptures which he accepts. This is a bold claim. I wonder what the Bishop of Churchmen would think if he happened to have married a widow, and a Comtist were to round upon him and say that, according to the doctrines of Positivism, by which all mankind were bound, he was living in sin? Or suppose he had married his first cousin in accordance with the laws of his country and his Church, and a Roman Catholic denounced it as an incestuous union because it was so regarded by his Church? Church of England ecclesiastics writing for the faithful do not always pause to consider the full implications of their arrogant claims.

The Bishop of Ely gives no very clear answer to the question he set out to solve as to what Christ did teach about divorce. He deals with Dr Charles; he talks of 'one modern answer'; he says: 'Two main arguments are brought forward'; again: 'It is maintained by some.' The one conclusion which he says is beyond doubt is this: 'There is not any version of Christ's judgment on divorce which does not forbid divorce except on the one and one ground of adultery'; but does not himself say whether divorce is permitted by his Church on this ground. The Bishops in 1857 said very definitely that it was not, and fought hard to preserve their Churches from having such marriages inflicted upon them.

The Archbishop of York, referring to Lord Braye, said that the views he expressed are not confined to the members of his communion, but were shared by the great multitude of the Archbishop's communion; and he later accepted in terms the conception of his marriage as dissoluble only with death. Again, further on in his speech he said: 'For better for worse until death us do part has become part of the common conscience of the community.' If this is what he really thinks, how did he find himself able to support Lord Gorell's Bill in 1921, which recognized divorce for simple adultery both for man and for woman? He said that he regarded it 'as involved in the teaching of Christ, and in the principles of the Church, that *marriage is dissoluble only by death, and that divorce, carrying with it the right of re-marriage, is not consistent with those principles*'; and yet he went on to say that with those convictions he was not precluded from trying to do what he could to amend the existing law in the interests of justice and morality where no essential principle is set aside. Indeed, he described Lord Braye as 'tilting at a windmill', and said that he could not see that any question of fundamental principle was involved. Really in that which, according to the Archbishop of York's own view, is not consistent with the teaching of Christ and not consistent with the principles of the Church, I am bound to say I should have thought a fundamental principle was involved. If the fact of its being contrary to the teachings of Christ and the teachings of the Church is not fundamental, and he is to be guided like any politician by his sense of justice and morality, he cannot be heard to advance the arguments of ecclesiastical tradition against divorce on any other ground.

The Bishop of Durham, on the other hand, with that good sense which makes him so distasteful to his brother prelates, said that Christ's words were not legislative; and he commented very justly upon the Archbishop of York's speech by saying that with the conviction that divorce is by the divine law altogether inadmissible it was very difficult 'to bring a candid and open mind to the question', but that the position consistently held by the Roman Catholic Church was 'taken up and maintained with equal assurance and less reason by those members of our Church who voluntarily adopt it.' He admitted, which is obvious to everyone who has studied the subject, that ecclesiastical authority is in a pitiable state of division, and those who are accustomed to appeal to the tradition of the Church are locked up in a hopeless position. Indeed, Dr Henson, with his characteristic courage, went further, and warned his colleagues 'not to take the name of the Lord thy God in vain and to urge the divine authority of Christ in support of a contention which outrages the sense of justice in the minds of many thousands of sincere and just men.' The Archbishop of Canterbury, in March, 1920, was much more careful. He entirely sheared off dealing with the religious ground, although he said he might talk about that aspect in a more appreciative assembly, presumably Convocation, and throughout his speech did not commit himself. The extreme contrast to this attitude is that of Dr Furse, whom we have recently imported from the Colonies to the Bishopric of St Albans. He stated that if the Bill were passed it would regularize polygamy, bigamy, and adultery; that it was a blasphemous farce and fatal to the true interests of family life. One is, I suppose, to assume that the present system, by which thousands of separated persons are driven to form adulterous unions, and by which those who remain chaste but find themselves unable to live together are forever forbidden to repair their initial mistake, is not blasphemous, is not a farce, and is in accordance with the spirit of Christ's teaching.

However, let us turn from these episcopal follies, the discussion of which is suited only to schoolmen, to a somewhat boarder view of the question.

Yet we must not forget these ecclesiastics, or be unprepared to rout them on their own ground, for the lies they tell are various and many-coloured, and the harm they do in impressing old women in cathedral towns, and even the other kind of old women who wear trousers, is great. Outside Parliament, where they cannot be challenged, at diocesan conferences, at meetings of Mothers' Union and the like, they gravely misrepresent the purpose of measures of reform, and, while relying nominally upon social considerations alone, make their appeal, in fact, to all the baser elements of hidebound superstition. And so long as these folk stand between the people of the country as a whole and reasonable measures of freedom and progress there must be no truckling to them, and they must be swept aside without any apologies or mincing of words.

On the broader ground, if we grant their premises that Christ is correctly reported, even perhaps if we grant their assumption that he is divine in some greater measure than other prophets, and if we make the very large assumption that in speaking to a select audience of Jews with their special traditions he was professing to legislate for all times and for all peoples, including unbelieving England in 1921, we are entitled to retort upon them that it is not for them to pick and choose which of these bits of divine legislation are to be forced down own throats. What of the Sermon on the Mount? Is that not divinely inspired? And yet I heard very few Bishops and parsons insisting on its teaching during the late War. What of the denunciation of rich men? What of the command to sell all and give to the poor? What of the warning to lay not up treasure upon earth? Yet I do not remember to have heard the Church so busy denouncing profiteers and ground landlords and the like. What about the duty of denouncing wickedness in high places – one in which Christ never failed? Yet in all my experience in the House of Lords I have never heard a single Bishop bearing spoken testimony to this law even in the most general terms. Bishops are ready enough to put difficulties in the way of letting the poor have access to the County Courts for the purposes of divorce, and they are always denouncing the right of the guilty party to marry again; but never once in an Irish Divorce Bill, which, owing to its expense, can be only a rich man's privilege, have they attended to resist the amendment which gives power to the guilty party to marry again. There is a deal of the dry husk of tradition, and Bishop Chase with gusto tithes mint and cumin, while Bishop Furse becomes lyrical in his lies; but precious little of the spirit of Christ, their nominal Master, is to be detected in any of these utterances. Let me conclude with a quotation which my Shakespeare Calendar brings pat before my notice:–

In religion
What damnéd error but some sober brown
Will bless it, and approve it with a text?[15]

Soothing the Sinner's Path, *John Bull*, 8 July 1922

The divorce laws of this country are absurd! This incontrovertible statement cannot be made too often. The reasons why they remain absurd are: one, the muddy mindedness of ecclesiastics whose outlook on life has not progressed since the Council of Trent; two, the incredible folly of those dupes who are organized into opposition to change; three, for supineness of the general public, who are indifferent about divorce while incontinence is easy; four, the cowardice of the Labour Party on this subject.

The Public and Press have allowed themselves to be stampeded into the idea that there is something discreditable in divorce, and that one should put aside all common sense when discussing it.

Look for a moment at the present actual position in practice. Any man or woman who is willing to commit adultery, or even pretend to have committed adultery, may be free in the minimum time at the minimum expense. The Church rewards the adulterer with both hands. Respectable people who care about the law, their personal purity, and their reputation, are tied for life however atrocious the circumstances.

Ronald True is a murderer, and has unfortunately escaped hanging;[16] Mrs True, a young woman, is condemned to celibacy for life. Colonel Rutherford's wife finds herself in the same position.[17]

Every object of marriage set out in the Prayer Book is destroyed by desertion, but there is no remedy. I decline even to speak of judicial separation as a remedy: it is a Roman curse imposed upon this country. If the wife who has run away refuses to be an adulteress, the husband can do nothing.

I ask: why is it discreditable to find a husband and wife to fail to agree or to find it impossible to live together? It is a misfortune for which they should be pitied; but, instead, they are both blamed and punished–while your gay and easy adulterer can do what he likes.

Is this the sanctity of the home that the Mothers' Union is always more maundering about? Is this the respect for marriage Bishop Furse seeks to give us? 'Marriage is a sacred institution, which cannot lightly be attacked without risk to the foundations of society,' say the more subtle opponents of divorce with their tongues in their cheeks.

I find it is quite impossible to speak calmly about the present state of things; all those members of the community who occupy responsible positions, all those who have good moral characters, and all those who have a care for the ordinances of society and the welfare of the state, are denied relief in this matter of divorce–while it is offered with both hands to the frivolous minded, the loose livers and the worthless.

John Bull is to be congratulated if it takes the lead among the Press of this country in exposing the cant and the mockery of the present dishonest attitude to this important question.

'The Ethics of Suicide', read before the Medico-Legal Society, 21 November 1922

It will be remembered that not long ago a nurse brought an action to recover damages for her detention as a lunatic, and that the principal allegation against her was that she had threatened to commit suicide.[18] She took up the challenge, and proceeded to argue with a good deal of force that a declared intention to commit suicide was no evidence of insanity, and she prayed in aid many classical examples. As her line of argument appeared to raise some interesting ethical questions, it occurred to me that the Society might like to have a paper on the subject.

As is usual in almost any question of human interest or moral conduct, one does not need to look beyond Shakespeare to find the subject adequately presented in language more perfect than we moderns can dare to use. All the questions upon which I propose to address you tonight are summed up in that well-known soliloquy of Hamlet:

To be, or not to be, that is the question:-
Whether 'tis nobler in the mind, to suffer
The slings and arrows of outrageous fortune;
Or to take arms against a sea of troubles,
And, by opposing, end them? To die, – to sleep, –
No more...
...
But that the dread of something after death,-
The undiscovered country, from whose bourn
No traveller returns, – puzzles he will;
And makes us rather bear those ills we have,
Than fly to others that we know not of?
Thus conscience does make cowards of us all;

And thus the native hue of resolution
Is sicklied o'er with the pale case of thought.[19]

In this wonderful speech Shakespeare gives in part the reason why suicide
has been condemned by Christianity and made a crime by laws of Christian
nations. This reason is, of course, ecclesiastical, and the logical outcome of
the Christian view that in the act of procreation a soul is born into the world
by the will of the Creator, and must remain in the world and tied to the body
until the Creator Himself sees fit to release it. In this view suicide does not
differ from homicide, and the man who slays himself is guilty of the same
crime as he who slays another, and no doubt if circumstances admitted of it
would receive the same punishment. In the ecclesiastical view the offences
are the same, and the punishment in the next world is the same, and it is the
thought of this punishment after death which Hamlet chiefly dwells on, and
it is this thought which is, to his mind, the deterrent to suicide. Grant this
view, and there remains no question to discuss to-night, for no circumstances
can justify, even if some may extenuate, so impious an interference with the
will of the Creator.

I am going to assume, however, that to the majority of educated people
the question is not capable of so simple a solution, and that they are prepared
rather to consider the question upon its merits and endeavour to arrive at
some sort of conclusion on the following points:

1. Ought the law to treat suicide as a crime?
2. Ought the law, when two people have agreed to commit suicide
together, to treat an accidental survivor as the murderer of the other?
3. Are there any circumstances, and, if so, what circumstances, which
make suicide justifiable?
4. As a sub-heading of the above, the question of euthanasia.
5. Is suicide a matter in which the individual alone is concerned?

In fact, I want rather to discuss the earlier question in Hamlet's speech as to
whether it is nobler in the mind to suffer its present ills or to shuffle off this
mortal coil, and so to still forever its doubts and its sufferings. For that
purpose it will be well, I think, to begin by considering certain specific cases
of suicide, and I have chosen many of the cases that I propose to discuss
tonight from works of fiction rather than from the columns of newspapers,
because in these cases the motives and antecedents can be better
apprehended than is possible in the bare details of a Coroner's inquest.

Even as I write, however, there comes a tragedy in the morning papers
which well illustrates one branch of the subject. It is the wilful murder of one
bank clerk by another, and the suicide of the murderer because they were
both enamoured of the same woman.[20] This is a clear case of diseased vanity,
and of that overweening egotism which insists upon obtaining from the world
the thing which it desires, even when that thing is so elusive and so little
subject to command as a woman's love. Failing to obtain it, it is ready to
destroy even though the end be its own destruction. In this case the diseased
egotism had passed the limits of sanity, and from the family history it is clear
that the suicide was of unsound mind, though for some reason the Coroner's
jury chose not to find him so. Exactly the same feelings and exactly the same

passions animated the breast of Sir Willoughby Patterne with regard to Clara Middleton in Meredith's novel *The Egoist*, but being in his case subject to the inhibitions of a sane and cultured man, they led to no violent action, but merely to a pained surprise. Somewhat similar in motive and in its undue prepossession with one particular matter of ambition and desire, though less ignoble because less personal, was the suicide of Herr Ballin at the beginning of the War, when he saw the destruction of that magnificent enterprise, the Hamburg-Amerika Line of steamers, which he had built up principally by his own ability.[21] It would have been well for the reputation of the Kaiser if at the end of his war he had sought the same way out, though nobler still had he decided to live and devote his remaining years to reparation and amendment of his former naughty life. As it is, when I contrast the contemporary portrait which has recently been in the newspapers with the face I remember at Kiel in 1913, it looks as if even that complacent egoist and blood-stained autocrat had received some punishment.

In a simpler class come the suicides of despair: a sudden crashing of all future hope, such as that which caused Whittaker Wright, who had hitherto lived soft and was in the act of building himself a great mansion on Hindhead, to take cyanide of potassium on hearing his sentence of penal servitude;[22] or the recent case of Kaye, who thinking himself ruined in business destroyed his family and then himself.[23] Or the more prolonged despair which leads a prisoner serving a long term to end it, or an unmarried mother outcast by her relations and deserted by her betrayer, with no prospect ahead but disgrace and poverty, or the very poor and homeless, to whom the rest of death seems an alluring alternative to hunger and exposure. The dominating emotion in these cases may, I think, be said to be fear: fear of disgrace, fear of hardships to be endured. If I am right in giving fear the cause, this can hardly be regarded as a noble motive, however adequate it may appear to the sufferers.

Then there are what one may call romantic suicides, of which there have been quite a number recently in the public press. To Brighton there fled a wife and her brother-in-law, the slaves to a quasi-incestuous intrigue, to whom the only practicable end appeared to be their joint suicide by poison.[24] At Walton-on-Thames a young railwayman has an affair with a still younger girl: moved by one knows not what tenebrous impulses of Swinburnian passion, they threw themselves in front of a train, and the man partially survives.[25] We can turn to Shakespeare for the two best-known examples. In *Romeo and Juliet* Romeo think his love is dead, and straightway poisons himself: Juliet, waking from her drugged sleep and finding Romeo dead, dispatches herself with his dagger. In *Othello*, the Moor, overcome with remorse for his unfounded vengeance on Desdemona, falls upon his sword. The mainspring of all these romantic suicides is love, and all we can say about them is that when the passion of love has possession of a man or woman, the scale of values is so altered that life without the beloved one becomes a valueless and idle thing, and the only possible course is to end it. Coroners' juries and the public, not infected by the passion, may see fit to describe it as a temporary insanity, but I can imagine the romantic retorting upon us that we suffer from permanent insanity in having a wrong scale of values.

This is perhaps an appropriate place to consider the law as to the survivor of a joint suicide. In the first two cases of romantic suicides given above there was a survivor, as there was in a third case of a different character, where an elderly man and his sister at Worksop agreed to commit suicide on account of poverty. In each of these cases the survivor has been charged with murder. I should have been disposed to say that the law was clear upon this point, and that the survivor of a joint compact to commit suicide was always technically guilty of murder. I see, however, that Mr Justice Lush, moved no doubt by merciful considerations, instructed the jury in the last case that in order to justify the charge of murder there must have been some incitement on the part of the survivor. My sympathies are entirely with the learned Judge, but I doubt if this is good law. These three cases, however, all raise one of the points that we desire to discuss tonight, as to whether the law in this respect should be amended. Most people would be inclined to answer the question in the affirmative without any hesitation, but the law is never quite so silly as the general public is apt to think it, and there are considerations on the other side. If the survivor of a joint attempt at suicide were guilty of no crime and liable to no punishment, this method might be used by a man to get rid of an inconvenient sweetheart whom he had got into trouble, by a husband to get rid of a wife, or by a jealous woman to get rid of a rival. In such cases, of course, the survivor would never have intended to take his life, and having fraudulently incited the other party to do so would be morally guilty of murder; and should, I think, also be legally guilty. If it is agreed that these considerations are not without weight, then the remedy should be sought in some amendment of the law on the lines suggested by Mr Justice Lush, limiting criminality to those cases where there was no real suicidal intention on the part of the survivor, and some incitement. Obvious difficulties of proof will, however, occur to any lawyer.

Now let us turn to suicides of a different character, provoked by altruistic motives, having the nature of sacrifice and often the result of a prolonged process of reasoning, even though the reasoning be somewhat distorted. A typical example is to be found at the end of Rebecca West's book *The Judge*. In this book a mother of great endurance and remarkable character has two sons, of whom one is in every way lovable and the very apple of her eye, while the other is hateful to her both on account of the degrading circumstances surrounding his birth and of his own character. But he loves her and depends upon her love, and she feels it her duty not to deny it to him. Between the two sons there exists a perpetual friction of jealousy, until at last the mother decides that the only solution to the problem is to remove herself, and so goes out on to the marshes and is drowned. Mr Hutchinson, whose psychology is less complex than Rebecca West's, gives us a simpler example of the sacrificial suicide in his book, *The Clean Heart*, when the preposterous but lovable Mr Puddlebox deliberately allows himself to be drowned in order to save his friend. There is again the heroic sacrifice with a gesture, as when Mettus Curtius leapt into the chasm of the Forum, declaring with a certain complacent vanity that Rome had no finer sacrifice to offer than the life of a virtuous and distinguished citizen. These sacrifices are more often made by women as a matter of instinct and without a gesture as in *If Winter Comes*. The tragic and awful ending of Conrad's *Victory* will be remembered, when the woman intercepts the bullet intended for the man she loves. A very similar incident occurs in Anthony Hope's *A Change of Air*, but here the woman did not intend her action and does not die of it, and the matter is treated lightly, as is that author's way.

There is yet another class, confined as a general rule to men, which may be described as the suicide of mere boredom, as that of the man who has had enough of life, and thinks it has no more to offer of sufficient interest to keep alive for. To this class belong most of the Roman suicides and, I dare say, a fair number of modern instances. A good illustration of the spirit which it exemplifies may be found in James Thomson's *City of Dreadful Night*, and readers will remember the little note in which he points out that over the wall of the garden of life hangs ever a cluster of the grapes of death, of which a man may pluck and eat when he has had enough of it. It is not a very creditable class, because the sensation on which suicide is founded can only arise in a man whose life has been lived entirely for himself, and who has not recognised any ties of duty or obligations of service to others. On the other hand, the members of this class cannot reasonably be described as insane – unless, indeed, it is an act of insanity to be a disillusioned cynic. Here, as in the case of the romantics, the would be suicides might well retort upon us that we deliberately go through life with our eyes closed and buoyed up by an entirely unwarranted optimism.

Having now collected a certain number of concrete cases in order that we may have before our minds the circumstances in which suicide actually does take place, we may proceed to consider the points raised at the beginning of the paper. The legal question need not long detain us, for I am inclined to think that we should all agree that there is no valid reason why the would-be suicide who has had the misfortune to be unsuccessful should be treated as a felon, although there may be some reason for putting him under medical observation and restraint. The more interesting question is as to what justification may exist for any suicide, and in my view the answer is irrevocably bound up in a further question as to whether suicide can in any case be regarded as a purely individual act. If it can be so regarded, then our lovers, who find life empty and meaningless, those who are destitute and disgraced, those who see nothing but sordid and hopeless misery before them and are world-weary, those who find no sufficient interest in life to make its continuance worthwhile, have only their own point of view to consider. In that view the decision rests with them, and with them alone, and is not open to revision by us. It is specious to say that a man has not been consulted as to his entry into this world, that he finds himself there without any volition or choice of his own, and that therefore he is at liberty to decide whether he shall remain in the world of life or not. But if we regard men and women as having certain reciprocal obligations to other men and women, some of which at least they have assumed voluntarily since they came into the world, the question becomes less simple.

In one of Swinnerton's novels a man marries a woman of whom he is not particularly fond; she has a child, and he finds the menage unendurable. Regardless of the fact that she has only his earnings to depend upon and will be reduced to penury by this death, he walks into a pond on Hampstead Heath. Here there seems a fairly clear obligation which the suicide shirks, and one may compare such people to soldiers of a conscript army who have become soldiers without any act of volition on their part, but who none the less finding themselves in the ranks have certain obligations which they cannot escape, and for whom desertion would be a crime. If this be a true view of the relations of an individual to the community of which he forms part, it would seem difficult to justify ethically the laying down of his burden, and though he found it a heavy one, so long as there remained even a prospect of service to those to whom he has obligations. These considerations hardly apply to actions such as those of Mr Puddlebox, or of a mother who gives her life for her child; but then, these are not true cases of suicide: they are cases of deliberate sacrifice at a moment which calls for rapid decision, like those which are habitually made by men who in a sinking ship give place in the boats to the women. Some reinforcement of the suggestion that suicide may be unjustifiable may even be found in its results. Thus Rebecca West's heroine, for all her altruism and all her reasoning, does not, in fact, by her self-destruction lead to happiness for her sons. As to those who are driven by the extreme of misery to bring an unwanted life to an end, we may pity, we may excuse: we may even go so far as to say that it was for them to choose, and yet pass a moral judgment upon their choice.

One exception most people are willing to make, and I do not know that I should dissent from their conclusion, and that is in the case of euthanasia. Where a person is suffering from an incurable cancer, where the end is certain, prolonged, and painful, few would be so hard-hearted as to deny the sufferer an earlier and easier passage. Even in cases such as these, however, we must remember the splendid example of Barbellion, who by his indomitable spirit triumphed over impending death and its agonies, and in that act asserted the nobility of man's soul.[26]

There is also the earlier example of Heine,[27] slowly dying in almost continuous pain, but conquering his body and remaining bright and inspired, although he too, like Barbellion, was without the consolations of religion to support him. There is always the possibility of a new life, of a fresh start, of the soul conquering the body and the spirit rising superior to its surroundings and refusing to let itself be the victim of temporal accidents. More than one example of a noble and uplifted soul defying fate brightens the record of human endeavour and human failure, and stirs the spirit to assent to that view as being more noble than surrender. At the end we come back to the question as Hamlet posed it, and in his very words, Which is the nobler in man? We should not punish, we need no condemn, the unfortunate; and yet we may come to the conclusion that nearly all suicides have some flavour of cowardice, some shirking from responsibility, some self-indulgence, and some aspect of desertion in the face of the enemy, which does render endurance to the end the nobler in the unconquered spirit.

In reply to the ensuing discussion, Frank said:

Mr Chairman, Ladies and Gentlemen,–I will not detain you very long at this hour of the night. I was anxious to avoid, as far as possible, questions of insanity. In discussing the Ethics of Suicide, of course, the thing inevitably comes in, because the question inevitably arises as to how far suicides are the acts of balanced minds; but we have had very frequent discussions on the subject of insanity, and I wanted rather to try and eliminate those cases of the clearly insane and the cases of those who were so diseased or so wasted as hardly to be responsible for their actions, and to discuss the cases of what

I might call serious suicides. I certainly desired to eliminate those people who come under the class of accidental suicides, and other people who are merely playing with the emotions and using them to excite pity. Sir Robert Armstrong-Jones raised a great many questions which one could spend an hour or two discussing, because among other things he raised the whole question of whether we have free will or not. He said that we have, and that we have certain definite ethical actions which are perfectly clear to us, and that we are guided by a moral sense which is nearly as definite and as clear as the sense of smell. It struck me as an unfortunate example, because in this instance of the senses, and particularly, perhaps, the sense of smell, two people have very different views and very different capacities. You would hardly get anything approaching an absolute standard if your moral views and moral senses depended upon something which varies so much among individuals. When I listened to Sir Robert Armstrong-Jones speaking so clearly about the non-abrogation of free will and the repudiation of the suggestion that we were the creatures of circumstances, and to the subsequent speaker, Mr Chadwick, who followed him, and who said quite definitely that we were here for a purpose, I was reminded of that anecdote of Mr Justice Maule. A small child was put into the witness-box, and the question arose of whether she was of an age to understand the nature of an oath; counsel desired to examine her upon it, and said: 'Do you understand what it means to take the oath and to be sworn?' She said: 'Oh yes.' Counsel said: 'What do you understand by it?' and she said: 'If I do not tell the truth I shall go to hell.' Whereupon Mr Justice Maule said: 'Swear her; she knows more than I do.' I quite agree to this extent with Sir Robert Armstrong-Jones and subsequent speakers, that whether it be true or not in actual fact that we have free will, it is quite essential that we should pretend we have, and that we could not continue life for one moment without keeping up that belief, whether that belief be actually a delusion, or whether it be not. However much our actions are dependent on environment, heredity, and so on, it may be that they are dependent also on the belief that we have free will, and that our surrounding people will punish us if we do not exercise it. Perhaps it comes back more or less to the same thing.

Mr Lieck, speaking with his valuable experience, told us that, in fact, attempted suicides were not generally actually punished nowadays. That, of course, I was aware of. I do agree with what Sir William Collins has said, that it is not the best way of treating an attempted suicide either to send him to a remand prison, or to have him in a hospital with a police-constable sitting alongside the bed, waiting to take him away as soon as he can be taken. I think there might perfectly well be an alteration in the law in that respect. Remand in custody of the hospital authority, or some other person who would look after the individual, would no doubt be an improvement. The trouble is that technically they are charged with practically murder, and that is a felony.

Dr Graham Grant spoke about insanity, and Dr Trever spoke about suicide in the insane and the reason they did it. I think it probably is true that the mind of a man who commits suicide, whether you are prepared to say he is sane, or whether you are prepared to say he is insane, is at the time abnormal. Of course, it is quite true that a sane and healthy human being is presumably also a happy human being, and would not have any desire to commit suicide, but it is the circumstances of people's environment in civilised life with the disadvantages of civilisation that lead to their not being healthy or happy, or in healthy or happy surroundings. Those are the circumstances in which they cannot feel the same desire of life. I do not suppose your savage, hunting his animals, would want to commit suicide unless to escape the extreme pain of a lacerated limb or something of that sort; you do not, in fact, find that in that state. You may have a person whose mind would be normal in circumstances that makes his mind and his outlook upon things abnormal.

Mr O'Sullivan was good enough to say a great deal with which I entirely agree, and after he had spoken I was asked a very difficult question. I was asked if I would say what I thought was the difference between horror and fear. I do not know that at this hour of the night I want to enter upon a sort of lecture of Aristotle on these subjects, but I may say shortly that horror is the emotion which is excited in you by something which is horrible, whether it at the times makes you afraid or not. It may be something which you see in another person which excites the emotion of horror. The sight of the tearing out of someone's eyes would excite horror even if you were in no danger; the sight of a horrible railway accident would excite the sensation of horror. Where it becomes fear is, I think, when having that horror before your eyes you have the fear of the horror happening to you; it seems to me that then it becomes fear, and is justly classed as an emotion.

I do not think there is very much more I have to say in reply to the discussion, except to thank the audience very much for the patience with which they listened to the paper, and to say that I am glad to think that we have provoked a discussion which has given very divergent points of view, but in which on the whole the preponderance of opinion has been rather what I indicated at the end of my paper – that it was not a specially noble thing to avoid the responsibilities of life by escape, coupled with that kindness of humanity, which most of us have now, which makes us tend to say that most of the people who commit suicide cannot be regarded as being absolutely normal at the time they do it.

House of Lords Debate 13 June 1923: Strength of Socialism

THE EARL OF BIRKENHEAD rose to draw attention to the growing strength of Socialism, and to ask His Majesty's Government whether they propose to take any steps to modify by legislation the power of trades unions to make compulsory levies for political purposes.

Frank's response:

...I gather that the noble Earl is in a state of considerable fear about the growth of Socialism, and what it may do, and he asked what was to happen if this House found itself void of constitutional power when matters came before it with which it did not agree. While the present law exists, and while the present Parliament Act exists, a Bill has to be passed in three separate Sessions before your Lordships' House can be disregarded, and that is a thing which the House of Commons finds it difficult to do, and only can do if it has public opinion behind it. Public opinion is a very great influence and no

Bill can be passed three times and made law over your Lordships' heads, unless the country, as a whole, is in favour of it.

Then the noble Earl made an admission, from my point of view, when he said that the Labour Party did not intend the same things as the Liberal Party. That is perfectly true, and that has been quite clearly recognised by the Labour Party. The Liberal Party have, in my view of the situation, managed to preserve the peace by giving sops to Cerberus–by passing ameliorative legislation, making concessions, and generally giving just what was needed for the moment, and no more. The ideals and objects of the two Parties are quite different, I agree. The Liberal Party, as such, is not in favour of nationalisation, and many Members are strongly opposed to it.

The noble and learned Earl went on to make what I thought was the extremely rash assertion that we all know what Socialism stands for. My experience, in listening to people discuss Socialism, is that that is precisely what very few people do know, and what, even among those of us who think we know, very few of us agree about. All one can say, and say legitimately, is, I think, that Socialism, as it is understood by the Labour Party, aims at improving the lot of the underdog, at improving the life and the conditions of life of the lower class in society, of giving them a better standard of life and, to enable them to obtain that better standard, higher remuneration for their work where the industry will stand it, and without feeling any regret that that higher remuneration leads to a smaller profit for the exploiter.

EARL OF BIRKENHEAD: Does Socialism, or does it not, mean the nationalisation of the means of production and exchange?

A: Certainly, Socialism in some forms means the nationalisation of all the means of production.

EARL OF BIRKENHEAD: But the Socialism that we are discussing in this country, as a practical political creed?

A: No, I think it extremely unlikely that the business of selling newspapers in the streets will be nationalised at an early stage.

EARL OF BIRKENHEAD: There is not a single leader of the Socialist Party in the House of Commons who has not stated that that Party combines upon all those propositions.

A: Certainly, I said that that was the ideal, and that we should be quite prepared–and are prepared if it is considered that that is the only way in which that can be attained–to nationalise the means of industry and the means of work, the tools of trade and the material wealth of the country. That seems to me to be not at all an unreasonable thing to do if a better economic result is obtainable from it. That is what the question really turns upon. It is an economic proposal. What is said by Socialists is that the present Capitalist system is a wasteful system and a very imperfect system, and that it might be much more perfect and therefore might bring much greater happiness to greater numbers. Not only is this question one of improving the conditions of life of the worker, but there is the much more important question, and the very vital question to him, of his having the means of living at all. There is for him the fearful bogey and spectre of unemployment which hovers over him from the cradle to the grave. He never knows for certain whether he will get his next week's wages, and that is a condition of things which, I think, public opinion has felt ought to be changed.

Employers have had ample opportunity of trying to combine and to make arrangements to change it, and I am not aware that very much has been done in that direction. I think many people now feel that that condition of things ought to be ended. That is the object, and that is the idea that underlies all the economic proposals that are made. I am the last person to say that the mere giving of a sufficient material prosperity and of a certainty of livelihood to every human being in this country is, in itself, sufficient to make a new heaven and a new earth. I am perfectly certain that it is not, but it helps towards it, just as, on the other hand, slums and overcrowding and disease and want of food tend to crime and misery. The noble and learned Earl said that he heard people at the street corners constantly saying– 'Why does one man starve while other people are going about in wealth?' He said the answers to that question were so abundant that it was not worth while giving them. I can only tell the noble Earl that if, in the course of the propaganda which he proposes, he can at the street corners answer that question successfully, and in such a way as to bring conviction to the working classes, I think he will be able to convert them to the Capitalist system, but till he does that I fear that he will fail. I confess that I do not myself know the answer to that question. He referred, apparently with approval, to a new democratic development which he called the page that Mussolini had written in history. I was not aware that it was a democratic development, and it seems to me that a page which consists partly of black ink smeared with castor oil is not a very helpful page in the development of the world's history. I cannot look upon that example as one that could be commended in this country.

If it be true that trades unions are desirable–and it was admitted by the noble Marquess opposite that he thought they were desirable, and that organised labour was desirable–then I think it is unfortunate that the noble Earl who raised this Question should have said that people were practically forced to join trades unions. That is, no doubt, to a certain extent true. But I would point out that, if it were not also true that that plan met with the general consent and agreement both of the employers and the employed, it could not last. It would be perfectly open to employers to open free and non-trade union shops, and it would be perfectly open to people to work there. But, in effect, that does not happen, because all good employers, and, indeed, almost all employers, except in some of the sweated industries, have now realised that collective bargaining is essential to the proper carrying on of trade. And I think you would find hardly any of them who would be willing to have labour again unorganised and disorganised in the way it was before. That there are evils connected with trades unions no one would deny; there are evils connected with any organisation.

... I am prepared to defend–though not to-night, because the hour is late, and it has not been the main subject of this debate–but I am prepared at any time and at any place to defend the nationalisation of the means of livelihood; that is, the placing of control not under the private employer but under some communal authority. That seems to me to be, under our present system, almost the only safe method for the worker. I was rather astonished to hear the noble and learned Earl say that all positions of wealth were achieved solely as the result of merit on the part of the persons who held them. I do not know personally what merit has been shown by people who have become millionaires, sufficient to reap such a reward. Nor do I know what demerit those have shown who are thrown out of employment by vicissitudes of trade over which they have no control—vicissitudes arising, perhaps, from economic causes forced upon them, either by capitalists, or by other countries—and who suffer bitterly in consequence.

Anybody who is able to say to himself, with the comfortable feeling of the noble and learned Earl, that these things are the just and fair allocation of the reward of merit naturally feels that there is no question to be solved, but many people do feel that there are most serious economic questions to be solved; that although they do not give us a new heaven and a new earth, their solution must be attempted; and that we must not hesitate to explore new methods even if there is a menace to the capitalist.

The Torture of Jail, *John Bull*, 4 July 1925

Mr Bernard Shaw has been speaking again, with the well-known Shavian accent, on the subject of the unprotected child and the law, and comments unfavourably on what he describes as the only two prevalent views—one of excessive punishment, preferably by flogging, and the other of treating the matter lightly with a short sentence of imprisonment—and asserts that there is no middle view held by the general public.

The former, according to him, merely advocate physical punishment in order to gratify their own particular vice, and the others he refers to contemptuously as sympathetic amorists. Mr Shaw does not, however, adopt the practical course telling us what he would do if he found himself in the position of a judge about to sentence a man who has been convicted of some peculiarly horrible crime upon a young girl.

You may be as thoughtful as you will, you may try to free yourself from prejudice as far as possible, and you may adopt all the most enlightened theories of punishment and reform, and still find it very difficult to answer the practical question as to what society is to do with such a criminal. From sentiments to which he has given expression on other occasions I am inclined to think that Mr Shaw would prefer a lethal chamber to a sentence of two years imprisonment, but I am not at all sure that the criminal would. I propose to consider shortly the nature and desirability of punishment, the authority by which it is inflicted, and its moral effect, not only upon the person punished, but also upon the individuals who inflict punishment and the society that authorises it.

Wrath in itself suggests a certain surrender of the faculty of judging dispassionately or of calmly envisaging all the surrounding circumstances. To say that it is righteous is only a self-satisfied way of putting the fact that it is excited by something of which you personally do not approve.

In modern times the objects of punishments inflicted by society are supposed to be to punish, to deter, and to reform—to punish the criminal by inflicting upon him something unpleasant, so that he personally may come to the conclusion that it is not worthwhile to commit the crime again; to deter other potential criminals by the knowledge of the punishment; to reform the individual criminal so that he may leave prison a better member of society than when he entered it.

Great thought, great care, and real passion for humanity have for some generations now been directed to achieving the last of these objects, but, so far, practically without any result. Few people will be found to assert that a man leaves prison better than when he entered it.

The truth is that the reform comes some twenty years too late: it was in his earlier education and his early surroundings that it might have operated effectually. The only really successful reform is that of the murderer who is hanged, because then it is certain that he will not commit another murder.

So far as the deterring of others is concerned, this is a matter upon which it is very difficult to come to any certain conclusion. Probably in calculated crimes, such as frauds, thefts, and to some extent, burglary, severe sentences may exercise a deterrent effect upon others, but, of course, this element never entered into crimes of impulse or passion.

Now, as to the punishment of the individual. Here also we are faced with innumerable difficulties. First of all, there is the necessary inequality as between the rich and the poor, one of the very few cases where the scales are weighed against the rich.

Six months' imprisonment with hard labour means a very different degree of suffering, both physical and social, for the man who is well-to-do than it does for the street ruffian. It might seem that if our object were to make it so unpleasant for the individual that he would not desire to commit the crime again our system should be much harsher than it is.

Yet it may be doubted whether at present our prisons are not almost too comfortable, so that we may seem to be a little half-hearted in our attempt to frighten the criminal into good ways of life. It is probably considerations of this sort that occasionally make people advocate, and more rarely persuade judges to impose, sentences of flogging, and trot out the old and discredited myth that garrotting was put down by the lash.

In the days when people were hanged for sheep-stealing and our prisons were abominations there was not less, but more, crime than there is now, particularly more crimes of violence, so that it looks as if humanity to the criminal paid after all.

The simple truth is that society is entitled in its own self-defence to protect itself against those who menace social order and security by whatever seems to be the most effective means, and although this justification is an ample one it is well to recognise that it is a purely selfish one and not to obfuscate it by grandiloquent terms about righteous wrath or justice.

I confess, however, that I shudder when I contemplate the meaning of a sentence of ten years' penal servitude and the very perfection of the English prison system which makes it so machine-like and inhuman, and I think of an unfortunate fellow-creature condemned day after day for all that space of time to pass some fifteen hours out of the twenty-four in a bare and uncomfortable cell, allowed no conversation during the day, and only for a few moments in each week treated like a rational human being.

This brings me to my final point: What is the moral effect both upon those concerned and upon society at large of inflicting such punishments? Happily for its peace, and happily for its moral character, society at large does not think much about it, but I am not sure that it would not be a good thing if it did, so long as it continued to think sanely.

I am sure that everyone at the Home Office, every judge, and every magistrate should have served a sentence of three months' hard labour before he inflicts it or authorises it.

When we come to those who have the actual carrying out of sentences, the warders at a convict prison, the governor, and, to a minor extent, the Home Office, one cannot help feeling that the exercise of this terrible inhuman power over a fellow-creature must have a deadening effect upon their moral sensibilities, unless, indeed, they succeed in sustaining themselves by the consolation of a vindictive religion.

It is certain that where floggings are frequently administered a somewhat more brutal type of warder is required, and although I am personally in favour of capital punishment, because I believe it is a deterrent, I should certainly not like to take part in a hanging.

Is crime, then, to be free from reprobation and is the criminal to escape scot-free? By no means, because true crime is an individualistic, an anti-social and an anarchic action, and as such deserves the strongest reprobation of civilised society. When we go on to enquire almost unconsciously if the criminal is to escape scot-free, we find at once that we are back at the vindictive idea.

Seclusion may be one of the proper remedies, but the only one that is going ultimately to count and to turn your criminal loose again as a fit member of society is that which will end by persuading him, in his own mind, that his crime has been an anti-social act which cannot be tolerated.

To cover him with obloquy, to expose him to degradation, to make him feel less of a human being, when his trouble already is a certain reversion to savagery, is emphatically not the way to restore his sense of balance and self-control.

If I am asked whether I suggest that no punishment should be inflicted in the present imperfect state of society, my answer can only be that I do not suggest it, but I do most emphatically suggest that every time a punishment is inflicted it is a confession of failure on the part of society, just as a schoolmaster would regard every flogging as a confession of failure with his boys.

The real cure must be sought, as I have already indicated, at a much earlier stage, in better education, in happier surroundings, and in a social sense of duty to the community and adjustment to a civilised environment which will make crime itself an unattractive folly.

Perhaps even a great deal may be done still, at the stage when we have caught and sentenced a criminal, to make our prisons as successful in curing criminals as our hospitals are in curing disease. Till we have achieved that, at any rate we can avoid anything in the nature of smug satisfaction in regarding ourselves as the instruments of divine justice, for until we do the moral effect upon those who inflict the punishment will be at least as bad as it is on the victims.

In support of Dr Marie Stopes

On 7 July 1921 Dr Anne Louise McIlroy delivered a paper to the Medico-Legal Society entitled 'Some Factors in the Control of the Birth-Rate'. In the ensuing discussion Frank gave some 'most cogent arguments against the enforced provision of further cannon-fodder and Empire Builders'.[28] As a consequence, Dr Marie Stopes, who had opened her Mother's Clinic in Holloway on 17 Mar 1921, wrote to Frank asking him to become a vice-president of her Society for Constructive Birth Control (CBC). Frank replied:

... I will be vice-president of your society with pleasure if you think it won't do you harm. I am told to my amusement that I have an entirely undeserved reputation as a profligate roué and it might be said I was controlling my own lapses! But I think serious people know me better...

This 'very charming and modest note' led Stopes to regretfully withdraw her request after two of her 'most useful supporters' threatened to resign if Frank was 'prominently associated' with the organisation. 'Aren't people funny?' replied Frank. 'You see I was right in the suggestion I made to you in my letter. I shall be quite prepared to do what I can to support the movement as indeed I have done for a year or two past...'

True to his word, Frank spoke at and chaired the occasional CBC meeting, offered Stopes legal advice in her bitter libel suit against Dr Halliday Sutherland and put the matter of the vice-presidency to Bertie at Stopes' request:

... and very much to my surprise he did not turn it down. On the contrary he is much interested in your work and a few words from you personally will get him. He seemed to think having a baby was against him but I pointed out the meaning of the word constructive. Am I not a good messenger? ...[29]

In addition, Frank publicly defended Stopes in the press against misconceptions concerning her clinic, and penned two articles for *John Bull* on the subject, this being the second:

'Why Not Birth Control?' *John Bull*, 29 January 1927

Some people's idea of civilisation seems to be the spawning of the codfish where millions of eggs are produced only a few of which come to maturity. Such a view ignores the suffering and death of the infantile and adolescent.

The idea of increasing the population seems to be a sort of fetish and to exercise a kind of magic spell over some people's minds as though it were something necessarily good in itself. They envisage with perfect calm the subsequent removal of any surplus population by infant mortality, by pestilence and famine, or by war: all of them avoidable by human foresight.

Among the considerations which appealed to earlier generations were the advantages of an ample supply of manual labour or of soldiers for cannon fodder. These ideas may have been natural enough to an oligarchy, but they are unlikely to appeal to an educated democracy.

A wise Government will not have its eyes permanently fixed upon war or the savage arbitrament of force, but will also consider the happiness of the lives led by its people while they are alive.

Our large populations have led to insanitary overcrowding in slum areas with an absence of light and air, specially harmful to the young and directly provocative of many avoidable epidemics and weak constitutions.

The war revealed the terrible fact that the majority of our adolescent male population had to be classed as C3, and anyone who desires to improve this state of things cannot fitly be described as an enemy of this country or a public danger. In an ideal State every house would have its own plot of land about it.

The specific evils of unrestrained breeding are worn out wives and mothers and sickly children, not only born weak, but also, frequently owing to economic conditions, under-nourished. For this the only practical remedy is what is known as Constructive Birth Control – that is to say the adoption of methods of contraception so that children may be conceived only if and when they are wanted.

Before proceeding to develop the matter further, let me deal with two main religious contentions. The view of the Roman Catholic Church, somewhat half-heartedly endorsed by the Church of England, is that the birth of children is an act of procreation by which is meant that the Almighty has delegated to mankind the power to create souls upon whom His blessing or damnation may operate, and that to misuse that trust is an impious act. The act of sexual reproduction is common to all animals and plants upon the earth for the sufficiently obvious object of continuing the species. I doubt if in these days more than a small fraction of my countrymen are prepared to believe that its object has been so specially differentiated in the one case of man.

The next Catholic contention would appear to conflict to some extent with the previous one, for it allows married couples to defraud the Almighty either by refraining from the necessary act or by performing it at a time when it is mistakenly supposed that it will not be effective. I pass over the argument that such abstention between married people is physiologically harmful, because I understand that there are a few doctors who take a contrary view. I will therefore merely confine myself to saying that even if such an unnatural practice were desirable it does not obtain, and no reasonable human being can expect that it ever will obtain among young married couples. Those who accept the Catholic view are of course bound to act upon it, but they have no more right to force their view upon others or to try to prevent their obtaining the necessary information than we have to compel them to use contraception.

The practice of getting rid of unwanted infants is not a new one. In ancient days it was done by the barbarous method of exposure, and in these days by the very dangerous method of abortion – particularly common in America, where birth control information is illegal. From the medical point of view it is far preferable to prevent conception than to endanger the mother's health, and even her life, by an artificially induced miscarriage, but the fact that these practices prevail, in spite of their danger and their criminality, bears witness of the strength of the motive.

It is probably true that contraception in one form or another is practiced by nearly all the educated classes, including the clergy. Among the poorer classes, struggling on the verge of subsistence, where the need is sorest, the remedy is least known.

The immediate political question, therefore, is how to bring the knowledge of constructive birth control to those who need it most and have the smallest opportunity of self-restraint or physical separation.

By constructive birth control is meant not the opportunity for unlicensed immorality, not the practice of abortion nor the preaching of childlessness, but the spacing of pregnancies of married women at such intervals (preferably three years) as will enable them to recover from their previous pregnancy and enable the child to have a reasonable chance of a healthy life. For be it noted that it is not the birth-rate that matters but the survival rate.

Doctor Stopes has analysed the whole of the first 5,000 cases at her free clinic, and I quote from her pamphlet[30] the following appalling figures – 90 women with between 10 and 12 pregnancies each, making a total of 968 pregnancies, had only 650 children surviving, while 18 women with from 13 to 17 pregnancies each, or a total of 260, had only 166 children surviving. This means that no fewer than 412 potential children have failed to survive, and the consequent suffering to both the mind and bodies of the mothers may be imagined.

It is to be remembered that in every one of these cases of excessive pregnancies in a few years, the mother has had no opportunity of avoiding the embraces of her husband, has too often had her health ruined and her vitality impaired so that she cannot adequately feed her child. It is to be remembered finally that even of the smallest number of children who survive the majority are C3 and will suffer throughout life from the conditions of their birth. I find it difficult to listen with patience to the suggestion that this result is in accordance with the Christian religion. It is against humanity, it is against medical science and common-sense, it is against the happiness and well-being of the race; and if indeed it be Christian then Christianity itself is against these things.

The idea of Birth Control as a respectable social institution has suffered a great deal from its prior association with the practice of prostitutes and the advocacy of atheists, although Malthus, its earliest advocate, was a clergyman. Fortunately it is now outgrowing these associations, and respectable and earnest men and women in every rank of life are combining in support of the demand that knowledge which is available to the rich should be at the disposal of the poor also. Clinics have been opened at the expense of private people to give first-hand information at numerous places, but the one place where such information should be obtainable free by expectant mothers is naturally the Infant Welfare Centre for their district. Yet strangely enough by some mental perversity of the Ministry of Health or its officials the doctors and nurses in charge of Infant Welfare Centres are expressly forbidden to give this information except in special cases.

In view of the suffering caused to mothers and the children for whom they are supposed to care, of which I have already given examples, it is impossible to understand the idea of an Infant Welfare Centre which refuses the first requisite for the health of the infant. The matter was debated in the House of Lords on a motion of Lord Buckmaster's that the Government be requested to withdraw such instructions, and even in that respectable and conservative assembly the motion was carried by 57 votes to 44.[31]

One of the most significant things in the debate was the statement of the Archbishop of Canterbury who said, 'I have never been able to take the stern and uncompromising view of some people on this subject who think that the thing *per se* is wrong and evil.'

In the face of this declaration, in the face of this resolution of the House, and in the face of all educated and well-informed opinion, this knowledge is still denied to potential mothers at the one place which professes officially to be the centre of information on the health of children and consequently on our future population.

Every human being and every newspaper that takes a stand in condemnation of this brutal folly will deserve well of all lovers in their country.

Spiritualism on Trial

In December 1928, the *Daily News* launched a campaign challenging spiritualists to prove their claims that the dead can commune with the living. In the post-war world, when so many stubbornly believe this unexplained phenomena, it argued, its serious investigation should not be considered 'beneath the dignity of formal science'.

The campaign consisted of 18 articles published from 7-31 December penned by some very familiar names. Proponents including Lord Gorell Barnes and Estelle Stead, daughter of puritanical newspaper editor W.T. Stead, who claimed she had spoken to her father since his death on the *Titanic*; those against included J.M. Robertson, Hilaire Belloc, Aldous Huxley, and, of course, Frank. Three questions were put to contributors:

1. Do you consider the spiritualists' claimed proved or disproved – or likely to be?
2. On what evidence or experience do you base your conclusion?
3. Do you consider the growth of spiritualistic practice a menace or otherwise to mind and body?

Earl Russell Denounces 'Spiritual Drug-Taking', *Daily News*, 12 December 1928.

I can say at once that I do not consider the claims of the spiritualists are either proved or disproved or are likely to be proved or disproved, in the sense that it will be impossible for anyone to maintain the contrary opinion.

For many centuries it was universally believed that the earth was flat instead of globular, but it would be difficult for anyone nowadays to maintain that opinion outside the walls of an asylum. The flatness of the earth is capable of disproof by anyone who goes always in the same direction east or west and yet finds that he has returned to his starting point. No such simple test is available in the case of the alleged communication with the dead.

Many people, a few of them repute, and still fewer of scientific attainments, have borne testimony to the fact that they have communicated with the dead and have received messages from them, and the question is often put to unbelievers, Why does this evidence not convince you? To this question the answers are many and I will endeavour to give some of them.

First of all, what is it that is usually alleged to have taken place? Not that believers have actually seen the figure of the dead person and spoken to it face to face, but that they have received communication through the medium of some third person which they have believed to emanate from the spirit of the departed. Their foundation for this belief is generally the nature of the messages transmitted.

On my mind in weighing human testimony (a very fallible thing at the best) these messages would have exactly the opposite effect; for as a rule they are trivial to a degree and reflect the mind and personality of the medium employed.

As an instance, I recollect one long account of the other world, published by the Psychical Society, as of great evidential value, in which, among other things, it was stated that the happy spirits possessed private bathing pools.

As a scoffer I desired to know with what liquid these pools were filled, for the only one I had hitherto heard of in the other world was liquid fire and, as a lawyer, I was very anxious to know under what particular law of real property the tenure of these private bathing pools was created. When I am told that they sometimes contain matter that could not possibly be known to the medium I am still not convinced, for the loose habits of mind and the absence of any sense of essential value discount heavily such statements.

Nor can we overlook the conscious and deliberate fraud and trickery practiced by many mediums from Hood and Madame Blavatsky and Eusapia Palladino to the present day. Nor again can we overlook that whenever unprejudiced scientific men have investigated these phenomena the phenomena have either not occurred or have proved susceptible by a simple physical explanation. On this head there seems nothing to be added to Tyndall's article on 'Science and the Spirits', written 60 years ago.

It must also be remembered that Mr Maskelyne asserted, and frequently proved, that he could produce by trickery all the manifestations which the mediums claim to produce by spirits. If a modern alchemist claimed that he had transmuted copper into gold I should hesitate to believe him and I should still hesitate even if he professed to perform the transmutation before my eyes. Yet modern chemists have definitely seen the transmutation of one element into another; but this is by experiments fully described, which anyone under the necessary conditions can reproduce, and having a solid base of intelligible theory.

To me, however, stronger reasons than any of these are afforded by the attitude of the scientific mind. No scientific man could in the past assert positively that the atom was the final subdivision of matter, nor would he now assert that the electron was; but he accustoms himself to an ordered universe in which certain things have a high degree of probability and certain theories not guaranteed to be final explain all the observable facts.

From that habit of mind, from chemistry, biology, and biochemistry, I am driven to the same conclusion as Sir Arthur Keith, that there can be no separate entity which can be called the soul or spirit of man, but only certain manifestations of complex chemical and electrical phenomena in the living body. From this it obviously follows that there cannot be any disembodied spirits to communicate with mortals. One cannot assert dogmatically that there are not, but one may be convinced that the probability of such spirits is even less than the probability of the sun not rising tomorrow.

At the time when the religion of the Churches was a live and definite thing, as well as being official, traffic with the spirits was discouraged and was generally regarded as a subtle device of the Evil One. With the diminution of the hold of organised religion upon the minds of the people, the growth of spiritualism has been very great, particularly in America, with its more neurotic temperament and its more complete break up of anything like an established religion.

In this country, no doubt, the Great War gave a certain stimulus to the practice owing to the very human and natural desire of the bereaved still to feel in touch with those whom they had lost. We have a current example in the lecture of Mrs Hinchliffe, who believes that she has received from her husband an account of his loss in the Atlantic.

This belief is a comfort to her, as similar beliefs are a comfort to many other people, but it is a form of spiritual drug-taking and the effect is no more wholesome than repeated doses of bromide for a case of sleeplessness.

The trouble with anodynes is that though they may be soothing for a time they ultimately have a debilitating effect and I cannot doubt that all this spiritual drug-taking diminishes the ability of those who practice it to cope with the realities or to maintain a healthy mind and a sane outlook on life. In extreme cases it may of course lead to actual insanity.

Incidentally, of course, it also gives the opportunity to a host of charlatans to flourish and to fraudulent people to impose upon the weak-minded for their own ends. No doubt in some cases it may lead to actual blackmail.

For all these reasons, I think that the growth of spiritualistic practices is a misfortune to the community and a peril to the mental health of the weak-minded. Let people, if they will, retain their belief in an immortal soul, and even in a reunion beyond the grave, but let them retain that belief subject to the old religious reverence and to the religious condition that death alone can open means of communication with another world, if such there be.

Notes

1. 'What Mr Bottomley Says', *John Bull*, 5 Mar 1921, p. 5.
2. *see* Obituary, *The Times* (Appendix I).
3. Robert Smillie (1857-1940) President of the Triple Alliance of Miners, Railwaymen and Transport Workers Unions and commissioner on the 1919 Coal Industry Commission.
4. RA1, Box 6.27, 46946.
5. Canon John Wakeford, Archdeacon of Stow was tried on 4 February 1921 and found guilty of immoral conduct, removed from his post but not from holy orders. His appeal was dismissed on 26 April and extensively reported in *Times*, 27 Apr 1921, p.7-8.
6. See HL Debate 28 Apr 1921 (*Hansard* 45, cols. 77-102).
7. Ruth Anderson, a possible paramour of Frank's.
8. National Council of Public Morals Venereal Disease Committee, *Prevention of Venereal Disease* (London: Williams & Norgate, 1921). Henry Russell Wakefield (1854-1933) was a good friend of Frank's from the Reform Club.
9. For more on this see Derham, 'Bible Studies: Frank Russell and the "Book of Books"', *Russell* 40, vol.1 (summer 2020): 43-51.
10. A Broadway comedy (1919) which came to London in 1921.
11. Charles Garvice (1850-1920), prolific romance writer.
12. *Hansard* 181, col. 367. Henry James (1828-1911), former attorney general, had represented Frank in his second divorce hearing, 1895.
13. Education Act 1902 (2 Edw. 7 c. 42).
14. Published by the Society for Promoting Christian Knowledge, 1921.
15. *Merchant of Venice*, act 3, sc.2, l.73.
16. On 5 May 1922, 30-year-old Ronald True was found guilty of wilfully murdering 25-year-old prostitute Gertrude Yates. True had pleaded not guilty on the ground of morphia-induced insanity. Despite the Appeal Court upholding the verdict, it was controversially overturned by Home Secretary Edward Shortt in June and True's sentence commuted to confinement in Broadmoor Criminal Lunatic Asylum (*Westminster Gazette*, 6 May, 10 & 14 Jun 1922).
17. Mrs Rutherford successfully sued her husband, Col. Cecil Rutherford, then in Broadmoor for the murder of Major Miles Seton, for divorce. Her decree *nisi* was reduced to a judicial separation after his alleged mistress appealed, leaving Mrs Rutherford 'bound to a madman' for life (*Pall Mall Gazette*, 13 Feb 1922).
18. *Gaul* v. *Spencer & others*. The action by Lilian Jane Gaul against the governors of St Andrew's Hospital for Mental Diseases was tried in June 1922 and failed. Her appeal was dismissed the day before Frank's speech (*Yorkshire Post*, 22 & 29 Jun 1922; *Pall Mall Gazette*, 20 Nov 1922).
19. *Hamlet*, act 3, sc.1. l.58-87.
20. 'Thwarted Lover's Terrible Crime of Revenge', *Reynolds's Newspaper*, 12 Nov 1922, p.9.
21. Albert Ballin (1857-1918) actually committed suicide on 9 Nov 1918.
22. James Whitaker Wright (1846-1904) committed suicide in the Royal Courts of Justice after being sentenced to seven years' imprisonment for fraud on 26 Jan 1904.
23. 'Murders in a Mansion', *Westminster Gazette*, 14 Sep 1922, p.1.
24. Mrs Maud Hibbert's sentence of nine months' hard labour provoked a petition for her release with many distinguished signatories, including Bertie ('Has Suffered Enough', *Daily Herald*, 1 Nov 1922, p.5).
25. 'Suicide Pact on Railway', *Daily Herald*, 6 Jul 1922, p.5.
26. Wilhelm Nero Pilate Barbellion (pseud. of Bruce Frederick Cummings), *The Journal*

of a Disappointed Man (London: Chatto & Windus, 1919).

27. Christian Johann Heinrich Heine (1797-1856).

28. Hall, p.195.

29. Correspondence between Frank and Marie Stopes, Aug 1921 – Jan 1922, Add MS 58556.

30. Marie Carmichael Stopes, *The First Five Thousand* (London: John Bale, 1925).

31. *Hansard* 63, cols. 996-1057.

Earl Russell
April - 1902.

8. Frank sketched by Eyre Crowe, 1902.

Appendix I

Obituary

The Times, 5 March 1931

Earl Russell: Under-Secretary for India

Earl Russell, who sudden death at Marseilles at the age of 65 is recorded on another page, was a man of real ability, whose bent was chiefly scientific, though his family traditions were all political. He was a practical engineer and a pioneer in motoring, and for nine years was a useful member of the London County Council.

Through his association with the Fabian Society Lord Russell had been a member of the Labour Party for many years, but he was not included in the first Labour Government. He was, however, included in Mr MacDonald's second administration on its formation after the last General Election in the summer of 1929 as Parliamentary Secretary to the Ministry of Transport, and helped in the preliminary arrangements for the passing of the Traffic Act. He was a most useful recruit to the scanty representation on the Government Front Bench, for he had a skill and adroitness in debate which few of his colleagues could approach. Indeed the late Lord Birkenhead, who paraded rather than concealed his contemptuous opinion of the abilities of some of its occupants, held him to be one of the first four debaters in the Lords. The Government turned to him constantly for the exposition or defence of the policy of such Departments as were not directly represented on the Front Bench, and with his genial humour he was wont to call himself the 'maid of all work' for the Cabinet.

Late in 1929 a studious country clergyman made the disconcerting discovery that the number of Under-Secretaries in the House of Commons exceeded by one the statutory limit. An Act of Indemnity was required, and the balance was redressed by transferring Dr Drummond Shiels to the Colonial Office and appointing Lord Russell to the Indian Under-Secretaryship. In this office his easy-going casualness gave him a bad start. At a Labour smoking at home at Cambridge he made some impromptu generalities on India, which, telegraphed in garbled form to that country, evoked angry comment from Nationalist newspapers. Here was a new Under-Secretary, they wrote, disparaging the Viceroy's famous declaration of some two months earlier by asserting that 'dominion status is not possible for a long time'. Lord Russell explained that this was a wholly unwarranted interpretation of his general statement. The evolution of democratic institutions had taken a long time in England, and even now was not perfect. The Under-Secretary, however, learned his lesson, and, much as he disliked being tied to the written word, he thereafter prepared his utterances on any question affecting his own Department with much care, though they were still characterised by a healthy outspokenness. While he was incapable by temperament of the sentimentalism prevalent in the Government, and not least in his own Department, he was in thorough accord with the policy of Indian political advance, and Indians soon came to recognise him as a real friend; nor did they object to the touch of cynicism which clothed his humour. In Departmental work he was quick and decisive, and his judgement was usually sound. His reputation was advanced at the Round-Table Conference, where he was a member of the Government delegation. He presided over two of the nine subcommittees – those on Burma and Sind – and the reports he drafted are models of concise and unambiguous statement. His easy friendliness, accessibility, and humour helped to create the cordial atmosphere which prevailed during the Conference.

John Francis Stanley Russell was born on August 12, 1865, the elder son of Viscount Amberley, MP, by his marriage to Katherine Louisa, daughter of the second Lord Stanley of Alderley, and grandson of the eminent Victorian statesman, Lord John Russell, who was created Earl Russell in 1861.

'I am a Stanley in appearance (he wrote in his reminiscences) and largely in temperament, although I have inherited from the Russells bad eyes, some sense of art, a certain capacity for speech and writing coupled with a certain inherent ineffectiveness and hesitation which prevent my being good at games, taking any interest in competition, and blustering my way through life with the superb assurance and self-satisfaction of the true Stanley.'

He had a strange upbringing, for when he was a child his parents turned from deep piety to agnosticism. They both died comparatively young, and at the age of 11 Frank Russell went to live with his grandparents at Pembroke lodge, and he was brought with more zeal than judgment under strong religious influences. He disliked the tutors provided for him and ran away, with the result that he was sent to Mr Tabor's famous preparatory school at Cheam. His grandfather died in 1878, and he became Earl Russell at the age of 12. Pembroke lodge was continued to his grandmother, Lady Russell, by Queen Victoria, and there he saw many distinguished people. Under the eye of his uncle, Mr Rollo Russell, he began those studies in electricity which afterwards bore much fruit. In 1879, when 14, he went to Winchester, to Mr Frederick Morshead's house. There he considered that the greatest individual influence of his life was his friendship with Lionel Johnson, but to his great sorrow his guardians took him away from Winchester in 1883, though he was already a house prefect. He went up afterwards to Balliol, where Evelyn Abbott was his tutor, and he made many friends. But his Oxford career was cut short by an accusation about a letter for which Jowett sent him down for a year. Russell's demands to be shown the letter, to be informed what was in it, and to have an inquiry with evidence, were all refused, and thereupon he took his name off the books. Afterwards, there was a reconciliation, and Jowett admitted he had made a mistake.

Yachting and travel occupied his time till his marriage in 1890 to Mabel Edith, daughter of Sir Claude Scott, fourth baronet. There is no need to recall the story of this unhappy union, which led to more than one trial. Russell, who was a member of the Institute of Electrical Engineers, had been conducting the electrical business of Swinburne and co. at Teddington, and an electrical contracting business at Westminster, and was an active member of the National Liberal Club when he was elected to the LCC for West Newington as a Progressive. He had already had some experience of local administration in the country, and he found the work of the various council committees absorbing. He was later elected an alderman, serving altogether for nine years. In 1899, having obtained an American divorce, he was married at Reno, in Nevada, to Marion, daughter of Mr George Cooke. They returned to England in 1900, and Russell's first wife obtained a decree *nisi*. In the spring of 1901, when he had been back a year, Russell, to his great surprise, was arrested for bigamy, and, the indictment being for felony he was tried by his peers. The late Lord Halsbury, then Lord chancellor, presided. On the advice of his Counsel Russell pleaded 'Guilty', but explained that he thought he had acquired a proper domicile in Nevada. He was sentenced to three months' imprisonment in the first division. In 1911 he received a free pardon under the Great Seal. While he was in Holloway his first wife's decree *nisi* was made absolute. She died in 1908.

Russell was called to the Bar by Gray's Inn in 1905 and practiced for about five years on the South-Eastern Circuit. He was one of the earliest motorists and members of the RAC, and helped in the development of the Motor Volunteers. He also went into the City and was concerned in various companies, some of which involved him in serious losses. In 1916, his second wife having obtained a divorce, he married Mary Annette, daughter of Mr H. Herron Beauchamp, and widow of Count Von Arnim. The Countess Russell is famous as the author of *Elizabeth and her German Garden*, and other delightful novels.

Lord Russell leaves no children. He is succeeded by his brother, the Hon. Bertrand Russell FRS, the distinguished mathematician, who is also a member of the Labour Party, and is known for his advanced views on social questions.

Appendix II

A Bibliography of
Frank Russell

This bibliography was first published in *Russell: the Journal of Bertrand Russell Studies* 41 (summer 2021): 62-76; now with eleven new entries marked*.

A. Books

Lay Sermons. London: Thomas Burleigh, 1901. Pp. vii, 244.

Reviews:

'Lay Sermons. By Earl Russell'. *The Times Literary Supplement*, no. 43 (7 Nov. 1902): 336.

'Minor Books'. *The Scotsman*, 7 Nov 1902, p. 7.

'Earl Russell's Sermons'. *The Daily News*, London, 28 Nov. 1902, p. 10.

Divorce. London: William Heinemann, 1912. Pp. iv, 218.

Reviews:

'Divorce. By Earl Russell'. *The Manchester Guardian*, 13 June 1912, p. 7.

'Some Books about Divorce'. *Sheffield Daily Telegraph*, 11 July 1912, p. 3.

'*Divorce*. By Earl Russell'. *The Academy and Literature* 83, no. 2,097 (13 July 1912): 45-6.

'Earl Russell on Divorce'. *Dublin Daily Express*, 25 Jul 1912, p. 7.

Some Winchester Letters of Lionel Johnson. London: George Allen & Unwin Ltd., 1919. Pp. 211. Published anonymously.

Reviews:

Harold Hannyngton Child. 'The Spiritual Progress of a Schoolboy'. *TLS*, no. 925 (9 Oct. 1919): 544.

'Lionel Johnson'. *The Yorkshire Post*, 26 Nov. 1919, p. 4.

'Some Winchester Letters'. *The Spectator*, 10 Jan. 1920, pp. 19–20.

My Life and Adventures. London: Cassell & Co. Ltd, 1923. Pp. xii, 360; 12 plates.[1]

Reviews:

E. E. Mavrogordato. 'A Conscientious Rebel'. *TLS*, no. 1,102 (1 Mar. 1923): 134.

'Piquant Memoirs: Autobiography of Earl Russell'. *Aberdeen Press and Journal,* 1 Mar. 1923, p. 5.

'Earl Russell's Term in Prison: Revelations in Book Issued Today. Racy Stories'. *Western Morning News,* 1 Mar. 1923, p. 4.

'Peer's Many Sides. Earl Russell's Story of Grandmother's Ears. Humour and Satire'. *Evening Telegraph,* 2 Mar. 1923, p. 10.

Desmond McCarthy. 'Books in General'. *The New Statesman* 20, no. 516 (3 Mar. 1923): 632.

'Earl Russell (By Himself)'. *Hull Daily Mail,* 20 Mar. 1923, p. 6.

Keble Howard. 'The Adventures of Earl Russell'. *The Sketch* 121, no. 1,573 (21 Mar. 1923): 576, 578.

'The Story of a Stormy Life'. *The Manchester Guardian,* 22 Mar. 1923, p. 7.

'An Earl's Adventures'. *The Cologne Post: Daily Newspaper Published by the Army of the Rhine,* no. 1,217 (24 Mar. 1923), p. 2.

Upton Sinclair. 'My Friends Write Books'. *Haldeman-Julius Journal,* Girard. ks, no. 1,431 (5 May 1923): 2.

B. Articles, Columns, Letters to the Editor

B1. Articles

'Electricity in Country Houses' (with B. H. Thwaite). *The National Review* 20, no. 120 (Feb. 1893): 764–6.

'The Legislative Problem: Memorandum Prepared by Lord Russell, Captain H. H. Deasy, and Mr. Robert Todd'. *Automobile Club Journal* 5, no. 55 (14 May 1903): 517–18.

'Preparing for the New Act: the Campaign'. *Automobile Club Journal* 6, no. 72 (10 Sept. 1903): 275–6.

'An Analysis of the New Act'. *The Autocar* 11, no. 412 (12 Sept. 1903): 338–40.

'Motor Volunteers at the Manoeuvres: with the Motor Volunteer Corps'. *Automobile Club Journal* 6, no. 74 (24 Sept. 1903): 314–16.

'Local Authorities and the Motor Car Act' [extract from a letter to a Rural District Council]. *Automobile Club Journal* 6, no. 79 (29 Oct. 1903): 427.

'Radiating Thoroughfares'. *Automobile Club Journal* 6, no. 88 (31 Dec. 1903): 728–30.

'Legal Aspects of the Motor Car Act'. *Automobile Club Journal* 7, no. 92 (28 Jan. 1904): 84–7.

'A Collision with a Military Car' (uncredited). *Automobile Club Journal* 7, no. 101 (31 Mar. 1904): 369.

'Royal Commission on London Traffic', summary of evidence given by Earl Russell. *Automobile Club Journal* 7, no. 102 (7 Apr. 1904): 384.

'The Monaco Meeting'. *Automobile Club Journal* 7, no. 105 (28 Apr. 1904): 459.

'Inconsiderate Driving: the Courtesies of the Road'. *Automobile Club Journal* 7, no. 112 (16 June 1904): 636.

'A Tour of Cornwall'. *Automobile Club Journal* 8, no. 123 (1 Sept. 1904): 174.

'Motor Notes'. *The Graphic*, 13 June 1908. Weekly column, continued until 26 Dec. 1908.

'Lord Russell Protests'. *The Syndicalist* 1, no. 3 (Mar.–Apr. 1912): 3.

'When Should Marriage Be Dissolved?'. *The English Review* 12 (Aug.–Nov. 1912): 133–41.[2]

'The Bible on the Film'. *The Nation & The Athenaeum*, no. 4,746 (16 Apr 1921): 106.

*'Modern Freedom *v.* Past Prudery', *Weekly Dispatch*, 15 May 1921, p. 6.

*'Manners of Our Younger Men', *Weekly Dispatch*, 7 Aug 1921, p. 6.

'The Difficulties of Bishops'. *The R.P.A. Annual* (1922): 25–31.[3]

*'The Tragic Martyrs of Marriage', *Sunday Illustrated*, 21 May 1922, p. 9.

'The Torments of Gaol'. *John Bull*, 27 May 1922. Advertised in *Birmingham Daily Gazette*, 24 May 1922, p. 6.

*'The Boy Murderers'. *John Bull*, 17 June 1922, p. 15.

*'Smoothing the Sinner's Path'. *John Bull*, 8 July 1922, p. 14.

*'"Old Beans" and Young Minxes'. *John Bull*, 12 July 1924, p. 19.

*'Birth Control Explained'. *John Bull*, 8 Nov. 1924, p. 21.

*'The Torture of Jail'. *John Bull*, 4 July 1925, p. 15.

*'Justice for the Poverty Court'. *John Bull*, 12 Dec 1925, p. 19.

'Why Not Birth Control?'. *John Bull*, 29 Jan 1927, p. 15.

'The Charabanc Peril'. *Daily Sketch*, 20 Sept. 1927, p. 7.

'Wireless Notes'. *The New Statesman* 31, no. 803 (15 Sept. 1928): 708, 710.

'Wireless Notes: the Radio Exhibition'. *The New Statesman* 32, no. 808 (20 Oct. 1928): 62, 64.

'Thermionic Valves'. *The New Statesman* 32, no. 817 (22 Dec. 1928): 366, 368.

'Spiritualism on Trial'. *Daily News*, 12 Dec. 1928. Advertised in *Nottingham Evening Post*, 10 Dec. 1928, p. 3.

B2. Letters to the Editor

'East London'. *The Leaflet*, n.s. no. 10 (March 1885): 121.

'Earl Russell and "Varsity Socialism"'. *St. Stephen's Review* 11, no. 475 (16 Apr. 1892): 6.

Letter to the Hon. Secretaries of the Royal Dublin Society. *Dublin Daily Express*, 12 June 1893, p. 4.

Letter to the Executive Committee of the Automobile Club concerning the

Motorcars Bill. *Automobile Club Journal* 4, no. 34 (18 Dec. 1902): 400.

*'The Duval Collapse', *Pall Mall Gazette*, 12 Jan. 1894, p. 5.

'Motor Cars in Hyde Park'. *Automobile Club Journal* 5, no. 38 (15 Jan. 1903): 58.

'Identification'. *Automobile Club Journal* 5, no. 47 (19 Mar. 1903): 293–4.

Memoranda to Legislative Committee of the Automobile Club concerning registration of motorcars prepared by Earl Russell, H. H. Deasy and Mr. Robert Todd, *Automobile Club Journal* 5, no. 56 (14 May 1903): 517–18.

'Identification'. *Automobile Club Journal* 5, no. 56 (21 May 1903): 545.

'The "Daily Express", Mr. Pearson, and The Club'. *Automobile Club Journal* 5, no. 59 (11 June 1903): 628.

'Attacks on Automobilists'. *Automobile Club Journal* 6, no. 81 (12 Nov. 1903): 491.

'The Road-Repairing Season'. *Automobile Club Journal* 6, no. 84 (3 Dec. 1903): 562. Follow-up letter on 24 Dec. 1903, p. 713.

'Heating of Long-Distance Trains'. *Evening Standard*, London, 16 Dec. 1903, p. 4.

'Hotels–and a Grumble'. *Automobile Club Journal* 7, no. 91 (21 Jan. 1904): 60.

'The Club and the Exhibition Question'. *Automobile Club Journal* 7, no. 93 (4 Feb. 1904): 118.

'The Inland Revenue to Earl Russell' and Earl Russell's reply, *Automobile Club Journal* 7, no. 94 (11 Feb. 1904): 146.

'The Exhibition Question'. *Automobile Club Journal* 7, no. 95 (18 Feb. 1904): 177.

'Newhaven to Dieppe'. *Evening Standard*, London, 20 May 1904, p. 7.

'A Point of Police Procedure in Offences under the Motor Car Act', Earl Russell to the Commissioner of Police, Scotland Yard. *Automobile Club Journal* 8, no. 115 (7 July 1904): 10.

'Lord Russell and the Pharos Club: Reply to Mr. Bart Kennedy'. *Daily News*, London, 10 Aug. 1904, p. 9.

'The Case for the Motorist', to the Editor of *The Times*. *Automobile Club Journal* 8, no. 127 (29 Sept. 1904): 246.

'The Size of Maps'. *Automobile Club Journal* 8, no. 131 (6 Oct. 1904): 265. Follow-up on 27 Oct. 1904, p. 319.

'Attacks on the Automobile Club', letter to the editor of *Morning Post* (refused). *Automobile Club Journal* 8, no. 131 (27 Oct. 1904): 309–10.

'Mutual Insurance Associations v. Propriety Insurance Companies', response by Earl Russell. *Automobile Club Journal* 9, no. 153 (30 Mar. 1905): 283.

[on Motors and Motoring]. *Truth*, 13 Nov. 1907, 'Special Motor Supplement', p. 8.

'The Suffragettes: Earl Russell's Support of By-Election Policy'. *Daily News*, London, 3 Apr. 1908, p. 4.

[On Bertrand Russell's 'Mr. Asquith's Pronouncement']. *Women's Franchise* 1 (28 May 1908): 587 (Bertrand being on o. 579).

'What the Militants have done: Earl Russell's Defence of a Principle'. *Daily News*, London, 8 Mar. 1912, p. 6.

'Lord Russell & "Fastidious Taxi Drivers"'. *Daily News*, London, 8 Jan. 1916, p. 3.

'A National Dishonour'. *The New Statesman* 6, no. 146 (22 Jan. 1916): 373. Reprinted in E.S.P. Haynes, *The Decline of Liberty* (London: Grant Richards, 1916), p. 25.

'Norman v. Brooke'. *The Times*, 10 Aug. 1917, p. 16.

'Excess Profits Duty'. *The Times*, 14 Dec. 1918, p. 14.

'The Tube–a Complaint'. *The Times*, 10 Nov. 1919, p. 38.

'Dr Stopes' Idea: the Battle of the First Clinic'. *Daily Herald*, 7 May 1923, p. 5.

'Séance Room Phenomena. Conan Doyle and Earl Russell. Inscribed Watch Mystery'. *Daily News*, London, 23 Jan. 1926, p. 4.

B3. Interviews

'Earl Russell's Book on Divorce: a Plea for Common Sense'. *The Observer*, 25 Feb. 1912, p. 11. Interview after completing 'the correcting of the last proof sheets'.

'Lord Russell's Release. Prison Experiences. The Life of a 'First-Classer'. Interview at His Chambers'. *Daily News*, London, 18 Oct. 1901, p. 5.

C. Speeches

C1. Major Speeches and Other Contributions in the House of Lords

'Lunacy Bill'. Proposed removal of clauses affecting regulation of asylums and adjustment of liabilities between local authorities and guardians. *Hansard* 51 (15 July 1897): cols. 135–43.

'Metropolitan Railway Bill'. Proposed amendments at third reading. *Hansard* 62 (19 July 1898): cols. 238–46.

'Trial of Earl Russell'. Brief summary and order that proceedings be printed. *Hansard* 97 (18 Jul 1901): col. 773. For the proceedings, see under D. Parliamentary Archives.

'Divorce Bill'. Second reading of Divorce Bill introduced by Earl Russell. *Hansard* 107 (1 May 1902): cols. 389–409.

'Divorce Bill'. Second reading of Divorce Bill introduced by Earl Russell. *Hansard* 124 (23 June 1903): cols. 202–13.

'Motor-Cars Bill'. Earl Russell proposed minor amendments. *Hansard* 126 (24 July 1903): cols. 212–22.

'Matrimonial Causes Bill'. Second reading of Divorce Bill introduced by Earl Russell. *Hansard* 150 (1 Aug. 1905): cols. 1,064–71.

'Metropolitan Police Commission Bill'. Move to resolve 'That in the opinion of this House the proposed inquiry is of too limited a character to serve any useful purpose'. *Hansard* 159 (19 June 1906): cols. 7–16.

'Education (England and Wales) Bill'. Response to right rev. Prelate that the proposed removal of clause 7 from this bill was intended to surreptitiously make religious instruction compulsory. *Hansard* 164 (8 Nov. 1906): cols. 655–719.

'Trade Disputes Bill'. Earl Russell proposed an amendment to clause 2. *Hansard* 167 (12 Dec. 1906): cols. 276–93. Earl Russell proposed an amendment to clause 2 to limit the number of strikers engaged in a picket to twenty.

'Divorce in Ireland'. Earl Russell rose to call attention to Private Bills for divorce in Ireland: and to move that a Return be made to this House of all Private Bills presented during the last five years for effecting divorces. *Hansard* 178 (16 July 1907): cols. 490–4.

'Matrimonial Causes Bill'. Second reading of Divorce Bill introduced by Earl Russell. *Hansard* 193 (22 July 1908): cols. 4–13.

'Prevention of Crimes Bill'. Move to insert a new subsection to clause 11, providing that persons undergoing preventive detention should 'enjoy the ameliorating and humanising influences of conversation with fellow-prisoners, reading and writing, visits from approved friends, and windows permitting a view of the sky'. *Hansard* 198 (15 Dec. 1908): cols. 1,529–40.

'Development and Road Improvement Funds Bill'. Speech in defence of motorists. *Hansard* 3 (14 Oct. 1909): cols. 1,225–83.

'The Income Tax'. Earl Russell questioned the rate of income tax for persons on low income and their opportunity for relief. *Hansard* 5 (14 July 1910): cols. 1,073–8.

'The House of Lords Reconstitution Bill'. Earl Russell questioned whether this was not an attempt to distract attention from the Parliament Bill. *Hansard* 8 (17 May 1911): cols. 489–574.

'Shooting Escaping Convicts'. Move to resolve 'That in the opinion of this House the infliction of the penalty of death or wounding upon convicts who are seeking to escape should no longer be authorised by law'. *Hansard* 12 (25 June 1912): cols. 190–4.

'Income Tax on Married Women's Property'. Earl Russell rose to call attention to the imprisonment of Mr. Mark Wilks at the instance of the Treasury for non-payment of his wife's Income Tax, and to move to resolve– That in the opinion of this House the present state of the law which renders a man liable to indefinite terms of imprisonment for matters over which he is by Statute deprived of any control is undesirable, and should be amended." *Hansard* 12 (14 Oct. 1912): cols. 823–34.

'Criminal Law Amendment Bill'. Debate concerning corporal punishment of convicted traffickers. *Hansard* 12 (28 Nov 1912): cols. 1,181–222.

'Criminal Law Amendment Bill'. Move to leave out clause 2. *Hansard* 13 (9 Dec. 1912): cols. 106–36.

'Immunity of Trade Unions'. HL debate on whether the concessions of the 1906 Act were going to continue to be supported by the House. *Hansard* 13 (22 Jan. 1913): cols. 410–12.

'Poor Law Amendment Bill'. A Bill to amend the Administration of the Poor

Law as to married women was presented by the Earl Russell; read 1ª, and to be printed (No. 108). *Hansard* 14 (9 July 1913): col. 802.

'Voluntary Mental Treatment Bill'. Earl Russell rose to call attention to difficulties in early treatment of mental cases, and to present a Bill. Bill read 1ª, and to be printed (No. 187). *Hansard* 17 (22 July 1914): cols. 89–92.

'Streatley and Goring Bridge Bill'. Move to resolve 'That in the opinion of this House new means of communication should be in the hands of local authorities and available for the free use of the public, and that it is undesirable to proceed with a Bill giving fresh powers for the levying of tolls by a private corporation'. *Hansard* 18 (4 May 1915): cols. 887–92.

'Military Prosecutions of Journalists'. Earl Russell rose to ask His Majesty's Government in what circumstances a reporter was prosecuted for sending a report to a newspaper editor, by whom the report was published, what damage was done to the interests of this country thereby, and what steps it is suggested that a reporter ought to take before communicating with his newspaper. *Hansard* 18 (4 May 1915): cols. 906–10.

'Military Service (No. 2) Bill'. Earl Russell spoke in opposition to conscription. *Hansard* 20 (25 Jan. 1916): cols. 1,014–16.

'Treatment of Conscientious Objectors'. Earl Russell spoke on the 'cavalier attitude' of tribunals. *Hansard* 21 (4 May 1916): cols. 919–24. In this second reading of the Military Service (No. 2).

'Military Service Bill'. Second reading. *Hansard* 21 (18 May 1916): cols. 1,114–16. Earl Russell questioned the methods of dealing with conscientious objectors.

'Military Service–Conscientious Objectors'. Earl Russell moved to resolve 'That in the opinion of this House it is undesirable to subject military prisoners to punishments not authorised by law'. *Hansard* 22 (4 July 1916): cols. 521–46.

'Conscientious Objectors'. Earl Russell had the question on the paper as to whether military conscientious objectors sentenced prior to Army Order X of 25 May 1916 will go into civil custody; and what had been the result of the second court-martial on C. H. Norman. *Hansard* 22 (18 July 1916): cols. 763–5.

'Internment of British Subjects'. Earl Russell rose to call attention to the Defence of the Realm Regulations under which British subjects are imprisoned without accusation or trial. *Hansard* 26 (24 July 1917): cols. 23–32.

'Maintenance of Public Order'. Notice on the Paper–Earl Russell called attention to the rioting in Hackney, and to ask what steps His Majesty's Government propose to take to maintain order in London. *Hansard* 26 (23 Oct. 1917): cols. 736–9.

'The Taxi-Cab Dispute'. Earl Russell rose to ask whether His Majesty's Government would make a statement on the questions at issue in the present taxi-cab dispute, and indicate their policy with regard to the admission of women to the ranks of licensed cab drivers. *Hansard* 26 (23 Oct. 1917): cols. 739–42.

'Conscientious Objectors'. Earl Russell continued to assert that absolutists should be treated in a manner that does not make them martyrs. *Hansard* 26 (11 Nov 1917): cols. 965–1,014.

'Coal Mines Control Agreement (Confirmation) Bill'. Earl Russell opined that the Bill missed an opportunity for 'a dramatic experiment in State Socialism'. *Hansard* 27 (13 Dec 1917): cols. 131–49.

'Representation of the People Bill'. Earl Russell spoke in favour of women's suffrage. *Hansard* 27 (17 Dec 1917): cols. 214–21.

'Military Service Bill'. Earl Russell questioned the need to extend military service to those under the age of 51, calling it 'a piece of panic legislation'. *Hansard* 29 (17 April 1918): cols. 705-62.

'Industrial Unrest'. Earl Russell opened the second day of debate with a long, eloquent speech in favour of a socialist policy. *Hansard* 33 (25 Feb. 1919): cols. 283–97.

'New Capital Issues'. Earl Russell rose to call attention to the new Regulation on Capital Issues, and to ask His Majesty's Government–1. Whether the present Regulation has been withdrawn. 2. Whether, in the promised modification of this Regulation, care will be taken to limit it to the purpose for which it is really required, and to avoid unnecessary and harassing interference with business. *Hansard* 33 (13 Mar. 1919): cols. 692–702.

'Martial Law in India'. Earl Russell rose to call attention to the sentences under Martial Law in India with special reference to the case of Harkissen Lal. *Hansard* 36 (6 Aug. 1919): cols. 490–504.

'Deportations to Ireland'. Earl Russell moved to resolve, That in the opinion of this House there is no justification for the retention by the Executive of any powers of arrest without trial. *Hansard* 54 (16 May 1923): cols. 199–227.

'Blasphemy Laws (Amendment) Bill'. Earl Russell moved for a second reading of this Bill. *Hansard* 54 (29 May 1923): cols. 253–66.

'Strength of Socialism'. Earl Russell responds to the question of modification of legislation concerning Trade Union political levies amid growing concerns over the rise of socialism. *Hansard* 54 (13 June 1923): cols. 475–525.

'The Government's Policy'. Earl Russell questioned the composition of the Parliamentary Labour Party. *Hansard* 56 (13 Feb 1924): cols. 121–54.

'Motor Vehicles Compulsory Insurance Bill'. Earl Russell introduced a Bill making third-party insurance compulsory. *Hansard* 62 (15 July 1925): 76–88.

'Motor Vehicles Compulsory Insurance Bill'. Earl Russell moved for second reading of his Bill to introduce compulsory third-party insurance. *Hansard* 64 (30 June 1926): cols. 686–711.

'Procedure of the House'. Earl Russell moved that interruptions were contrary to the Rules of Order of the House and a precedent of closure was being set in a heated response to accusations of obstruction by Labour peers during the debate on the Coal Mines Bill on 8 July 1926. *Hansard* 64 (14 July 1926): cols. 1,090–141.

'Lunacy and Mental Disorder'. Earl Russell rose to call attention to the Report of the Royal Commission on Lunacy and Mental Disorder, and to ask whether it is proposed to introduce legislation on the subject. *Hansard* 66 (24 Feb. 1927): cols. 232–57.

'House of Lords Reform'. Earl Russell expressed Labour's concerns that the proposed reform would put them in a permanent minority and that the

Government trod a dangerous path that will lead to revolution. *Hansard* 67 (23 Jun 1927): cols. 954–1,010.

'House of Lords Reform'. Earl Russell set out Labour's position on proposed Government reforms to the Parliament Act. *Hansard* 72 (13 Dec 1928): cols. 613–57.

'Select Vestries: Address in Reply to His Majesty's Most Gracious Speech'. Earl Russell was chosen against convention to reply to the King's Speech. *Hansard* 75 (2 July 1929): cols 9–50.

'Road Traffic Bill'. Earl Russell introduced the Bill and moved for second reading. *Hansard* 75 (5 July 1929): cols. 931–94.

'Mental Treatment Bill'. Earl Russell led the second reading of the Bill, which was committed to a committee of the whole House. *Hansard* 75 (28 Nov. 1929): cols. 724–67.

'Workmen's Compensation (Silicosis) Bill'. Earl Russell introduced the Bill and moved for second reading. *Hansard* 76 (3 Apr 1930): cols. 1,187–95.

'Unemployment Insurance (No. 3) Bill'. Earl Russell introduced the Bill and moved for second reading. *Hansard* 77 (15 Apr 1930): cols. 115–24.

'Coal Mines Bill'. Earl Russell led the second day of debate. *Hansard* 77 (30 Apr 1930): cols. 222–84.

C2. Reports of Speeches other than in the House of Lords and London County Council Meetings

Address to Brixton Liberals, 24 Apr. 1895. *South London Press*, 27 Apr. 1895, p. 1.

'What Is Morality?'. Newington Reform Club, 5 June 1895. *South London Press*, 8 June 1895, p. 7.

Address to Newington Liberals, 9 Oct. 1895. *South London Press*, 12 Oct. 1895, p. 5.

'Politics in Portugal'. Newington Reform Club, 24 Nov. 1895. *South London Press*, 23 Nov. 1895, p. 3.

'The Government's Water Bill'. Newington Liberal and Radical Association, 26 Mar. 1896. *South London Press*, 28 Mar. 1896.

'The Work of Darwin'. Newington Reform Club, 17 May 1896. *South London Press*, 17 May 1896.

Address to Newington Liberals, Trinity Ward, 31 Mar. 1897. *South London Press*, 3 Apr. 1897.

Address to West Newington Liberal and Radical Association, Annual Meeting, 24 May 1897. *South London Press*, 29 May 1897.

'Lord Russell on Prison Life'. Pharos Club, 26 Nov. 1901. *Morning Post*, 27 Nov. 1901, p. 2.

'Marriage and Divorce: Earl Russell as a Reformer'. Inaugural speech for Society for Promoting Reforms in the Marriage & Divorce Laws of England. Clifford's Inn, 15 Dec. 1902. *Daily News*, London, 16 Dec. 1902, p. 11.

'London Government'. Pharos Club, 10 Feb. 1903. *Daily News*, London, 10 Feb. 1903.

'Legal Aspects of the Motor Car Act'. Automobile Club, 21 Jan. 1904. *Automobile Club Journal* 6, no. 80 (5 Nov. 1903): 453.

'The Weight to be Attached to Medical Evidence', 1904. *Transactions of the Medico-Legal Society* 1 (1902-04): 94–103.

'The Scientific Regulation of Traffic'. Automobile Club, 21 Mar 1907. *The Observer*, 24 Mar 1907, p. 6.

Speaker at 'Great Demonstration in support of Women's Suffrage'. Men's League for Women's Suffrage, Queen's Hall, Langham Place, 17 Dec. 1907. *Women's Franchise* 1 (12 Dec. 1907): 280. Follow-up report, 26 Dec. 1907, pp. 302–3.

Address to Women's Freedom League, Memorial Hall, 1 Feb. 1908. *Women's Franchise* 1 (23 Jan. 1908): 346. Follow-up report, 6 Feb. 1908, p. 369.

Address to Women's Freedom League, Town Hall, Haverstock Hill, 19 Feb. 1908. *Women's Franchise* 1 (13 Feb. 1908): 378. Follow-up report, 27 Feb. 1908, p. 404.

Address to Women's Freedom League, Town Hall, High Wycombe, Bucks., 19 Mar. 1908. *Women's Franchise* 1 (12 Mar. 1908): 430. Follow-up report, 2 Apr. 1908, p. 465.

Debate: 'That the grant of the suffrage to women has been indefinitely postponed by the violent methods of some of its supporters' (opposer), Hardwicke Society, 20 Mar. 1908. *Women's Franchise* 1 (19 Mar. 1908): 437. Follow-up report, 26 Mar. 1908, p. 452.

Address to Women's Freedom League, Synod Hall, Edinburgh, 22 May 1908. *Women's Franchise* 1 (7 May 1908): 532. Follow-up report, 4 June 1908, p. 584.

Address to Women's Freedom League, Glasgow, 22 May 1908. *Women's Franchise* 1 (7 May 1908): 532. Follow-up report, 11 June 1908, p. 596.

Address to Women's Freedom League, Town Hall, Wandsworth, 19 Nov. 1908. *Women's Franchise* 2 (29 Oct. 1908): 198.

Address to Women's Freedom League and Men's League for Women's Suffrage, Cory Hall, Cardiff, 18 Jan. 1909. *Women's Franchise* 2 (18 Jan. 1909): 374. Follow-up report, 28 Jan. 1909, p. 374.

Address to Women's Freedom League, Caxton Hall, Westminster, 4 Mar. 1909. *Women's Franchise* 2 (18 Feb. 1909): 413.

Address to Women's Freedom League, Sydenham, 8 Mar. 1909. *Women's Franchise* 2 (18 Mar. 1909): 467. Follow-up report, 18 Mar. 1909, p. 467.

Address at King's Speech Meeting, Women's Freedom League, 13 Mar. 1909. *Women's Franchise* 2 (18 Feb. 1909): 414.

Address to Women's Freedom League, Earlsmead Council School, Tottenham, 23 Mar. 1909. *Women's Franchise* 2 (1 Mar. 1909): 452.

Address to Sussex Men's League, Town Hall, Hove, Sussex, 1 May 1909. *Women's Franchise* 2 (13 May 1909): 582–3.

Address to Women's Freedom League, Caxton Hall, Westminster, 10 June 1909. *Women's Franchise* 2 (10 June 1909): 628. Follow-up report, 17 June 1909, p. 639.

Address to Women Writers' Suffrage League, Richelieu Palace Hotel, Oxford St., 28 Mar. 1911. *The Vote* (25 Mar. 1911): 265.

Address to Men's League for Women's Suffrage in support of the Conciliation Bill, Town Hall, Chelsea, 2 Nov. 1911. *The Vote* (21 Oct. 1911): 315. Follow-up report, 16 Mar. 1911, p. 244.

'Toast [to John Hampden]'. John Hampden Dinner, Committee of the Women's Tax Resistance League, Hotel Cecil, 12 Dec. 1911. Programme.

Debate: 'That women are favoured by the law' (opposer). International Women's Franchise Club, 13 Dec. 1911. *Common Cause* 3 (19 Oct. 1911): 20.

'The Relationship Between Medicine and Law', 1912. *Transactions of the Medico-Legal Society* 10 (1912–13): 1-6.

Evidence given by Earl Russell, 19 Dec 1910. Royal Commission on Divorce and Matrimonial Causes. In *Minutes of Evidence Taken before the Royal Commission on Divorce and Matrimonial Causes*, Vol. 3. London: His Majesty's Stationary Office, 1912. Pp. 450–5.

Address to Men's League for Women's Suffrage, St. Peter's Hall, Bournemouth, Sussex, 14 Feb. 1913. *Common Cause* 4 (7 Mar. 1913): 826.

'Women's Suffrage'. Cambridge University Men's League for Women's Suffrage, Guildhall, Cambridge, 20 Feb. 1913. *Cambridge Independent Press* (21 Feb. 1913): 7.

Address to The Liberal Club, Petersfield, 28 Feb. 1913. *Portsmouth Evening News*, 1 Mar. 1913, p. 5.

'The attitude taken up in regard to the taxation of married women in the forthcoming Finance Bill'. Women's Tax Resistance League, Caxton Hall, Westminster, 28 Apr. 1913. *The Vote* (18 Apr. 1913): 423.

'The Business Aspect of Socialism'. C.E.Y.M.S. [Church of England Young Men's Society] Rooms, Cambridge University, 1 May 1913. *Cambridge Independent Press*, 2 May 1913, p. 11.

'Control of Industry'. Sheffield Fabian Society, Cutler's Hall, 3 Oct. 1913. "Earl Russell in Sheffield". *Sheffield Daily Telegraph*, 4 Oct. 1913, p. 6.

'The Minority Report of the Divorce Commission'. Fabian Society, Memorial Hall, 4 Nov. 1913. 'Divorce by Consent', *Yorkshire Telegraph and Star*, 15 Nov. 1913, p. 4.

'The Socialist Position'. Portsmouth Fabian Society, 23 Jan. 1914. 'Socialist Ideals: Earl Russell at Portsmouth'. *Portsmouth Evening News*, 24 Jan. 1914, p. 7.

'Some Morals of the War'. Fitzwilliam Street Social Union, Town Hall, Huddersfield, 22 Nov. 1916. 'Earl Russell on the War', *Leeds Mercury*, 23 Nov. 1916, p. 4; also as 'Earl Russell on the War: a Man's Right to Say What He Likes', *Manchester Guardian*, 23 Nov 1916, p. 6.

'Medicine and Law'. Annual Dinner of the Medico-Legal Society, Holborn Restaurant, 10 Dec 1920. *Transactions of the Medico-Legal Society* 15 (1921–22): 15–17.

'The Ethics of Suicide', 1922. *Transactions of the Medico-Legal Society* 17 (1922–23): 24–33.

'Crime and Character'. The Ethological Society, 90 Buckingham Palace Road, London, 8 May 1922. 'The Prison Taint. a Perfected Dehumanising System. Lord Russell's Suggestions for Reforms'. *Manchester Guardian*, 9 May 1922, p. 8.

Speech to Society of Constructive Birth Control in defence of Marie Stopes' publications, Essex Hall, Strand, London, 16 May 1923. *Daily Herald*, 17 May 1923, p. 2.

Speech to Labour Party in defence of Ramsay MacDonald's first government, Haywards Heath Council Schools, 23 Oct. 1924. *Mid Sussex Times*, 28 Oct. 1924, p. 3.

*'Conduct and Discipline', Soroptimist Club, Criterion Restaurant, London, 7 May 1925. 'Love By Numbers: Lord Russell Deprecates the Sergeant-Major Style', *Evening Standard*, 7 May 1925, p.8.

'National Finance'. The Sunday Lecture Society, Assembly Room, Fratton Hotel, Portsmouth, 18 Apr. 1926. *Portsmouth Evening News*, 19 Apr. 1926, p. 2.

Speech to Cambridge Labour Party on Indian Independence, 4 Jan. 1930. *The Observer*, 5 Jan. 1930, p. 19. See also 'Earl Russell on India: Misleading Summary What He Said at Cambridge; Dangers of Impatience'. *Manchester Guardian*, 9 Jan 1930, p. 4.

Cambridge Union Debate: 'That this House sees no reason for the continued existence of the Liberal Party'. Cambridge University, 21 Jan. 1930. *Yorkshire Post*, 22 Jan. 1930, p. 4.

Speech referring to India, Gandhi and civil disobedience at Annual Banquet of Southampton Chamber of Commerce, 2 May 1930. *Western Morning News*, 3 May 1930, p. 9; 'The Government And Mr. Gandhi: End Must Be Put to Passive Resistance; Speech by Earl Russell'. *Manchester Guardian*, 3 May 1930, p. 19; *The Hindu Illustrated Weekly*, 11 May 1930, p. 19.

D. Unpublished Letters, Diaries, Articles, etc.

D1. Libraries

The British Library. Stopes Papers, Correspondence between Marie Stopes and Frank Russell, Add MS 58556 (also includes correspondence with Bertrand).

Columbia University, New York, Rare Book & Manuscript Library. George Santayana Collection: Autobiography (Notebook IV) contains Santayana's notes for his chapter on Frank Russell in *Persons and Places*.

Huntington Library, California. Elizabeth Mary Russell, Countess Russell Papers: Journal [typescript] ER98–103 (1912–1918); Correspondence: 8 letters from Frank to Elizabeth Russell, ER1735-1742.

McMaster University, Ontario. Bertrand Russell Archives (RC0096), extensive correspondence prefix RA1–RA3; Frank Russell diaries, RA1 731.080042-4.

D2. The National Archives

Central Criminal Court: Depositions: Defendants: William Aylott, John Cockerton, Frederick Kast, Dame Maria Selina Elizabeth Scott (Lady Scott). Charge: Libel. Session: Nov 1896, CRIM 1/46/4,

Central Criminal Court: Depositions: Defendant: Russell, JFS, Earl. Charge: Bigamy, Session: Jun 1901, CRIM 1/67/4.

Home Office files: Criminal: Maria Selina Elizabeth Scott convicted at Central Criminal Court for Libel, 16 Nov 1896, HO 144/270/A58558.

Home Office files: Criminal: Earl Russell. Offence: Bigamy. Sentence: 3 Months–Granted Free Pardon in 1911, HO 144/951/A62795.

Lord Chancellor's Office: Registered files: House of Lords: Trial of Earl Russell for Bigamy, LCO 2/173.

Office of Works & Successors: Registered files: House of Lords: Royal Gallery: Preparation for Trial of Earl Russell, WORK 11/96.

D3. Parliamentary Archives

House of Lords Appeal Cases and Writs of Error [1897], HL/PO/JU/4/3/467.

House of Lords Journals [1895], HL/PO/JO2/127.

Record of the Trial of Earl Russell, HL/PO/DC/CP/33/6.

Correspondence and Departmental orders regarding the Trial of Earl Russell, HL/PO/1/183; HC/SA/SJ/11/31; HL/PO/1/79/13.

Ticket to the Trial of Earl Russell, HL/PO/RO/1/95.

Photographs of Royal Gallery set out as Court for the Trial of Earl Russell, FAR/4/16-17, HC/LB/1/111/4/18-21.

Address to the Sovereign on the Trial of Earl Russell, HL/PO/CP/2/1/69.

D4. Universities and College Archives

Oxford University. Balliol College Archives: Jowett Papers, letters to and concerning Earl Russell, IF6/61, IIC/C1/158, IV/A8/24.

University of Texas, Harry Ransom Centre. George Santayana Collection: Correspondence: Frank Russell to George Santayana, MS-3699, Box 3.8.

Winchester College Archives. George and Sarah Richardson Collection, E17/3-12. Includes letters from Frank Russell to Sarah Richardson, 1885–86; Evidence of Mrs Sarah Richardson in R. v. Scott & others, 27 Nov 1896.

Notes
1. The index omits many references to Bertrand. Altogether they are on pp. 5, 9, 11, 17, 18, 19–20, 25, 28, 30, 31, 34, 38, 43, 44, 46 (Granny's poem), 48, 51, 82, 83, 85, 101, 330, 338, 343.
2. Mistakenly ascribed to Bertrand in Lester E. Denonn's bibliography of him in P. A. Schilpp, ed., *The Philosophy of Bertrand Russell*, revised ed. (New York: Harper & Row, 1963), p. 816.
3. *ibid.*, p. 755.

Bibliography

Archival Material

British Library
Stopes Papers: Add MS 58556
Cheshire Archives
Stanley Family Collection: DSA 104/2, 175/2.
McMaster University, Ontario, Canada, William Ready Division:
Bertrand Russell Archives:
Correspondence: see notes for references.
Frank's Private Journals: RA1, Box 6.27, 080042-4.
University of Texas, USA, Harry Ransom Centre:
George Santayana Collection: MS-3699.
Winchester College Archives:
George and Sarah Richardson Collection (E17).

Published Material

Anson, Sir William R. *The Law and Custom of the Constitution, Part 2: The Crown*, 2nd ed. Oxford: Clarendon Press, 1896; and 3rd ed., 1907.

Ball, Sidney. 'The Moral Aspects of Socialism'. In Sidney Webb *et al.*, eds. *Socialism and Individualism*. New York: John Lane, 1911.

Blackwell, Kenneth & Ruja, Harry. *A Bibliography of Bertrand Russell Vol.1: Separate Publications 1896-1900*. London: Routledge, 1994.

Clark, Ronald. *The Life of Bertrand Russell*. London: Jonathan Cape and Weidenfeld & Nicholson, 1975.

Cretney, Stephen Michael. *Family Law in the Twentieth Century: A History*. Oxford: Oxford University Press, 2003.

Derham, Ruth. *Bertrand's Brother: The Marriages, Morals and Misdemeanours of Frank, 2nd Earl Russell*. Stroud: Amberley Publishing, 2021.

Forster, Joseph. *Oxford Men 1880-1892*. Oxford: James Parker, 1893.

Hall, Ruth. *Marie Stopes: A Biography*. London: Andre Deutsch, 1977.

Hardy, Henry John. *Winchester College 1867-1920: A Register*. Winchester: P&G Wells, 1923.

Hvolboll, Eric. *The Property God Has Given Me: A Brief and Unfinished Story of* the *Orgeta Family and their Rancho Nuestra Senora del Refugio, Santa Barbara County*. Stanford University, 1978.

Lippiatt, Graham. 'Liberal Party Colours'. *Journal of Liberal History* 84 (2014): 37-39.

Lucretius. *De Rerum Natura*. William Ellery Leonard, trans. London: J. M. Dent, 1916.

Modugno, Tom. 'Who's Ellwood?' *Goleta History*, 19 Oct 2014. https://goletahistory.com/whos-ellwood/ accessed 22 Aug 2021.

Murray, Gilbert. *The Foreign Policy of Sir Edward Grey, 1906-1915*. Oxford: Clarendon Press, 1915.

Paine, Thomas *The Age of Reason*. London: Freethought Publishing, 1880.

Olivier, Sydney. 'Moral'. In Shaw *et al*, eds. *The Fabian Essays in Socialism*. Boston: Ball Publishing, 1911.

Russell, Earl [John Francis Stanley]. *Divorce*. London: William Heinemann, 1912.

Russell, Earl [John Francis Stanley]. *Lay Sermons*. London: Thomas Burleigh, 1902.

Russell, Earl [John Francis Stanley]. *My Life and Adventures*. London: Cassell, 1923.

Santayana, George. *Persons and Places*. Critical edn. W. G. Holzberger & H. J. Saatkamp eds. Cambridge, MA: MIT Press, 1896.

Savage, Gail. '"… the instrument of an animal function": Marital Rape and Sexual Cruelty in the Divorce Court'. In Delap *et al*, eds. *The Politics of Domestic Authority in Britain since 1800*. Palgrave Macmillan, 2009.

Shakespeare, William. *The Complete Works of William Shakespeare*. Stanley Wells & Gary Taylor, eds. Oxford: Clarendon Press, 1986.

Shaw, George Bernard. *Bernard Shaw: Collected Letters vol. 1: 1874-1897*. Dan Laurence, ed. London: Max Reinhardt, 1965.

Stevens, Charles. *Winchester Notions*. London: Athlone Press, 1998.

Newspapers & Journals

London
Daily Herald
Daily News
John Bull
The Graphic
Pall Mall Gazette
Reynolds's Newspaper
St James's Gazette
The Times
Westminster Gazette

Regionals, Journals and US Papers
Automobile Club Journal
Manchester Guardian
New York Times
The Scotsman
The Wykehamist (Winchester College)
Yorkshire Post

Reference Works & Websites

Additional biographical information: https://www.ancestry.co.uk/
Brixton Letters of Bertrand Russell: https://russell-letters.mcmaster.ca/
Classical texts: https://www.perseus.tufts.edu/hopper/
King James Bible: https://biblehub.com
Motoring: https://www.gracesguide.co.uk
Parliamentary Debates: https://hansard.parliament.uk
Stylographic Pens: https://vintagepens.com/stylos.shtml
UK Case Law: https://www.casemine.com/

Index